DATE DUE

MAR 22 1993	
APR 2 2 1993	

|

CHELSEA HOUSE PUBLISHERS
Modern Critical Views

Further titles in preparation.

Modern Critical Views

HOMER

Modern Critical Views

HOMER

Edited with an introduction by

Harold Bloom

Sterling Professor of the Humanities
Yale University

CHELSEA HOUSE PUBLISHERS
New York
Philadelphia

PROJECT EDITORS: Emily Bestler, James Uebbing
ASSOCIATE EDITOR: Maria Behan
EDITORIAL COORDINATOR: Karyn Gullen Browne
EDITORIAL STAFF: Perry King, Bert Yaeger
DESIGN: Susan Lusk

Cover design by Carol McDougall

10 9 8 7 6 5 4 3 2

Library of Congress Cataloging in Publication Data

Homer.
     (Modern critical views)
     Bibliography: p.
     Includes index.
     1. Homer—Criticism and interpretation—Addresses,
essays, lectures.   I. Bloom, Harold.   II. Series.
PA4037.H774   1986   883′.01   85–29896
ISBN 0–87754–723–8

Contents

Editor's Note

This volume brings together a representative selection of the best criticism available in English upon Homer, arranged in the chronological order of its publication. The time span covered is from 1933 to the present, so that the movement of more than a half-century in Homeric commentary can be studied here. Without the erudition of Ms. Cathy Caruth, and her keen judgment, the editor's task would have been considerably heavier.

A comparison and contrast between the poet of the *Iliad* and the Yahwist or J writer, author of the oldest strand in the Torah, is attempted in the editor's "Introduction." The historical sequence of speculation upon and analysis of the Homeric poems necessarily begins with three pioneering discussions by Milman Parry, the father of modern critical views of Homer. These discussions introduce us to the relations between the formulae of oral poetry and the poetic language of Homer, his traditional epithets and metaphors. A very different mode of criticism, moral and compassionate, is exemplified by Rachel Bespaloff's meditation upon the courtliness and poetic sensibility of Achilles in the great scene that closes the *Iliad*, when the slayer of Hector shares a meal with Hector's father, Priam.

A third mode, dialectical and metaphysical, appears in Maurice Blanchot's excursus upon the song of the Sirens as a fiction of duration, a temporal manifestation of the imaginary. In another dialectical investigation, by the Frankfurt philosophers Horkheimer and Adorno, the Sirens episode is read in a very different spirit, one that relates the protective measures taken against the song to that element in "the dialectic of enlightenment" that is seen as stopping the ears of the proletariat. This sociopolitical allegory is followed by a very antithetical performance, Simone Weil's extraordinarily personal and intense essay on the *Iliad* as "the poem of force," in which the poem is indubitably Christianized, but with striking moral exuberance.

Still another approach, profoundly influential in opening modern readers to nonrational factors in Homer's view of man, is presented in the essay by E. R. Dodds, who bases his work partly upon that of Bruno Snell, translated into English soon afterward. Taken together, they provide a necessary correction to anachronistic if relevant moralizings, such as those by Bespaloff and Weil. To my mind, they also call into question the celebrated account of Homeric mimesis by Erich Auerbach, printed here between Dodds and Snell.

The next four critical selections have enough in common to suggest the contours of yet another mode in modern analysis of Homer's epics. Adam Parry, considering the language of Achilles, finds in it the unique Homeric instance of the conscious gap between words and reality. In Cedric H. Whitman's tracing of the *Iliad*'s "geometric structure," there is a parallel concern with the ways in which Homer's forms expose a realization of the presence of self-deception in language. Thomas Greene, investigating form in the *Odyssey*, relates the tension of the poem's language to what he subtly calls its "emotional hardness," its lack of concern with personal sentiment. Eric Havelock also emphasizes a formalist orientation in showing that the Homeric epic was as much encyclopaedic storehouse and record as it was narrative.

With the next eight essays, another critical project emerges as a unifying factor in the enterprise of Homeric analysis. This can be called a newer and sharper sense of everything that is problematic about Homer's concepts of the epic hero. Norman Austin finds the function of digressions in the *Iliad* to be defensive and pragmatic, invariably connecting present behavior to past heroisms. In Hermann Fränkel's reading of the difference between the *Odyssey* and the *Iliad*, the greater detachment and shrewdness of the *Odyssey* is judged as an insulation of the hero against the outward world, a new realization of the distinction between what is the self and the non-self. With James M. Redfield's meditations upon the hero, structuralism as a critical mode makes a belated entrance, illuminating the Homeric social anthropology as a system of mutual support against the hostile context of nature. The focus moves back to the *Odyssey* with Douglas J. Stewart's analysis of the social basis of identity in the Homeric structure. This sequence of ruminations upon qualified heroism culminates with two brief considerations, by Gregory Nagy, of Achilles as the best of the Achaeans and Thersites as the worst.

The volume concludes with two recent observations upon the Homeric simile by Martin Mueller and by David Marshall. Mueller is concerned with the narrative function of the similes, in carrying the action of the poem forward, while Marshall more dialectically reads their frequent role as being antithetical, enforcing deferral and delay. With this more-than-technical difference exposed in the most basic of Homer's rhetorical gestures, we are returned full circle to Milman Parry's pathbreaking speculations on the superb and evasive balance in Homer between oral tradition and written artifice.

Introduction

. . . Hektor in his ecstasy of power/is mad for battle, confident in Zeus,/ deferring to neither men nor gods. Pure frenzy/fills him, and he prays for the bright dawn/when he will shear our stern-post beaks away/and fire all our ships, while in the shipways/amid that holocaust he carries death/ among our men, driven out by smoke. All this/I gravely fear; I fear the gods will make/good his threatenings, and our fate will be/to die here, far from the pastureland of Argos./Rouse yourself, if even at this hour/ you'll pitch in for the Akhaians and deliver them/from Trojan havoc. In the years to come/this day will be remembered pain for you/if you do not.

(The Iliad, Book Nine, Fitzgerald translation, p. 211)

For the divisions of Reuben there were great thoughts of heart.
Why abidest thou among the sheepfolds, to hear the bleatings of the flocks? For the divisions of Reuben there were great searchings of heart.
Gilead abode beyond Jordan: and why did Dan remain in ships? Asher continued on the sea shore, and abode in his breaches.
Zebulun and Naphtali were a people that jeoparded their lives unto the death in the high places of the field.

(Judges 5:15–18, King James version)

I

Simone Weil loved both the Iliad and the Gospels, and rather oddly associated them, as though Jesus had been a Greek and not a Jew:

The Gospels are the last marvelous expression of the Greek genius, as the Iliad is the first . . . with the Hebrews, misfortune was a sure indication of sin and hence a legitimate object of contempt; to them a vanquished enemy was abhorrent to God himself and condemned to expiate all sorts of crimes—this is a view that makes cruelty permissible and indeed indispensable. And no text of the Old Testament strikes a note comparable to the note heard in the Greek epic, unless it be certain parts of the book of Job. Throughout twenty centuries of Christianity, the Romans and the Hebrews have been admired, read, imitated, both in deed and word; their masterpieces have yielded an appropriate quotation every time anybody had a crime he wanted to justify.

• 1 •

Though vicious in regard to the Hebrew Bible, this is also merely banal, being another in that weary procession of instances of Jewish self-hatred, and even of Christian anti-Semitism. What is interesting in it however was Weil's strong misreading of the *Iliad* as "the poem of force," as when she said: "Its bitterness is the only justifiable bitterness, for it springs from the subjections of the human spirit to force, that is, in the last analysis, to matter." Of what "human spirit" did Weil speak? That sense of the spirit is of course Hebraic, and not at all Greek, and is totally alien to the text of the *Iliad*. Cast in Homer's terms, her sentence should have ascribed justifiable bitterness, the bitterness of Achilles and Hector, to "the subjections of the human force to the gods' force and to fate's force." For that is how Homer sees men; they are not spirits imprisoned in matter but forces or drives that live, perceive, and feel. I adopt here Bruno Snell's famous account of "Homer's view of man," in which Achilles, Hector and all the other heroes, even Odysseus, "consider themselves a battleground of arbitrary forces and uncanny powers." Abraham, Jacob, Joseph and Moses clearly do not view themselves as a site where arbitrary forces clash in battle, and neither of course does David or his possible descendant, Jesus. The *Iliad* is as certainly the poem of force as Genesis, Exodus, Numbers is the poem of the will of Yahweh, who has his arbitrary and uncanny aspects, but whose force is justice and whose power is also canny.

II

The poet of the *Iliad* seems to me to have only one ancient rival, the prime and original author of much of Genesis, Exodus, Numbers, known as the Yahwist or J writer to scholars. Homer and J have absolutely nothing in common except their uncanny sublimity, and they are sublime in very different modes. In a profound sense, they are agonists, though neither ever heard of the other, or listened to the other's texts. They compete for the consciousness of Western nations, and their belated strife may be the largest single factor that makes for a divided sensibility in the literature and life of the West. For what marks the West is its troubled sense that its cognition goes one way, and its spiritual life goes in quite another. We have no ways of thinking that are not Greek, and yet our morality and religion—outer and inner—find their ultimate source in the Hebrew Bible.

The burden of the word of the Lord, as delivered by Zechariah (9:12–13) has been prophetic of the cultural civil war that, for us, can never end:

Turn you to the stronghold, ye prisoners of hope: even today do I declare
that I will render double unto thee;
  When I have bent Judah for me, filled the bow with Ephraim, and
raised up thy sons, O Zion, against thy sons, O Greece, and made thee
as the sword of a mighty man.

Like the Hebrew Bible, Homer is both scripture and book of general
knowledge, and these are necessarily still the prime educational texts, with
only Shakespeare making a third, a third who evidences most deeply the
split between Greek cognition and Hebraic spirituality. To read the *Iliad*
in particular without distorting it is now perhaps impossible, and for reasons
that transcend the differences between Homer's language and implicit so-
cioeconomic structure, and our own. The true difference, whether we are
Gentile or Jew, believer or skeptic, Hegelian or Freudian, is between Yahweh, and the tangled company of Zeus and the Olympians, fate and the
daemonic world. Christian, Moslem, Jew or their mixed descendants, we
are children of Abraham and not of Achilles. Homer is perhaps most
powerful when he represents the strife of men and gods. The Yahwist or J
is as powerful when he shows us Jacob wrestling a nameless one among the
Elohim to a standstill, but the instance is unique, and Jacob struggles, not
to overcome the nameless one, but to delay him. And Jacob is no Heracles;
he wrestles out of character, as it were, so as to give us a giant trope for
Israel's persistence in its endless quest for a time without boundaries.

The *Iliad,* except for the Yahwist, Dante, and Shakespeare, is the
most extraordinary writing yet to come out of the West, but how much of
it is spiritually acceptable to us, or would be, if we pondered it closely?
Achilles and Hector are hardly the same figure, since we cannot visualize
Achilles living a day-to-day life in a city, but they are equally glorifiers of
battle. Defensive warfare is no more an ideal (for most of us) than is
aggression, but in the *Iliad* both are very near to the highest good, which
is victory. What other ultimate value is imaginable in a world where the
ordinary reality is battle? It is true that the narrator, and his personages,
are haunted by similes of peace, but, as James M. Redfield observes, the
rhetorical purpose of these similes "is not to describe the world of peace
but to make vivid the world of war." Indeed, the world of peace, in the
Iliad, is essentially a war between humans and nature, in which farmers rip
out the grain and fruit as so many spoils of battle. This helps explain why
the *Iliad* need not bother to praise war, since reality is a constant contest
anyway, in which nothing of value can be attained without despoiling or
ruining someone or something else.

To compete for the foremost place was the Homeric ideal, which
is not exactly the Biblical ideal of honoring your father and your mother.

I find it difficult to read the *Iliad* as "the tragedy of Hector," as Redfield and others do. Hector is stripped of tragic dignity, indeed very nearly of all dignity, before he dies. The epic is the tragedy of Achilles, ironically enough, because he retains the foremost place, yet cannot overcome the bitterness of his sense of his own mortality. To be only half a god appears to be Homer's implicit definition of what makes a hero tragic. But this is not tragedy in the Biblical sense, where the dilemma of Abraham arguing with Yahweh on the road to Sodom, or of Jacob wrestling with the angel of death, is the need to act as if one were everything in oneself while knowing also that, compared to Yahweh, one is nothing in oneself. Achilles can neither act as if he were everything in himself, nor can he believe that, compared even to Zeus, he is nothing in himself. Abraham and Jacob therefore, and not Achilles, are the cultural ancestors of Hamlet and the other Shakespearean heroes.

What after all is it to be the "best of the Achaeans," Achilles, as contrasted to the comparable figure, David (who in Yahweh's eyes is clearly the best among the children of Abraham)? It is certainly not to be the most complete man among them. That, as James Joyce rightly concluded, is certainly Odysseus. The best of the Achaeans is the one who can kill Hector, which is to say that Achilles, in an American heroic context, would have been the fastest gun in the West. Perhaps David would have been that also, and certainly David mourns Jonathan as Achilles mourns Patroklos, which reminds us that David and Achilles both are poets. But Achilles, sulking in his tent, is palpably a child, with a wavering vision of himself, inevitable since his vitality, his perception, and his affective life are all divided from one another, as Bruno Snell demonstrated. David, even as a child, is a mature and autonomous ego, with his sense of life, his vision of other selves, and his emotional nature all integrated into a new kind of man, the hero whom Yahweh had decided not only to love, but to make immortal *through his descendants,* who would never lose Yahweh's favor. Jesus, *contra* Simone Weil, can only be the descendant of David, and not of Achilles. Or to put it most simply, Achilles is the son of a goddess, but David is a Son of God.

III

The single "modern" author who compels comparison with the poet of the *Iliad* and the writer of the J text is Tolstoy, whether in *War and Peace* or in the short novel which is the masterpiece of his old age, *Hadji Murad.*

Rachel Bespaloff, in her essay, *On the Iliad* (rightly commended by the superb Homeric translator, Robert Fitzgerald, as conveying how distant, how refined the art of Homer was) seems to have fallen into the error of believing that the Bible and Homer, since both resemble Tolstoy, must also resemble one another. Homer and Tolstoy share the extraordinary balance between the individual in action and groups in action that alone permits the epic accurately to represent battle. The Yahwist and Tolstoy share an uncanny mode of irony that turns upon the incongruities of incommensurable entities, Yahweh or universal history, and man, meeting in violent confrontation or juxtaposition. But the Yahwist has little interest in groups; he turns away in some disdain when the blessing, on Sinai, is transferred from an elite to the mass of the people. And the clash of gods and men, or of fate and the hero, remains in Homer a conflict between forces not wholly incommensurable, though the hero must die, whether in or beyond the poem.

The crucial difference between the Yahwist and Homer, aside from their representations of the self, necessarily is the indescribable difference between Yahweh and Zeus. Both are personalities, but such an assertion becomes an absurdity directly they are juxtaposed. Erich Auerbach, comparing the poet of the *Odyssey* and the Elohist, the Yahwist's revisionist, traced the mimetic difference between the *Odyssey*'s emphasis upon "foregrounding" and the Bible's reliance upon the authority of an implied "backgrounding." There is something to that distinction, but it tends to fade out when we move from the *Odyssey* to the *Iliad* and from the Elohist to the Yahwist. The *Iliad* may not demand interpretation as much as the Yahwist does, but it hardly can be apprehended without any reader's considerable labor of aesthetic contextualization. Its man, unlike the Yahwist's, has little in common with the "psychological man" of Freud.

Joseph, who may have been the Yahwist's portrait of King David, provides a fascinating post-Oedipal contrast to his father Jacob, but Achilles seems never to have approached any relation whatever to his father Peleus, who is simply a type of ignoble old age wasting towards the wrong kind of death. Surely the most striking contrast between the *Iliad* and the J text is that between the mourning of Priam and the grief of Jacob when he believes Joseph to be dead. Old men in Homer are good mostly for grieving, but in the Yahwist they represent the wisdom and the virtue of the fathers. Yahweh is the God of Abraham, the God of Isaac, the God of Jacob, even as He will be the God of Moses, the God of David, the God of Jesus. But Zeus is nobody's god, as it were, and Achilles might as well not have had a father at all.

Priam's dignity is partly redeemed when his mourning for Hector is joined to that of Achilles for Patroklos, but the aged Jacob is dignity itself, as his grandfather Abraham was before him. Nietzsche's characterization is just. A people whose ideal is the agon for the foremost place must fall behind in honoring their parents, while a people who exalt fatherhood and motherhood will transfer the agon to the temporal realm, to struggle there not for being the best at one time, but rather for inheriting the blessing, which promises more life in a time without boundaries.

Yahweh is the source of the blessing, and Yahweh, though frequently enigmatic in J, is never an indifferent onlooker. No Hebrew writer could conceive of a Yahweh who is essentially an audience, whether indifferent or engrossed. Homer's gods are human—all-too-human particularly in their abominable capacity to observe suffering almost as a kind of sport. The Yahweh of Amos and the prophets after him could not be further from Homer's Olympian Zeus.

It can be argued that the spectatorship of the gods gives Homer an immense aesthetic advantage over the writers of the Hebrew Bible. The sense of a divine audience constantly in attendance both provides a fascinating interplay with Homer's human auditors, and guarantees that Achilles and Hector will perform in front of a sublimity greater even than their own. To have the gods as one's audience enhances and honors the heroes who are Homer's prime actors. Yahweh frequently hides Himself, and will not be there when you cry out for Him, or He may call out your name unexpectedly, to which you can only respond: "Here I am." Zeus is capricious and is finally limited by fate. Yahweh surprises you, and has no limitation. He will not lend you dignity by serving as your audience, and yet He is anything but indifferent to you. He fashioned you out of the moistened red clay, and then blew his own breath into your nostrils, so as to make you a living being. You grieve Him or you please Him, but fundamentally He is your longing for the father, as Freud insisted. Zeus is not your longing for anyone, and he will not save you even if you are Heracles, his own son.

IV

In Homer, you fight to be the best, to take away the women of the enemy, and to survive as long as possible, short of aging into ignoble decrepitude. That is not why you fight in the Hebrew Bible. There you fight the wars of Yahweh, which so appalled that harsh saint, Simone Weil. I want to

close this introduction by comparing two great battle odes, the war song
of Deborah and Barak, in Judges 5, and the astonishing passage in Book
18 of the *Iliad* when Achilles reenters the scene of battle, in order to recover
his arms, his armor, and the body of Patroklos:

> At this,
> Iris left him, running downwind. Akhilleus,
> whom Zeus loved, now rose. Around his shoulders
> Athena hung her shield, like a thunderhead
> with trailing fringe. Goddess of goddesses,
> she bound his head with golden cloud, and made
> his very body blaze with fiery light.
> Imagine how the pyre of a burning town
> will tower to heaven and be seen for miles
> from the island under attack, while all day long
> outside their town, in brutal combat, pikemen
> suffer the wargod's winnowing; at sundown
> flare on flare is lit, the signal fires
> shoot up for other islanders to see,
> that some relieving force in ships may come:
> just so the baleful radiance from Akhilleus
> lit the sky. Moving from parapet
> to moat, without a nod for the Akhaians,
> keeping clear, in deference to his mother,
> he halted and gave tongue. Not far from him
> Athena shrieked. The great sound shocked the Trojans
> into tumult, as a trumpet blown
> by a savage foe shocks an encircled town,
> so harsh and clarion was Akhilleus' cry.
> The hearts of men quailed, hearing that brazen voice.
> Teams, foreknowing danger, turned their cars
> and charioteers blanched, seeing unearthly fire,
> kindled by the grey-eyed goddess Athena,
> brilliant over Akhilleus. Three great cries
> he gave above the moat. Three times they shuddered,
> whirling backward, Trojans and allies,
> and twelve good men took mortal hurt
> from cars and weapons in the rank behind.
> Now the Akhaians leapt at the chance
> to bear Patroklos' body out of range.
> They placed it on his bed,
> and old companions there with brimming eyes
> surrounded him. Into their midst Akhilleus
> came then, and he wept hot tears to see
> his faithful friend, torn by the sharp spearhead,

lying cold upon his cot. Alas,
the man he sent to war with team and chariot
he could not welcome back alive.
(*The Iliad*, Fitzgerald translation)

Exalted and burning with Athena's divine fire, the unarmed Achilles is more terrible even than the armed hero would be. It is his angry shouts that panic the Trojans, yet the answering shout of the goddess adds to their panic, since they realize that they face preternatural powers. When Yahweh roars, in the prophets Isaiah and Joel, the effect is very different, though He too cries out "like a man of war." The difference is in Homer's magnificent antiphony between man and goddess, Achilles and Athena. Isaiah would not have had the king and Yahweh exchanging battle shouts in mutual support, because of the shocking incommensurateness which does not apply to Achilles and Athena.

I began this introduction by juxtaposing two epigraphs, Odysseus shrewdly warning Achilles that "this day," on which Hector may burn the Achaean ships, "will be remembered pain for you," if Achilles does not return to the battle, and a superb passage from Deborah's war song in Judges 5. Hector's "ecstasy of power" would produce "remembered pain" for Achilles, as power must come at the expense of someone else's pain, and ecstasy results from the victory of inflicting *memorable* suffering. Memory depends upon pain, which was Nietzsche's fiercely Homeric analysis of all significant memory. But that is not the memory exalted in the Hebrew Bible. Deborah, with a bitter irony, laughs triumphantly at the tribes of Israel that did not assemble for the battle against Sisera, and most of all at Reuben, with its scruples, doubts, hesitations: "great searchings of heart." She scorns those who kept to business as usual, Dan who remained in ships, and Asher who continued on the sea shore. Then suddenly, with piercing intensity and moral force, she utters a great paean of praise and triumph, for the tribes that risked everything on behalf of their covenant with Yahweh, for those who transcended "great thoughts" and "great searchings of heart":

Zebulun and Naphtali were a people that jeoparded their lives unto the death in the high places of the field.

The high places are both descriptive and honorific; they are where the terms of the covenant were kept. Zebulun and Naphtali fight, not to be the foremost among the tribes of Israel, and not to possess Sisera's women, but to fulfill the terms of the covenant, to demonstrate *emunah*, which is trust in Yahweh. Everyone in Homer knows better than to trust in Zeus. The aesthetic supremacy of the *Iliad* again must be granted. Homer is the best of the poets, and always will keep the foremost place. What he lacks, even aesthetically, is a quality of trust in the transcendent memory of a covenant fulfilled, a lack of the sublime hope that moves the Hebrew poet Deborah:

> They fought from heaven; the stars in their courses fought against Sisera.
>
> The river of Kishon swept them away, that ancient river, the river Kishon. O my soul, thou hast trodden down strength.

MILMAN PARRY

The Traditional Epithet
in Homer

The experience of a member of Homer's audience must have been fundamentally the same as that of a modern student, only much wider and deeper. From their earliest childhood, his audience must have heard again and again long recitations of epic poetry, poetry composed always in the same style. The diction of this poetry, accessible to the modern reader only by way of long study, was familiar to them in its smallest details. The experience . . . of the beginner, who learns how to understand "fast" in "fast ship" . . . must have come quickly to a member of Homer's audience, and long before he heard a line sung by Homer. And so with other noun–epithet combinations which a modern student learns to associate in thought after years of reading: Homer's audience would have made these associations easily. If we today, using dictionary and grammar to go slowly through the text of only two poems, can acquire a complete indifference to the particular meaning of an epithet in certain combinations, the original audience of those poems, who had become familiar with their style by no conscious effort but by having heard a quantity of epic verse countless times greater, must have already acquired this indifference even for expressions which appear but twice or thrice in the *Iliad* and *Odyssey*, too rarely for us to regard in this way. This problem of the assimilation of the noun–epithet combination cannot be reduced to

From *The Making of Homeric Verse: The Collected Papers of Milman Parry*, edited by Adam Parry. Copyright © 1971 by Oxford University Press. Translations by Richmond Lattimore from *The Iliad*, Chicago: The University of Chicago Press, 1951 and by Albert Cook from *The Odyssey*, New York: W. W. Norton, 1974.

a definite equation; for our desire to find a particularized meaning varies according to the idea of the epithet and the meaning of the sentence. But the question, whether, in a given case, Homer's audience had become thoroughly indifferent to any particular meaning of an epithet, is ultimately one of numbers. It is a question of knowing whether or not that audience had heard the expression a *sufficient number of times* to acquire this indifference. The fact that a reader attributes a particularized meaning to an epithet indicates simply that the reader has not encountered this combination of noun and epithet often enough to have fused into one the two ideas represented by the two words. But if we could know that Homer's audience had heard the expression often enough, there could be no doubt that the function of the epithet was ornamental.

For us there is but one way of finding the terms of this hypothetical equation. We must be in a position to suppose that Homer's audience had heard a given expression not twice, and not thrice, but twenty and thirty times, as many times as the most ardent champion of the particularized meaning could demand. To be able to make such a supposition, we must go back to the evidence of noun–epithet formula systems: they alone can give us unambiguous information concerning the frequency of such expressions. We are not mistaken in believing that Homer's audience had previously heard many another epic poem. Therefore, once it is established that a given noun–epithet expression forms part of a traditional system designed for the use of a given noun, or in other words that it is a *fixed* epithet, we can be certain that this audience, long before they ever heard the *Iliad* and the *Odyssey*, were too familiar with the expression to think of finding in it any particularized meaning.

We are thus led to conclude that no noun–epithet formula which *certainly* forms part of a traditional system of noun–epithet formulae can contain an epithet whose meaning is particularized. And this conclusion should be categoric, should admit of no exception. To know that a noun–epithet formula includes a traditional epithet which is also a fixed epithet, is to know that those who first heard the songs of Homer had already had the experience at which the modern reader so easily arrives in the case of "fast ship."

The trouble which Alexandrian scholars gave themselves to explain cases where an epithet seems to be used illogically shows us how much they felt such usages to be unusual and even strange. But like the scholars of modern times, they never asked themselves why Homer did not regard these usages as they did. The answer is that the kind of interpretation which, in the course of reading, occurs to a man accustomed to a literature in which every adjective is used for a particular reason simply never occurred to Homer at all. A total indifference is the only possible explanation, and so every case of what seems an illogical use of an epithet proves how much the poet and his listeners had become familiar with the noun–epithet formulae of a traditional style. These usages are so many independent confirmations of the conclusion we reached by examining the reaction of the novice reader to "fast ship." . . .

We have seen, on the one hand, that in a great many cases it is impossible to find a particularized meaning in an epithet. On the other hand, almost all substantives in Homer are used, in varying proportions, both with and without epithets. These two points are perfectly obvious, but putting them together raises a question of capital importance: why does the poet omit the epithet in one place and put it in in another? Why, for example, does Odysseus have an epithet in 344 cases and not have one in 343 cases? Let us leave in abeyance the question of metrical convenience and concern ourselves instead with the bard's aesthetic sense. Obviously the poetry would be too weighed down if the poet provided each and every noun with an epithet. But while this may, up to a point, explain the quantity of epithets in a given number of lines, it is not always easy to explain a specific case. We are still in the dark, for example, as to why Sparta does not deserve an epithet quite as much as Pylos in *Odyssey* 1.93,

> I shall send him on to Sparta, and also to sandy Pylos.

considering that the two lands are equally favoured in *Odyssey* 4.702,

> To divine Pylos, and also to godly Lacedemon.

There are hundreds of other examples where there are two or more nouns and only one has an epithet. Usually, as in the case just cited, the reader will pay no attention; but there are cases where an attentive reader will find some explanation almost indispensable. When there are several heroes, as in *Iliad* 14.425,

> Polydamas and Aeneas and brilliant Agenor.

Why does Agenor get the epithet rather than Aeneas, who is certainly the stoutest warrior of the three, or even rather than Polydamas? Likewise *Iliad* 12.88–9,

> They who went with Hector and Polydamas the blameless,
> these were most numerous, and bravest.

Hector has certainly as much right as Polydamas to an ennobling epithet. This fashion of favouring one hero over another is yet more inexplicable in *Iliad* 17.534,

Hector and Aeneas and godlike Chromius.

Chromius, a Mysian chieftain, is in fact mentioned only in this book, and in it, thrice: encouraged by Hector he enters the fray along with Aretus, hoping to capture the body of Patroclus; beaten back by the valour of the two Ajaxes, he withdraws, leaving on the field of battle the body of his comrade, slain by Automedon. The record of his deeds hardly requires that the poet show him greater honour than the bravest warriors of Troy. Finally consider *Iliad* 24.249–51 where Priam accuses his sons of cowardice,

> cursing Helenos, and Paris, Agathon the brilliant,
> Pammon and Antiphonos, Polites of the great war cry,
> Deïphobos and Hippothoös and proud Dios.

Agathon is mentioned nowhere else by Homer; nor is Dios. Polites, who the poet has told us (*Iliad* 2.792) was noted for his swiftness of foot, appears elsewhere in the poem only in *Iliad* 13.533, when he leads his wounded brother Deiphobus from the battle. What makes the heroic epithets used here stranger still is that a few lines later Priam qualifies the most valiant of his sons with epithets which seem in no way more honorific:

> Mestor like a god and Troilos whose delight was in horses,
> and Hector, who was a god among men.
> (*Iliad* 24.257–8)

It is clear that we have here examples of usage in some ways akin to the illogical usages that drew the attention of ancient scholars. There, it was a matter of the meaning of the epithet. In the cases we have just been considering, there is no question of meaning, but we still want to know why the poet chose to use an epithet at all. There is but one explanation, the indifference of the audience, not only to the meaning of the epithet, but also to its connotations of nobility.

A more general proof of this indifference is the frequency with which certain names of heroes are variously accompanied by epithets. Why is the name of Agamemnon used in the nominative case as often as the name of Patroclus, but seven times more often with an epithet? Because he is the commander-in-chief of the Achaean army? Why then does Diomedes in the nominative case appear without an epithet only once out of 42 times, whereas out of an equal number of occurrences Agamemnon in the nominative appears without epithet twelve times? Again why does Menelaus, fine warrior that he was, but clearly no Achilles or Odysseus, deserve the epithet four times as often as they? So with the gods: possibly reasons could be given to explain why Apollo, Athena, Hera, and Ares have approximately the same proportion of epithets when their names appear in the nominative case. But why then should not Zeus, the greatest of all the gods, not have still more of them? For in actuality, the epithet is found with his name in this grammatical case less than with the names of the other gods. We might also have to explain why Iris enjoys the epithet more than any other deity (24 times out of 27).

Metrical convenience alone can explain these differing proportions; and therefore we must abandon the idea which offers itself so naturally to us that the courage or the majesty of a hero or a god led the poet to attribute the epithet to him more often. Anyone inclined to believe that Homer chose an epithet in a given passage in order to honour a particular character, will have to concede that, far from indicating the virtues and the deserts of his heroes and gods, the poet has actually falsified our conception of their character. Surely Homer did not believe, as the use of the epithets would suggest, that Menelaus was a braver warrior than Achilles or even Ajax, or that Diomedes surpassed Ajax, or that Patroclus merited fewer titles of honour than any other hero.

Let us return to the Homeric audience's indifference to the fixed epithet. It is to be sure a relative indifference, as becomes evident if we imagine a Homeric hero who has some importance in the story, but is never described by an epithet at all: the hearers would not notice the absence at first, but eventually it would ring strange to them. But these same hearers, as we have just seen, were undisturbed by even considerable variations in the frequency of the use of epithets, and never looked for the specific motivation of an honorific epithet in a given case. This must have been so. How, for example, could a member of Homer's audience hear the epithet *divine* an average of about once every 68 lines, and find in it any particularly ennobling significance? Or, in the case of a less usual epithet, say, "warlike" or "steadfast," how could he distinguish between this epithet and so many others which equally evoked a general heroic quality? If we look at the question in a different light, that of the totality of epithets, consider what a grave impediment to the fine rapidity of Homeric style would be created by the requirement that we find in every fixed epithet a specific motivation for its use. Let us note by the way that most of such specific motivations as have been pointed out were found not in a continuous reading of Homer, but rather in the process of annotation or criticism, or in the course of translation, by applying to the text that search for subtleties of thought which is so essential for our authors and even for Pindar, but inappropriate to an author who has no individual style.

It is easy to understand why Homer was able to dispose his epithets so unevenly. For him and for his audience alike, the fixed epithet did not so much adorn a single line or even a single poem, as it did the entirety of heroic song. These epithets constituted for him one of the familiar elements of poetry, elements which we of a later age find it so difficult to appreciate, but the importance of which, for both poet and audience, is shown by everything in Homer: by the story, by the characters, by the style. In this respect, fixed epithets were just like the other familiar elements of poetry. The audience would have been infinitely surprised if a bard had left them out; his always putting them in hardly drew their attention. Epic lines without epithets would have seemed to them like a heroic character without his traditional attributes. But even now, who among those of us who have any knowledge of the legend has asked why Odysseus should be *crafty* in this or that particular episode? Just so, Homer's listeners demanded epithets and paid them no attention, showing thereby the same lack of exact observation that becomes a habit with the modern reader. And it is this lack of exact observation that explains uses of the epithet which appear to us unmotivated, because we look for their motivation in the lines where they occur, rather than in all the poetry Homer's audience had already heard before they ever heard him sing.

We have considered the epithet as a word chosen to emphasize the heroic quality of a person or thing. If we take as point of departure another way of using the epithet, which again shows how Homer sacrificed precision of thought to ease of versification, we shall see that it is impossible to understand how the audience felt about the meaning of the epithet as long as we are unaware of the principle that the epithet adorns all epic poetry rather than a single line. There is a large group of epithets which Homer uses for a character in only one grammatical case. Why, we may ask, does Homer, with but one exception, call Odysseus *divine* only in the nominative case? Here is an epithet which describes Odysseus 99 times in the *Iliad* and *Odyssey*; had the poet selected it, even occasionally, with a view to the momentary circumstances of his narrative, it would inevitably have to appear in the oblique cases more often than it does since Homer mentions Odysseus 302 times in the oblique cases and 385 times in the nominative. Here we cannot adduce the exigency of metre, as we can elsewhere, as for *polytlas* [much-enduring] for example, which would have a genitive form *polytlantos*. The poet is able to put *dios* in the oblique cases in a great many positions in the hexameter. This limitation of the epithet to a single case is too widespread to be the work of chance. Achilles is qualified by the same epithet, *dios* [divine], 55 times in the nominative and twice only in an oblique case. Odysseus is "crafty" 81 times, but only in the nominative, ... Similarly, we find in the nominative case only "swift" (5 times) or "swift footed" (32 times) for Achilles; "helmet-shaking" (37 times) or "shining" (29 times) for Hector; "ruler" (30 times) for Agamemnon; "sensible" (35 times) for Telemachus; "horseman" (32 times) for Nestor. Going on to the genitive, "godlike" is said of Odysseus solely in this grammatical case (31 times), likewise "stout-hearted" (11 times). With one exception the Achaeans are "bronze-shirted" only in the genitive (24 times). Hector is "man-slaying" only in this form (11 times). Ships are described as "curved" only in the dative plural (17 times). Odysseus is "shrewd" (22 times) and "shining" (5 times) only in the vocative. These are some of the most striking examples; others could be cited, and if we added all the cases where an epithet is used for a particular person or thing only in either the nominative or the vocative, or in either the nominative or the accusative, or only in the oblique cases—for many nouns and epithets have identical metrical quantities in these sets of grammatical cases—we have a list comprising almost every fixed epithet.

Perhaps it will be thought that this restriction is one in appearance only, and that in reality a single idea is expressed by several epithets. Thus the idea of "much-enduring" which appears only in the nominative, would be expressed by "stout-hearted" in the genitive; "divine" in the nominative would correspond to "godlike" [theiou] in the genitive, to "godlike" [antith-eiou] in the dative; "crafty" in the nominative would correspond to "shrewd" in the vocative . . . etc. But this hypothesis is too little in accordance with what we find in Homer. What other epithet has Hector to correspond to "helmet-shaking," or to "shining," or to "man-slaying"? What epithet of Telemachus can we find to compare with "sensible"? Which among all the epithets of Zeus answers to "counselor" and "father of men and gods"? Among the epithets of the Achaeans, "bronze-shirted" expresses a unique idea, and likewise "curved" among the epithets of ships. What nominative epithet of Odysseus can be compared with "blameless" or "proud" which are given to the hero only in the oblique cases? It is evident that the similarities of meaning which we can find among different epithets are not the result of a plan. They depend solely on the bards' desire to designate, in one way or another, either a salient characteristic of a single hero, or else one of the characteristics of the hero in general. These characteristics are in fact very few. A close examination of the 61 generic epithets of heroes [which appear on Table III] reveals that they all refer to five qualities: courage, strength, fame, royalty, and that heroic but vague concept, "divinity."

There is therefore but one way to account for the frequent limitation of an epithet to one or more grammatical cases: by the ornamental meaning of the fixed epithet. Otherwise only a fantastic coincidence would explain why, every time the poet wanted to complete the thought of his sentence by means of an epithet, the substantive described by this epithet was in the one grammatical case in which this epithet appears. Hence we see that the circumstances of the moment, even if they are perfectly consonant with the meaning of the epithet, never suggest that epithet to the poet. And so we are led once more to the same conclusion which we reached both by the study of illogical uses of the epithet, and by considering the reader's actual experience of the constantly recurring noun–epithet formula.

Still, the question can always be asked whether, even granted the particularized meaning of the epithet, this limitation of its use to one or a few grammatical cases is not a fault. For the poet, it would seem, was quite unaware of the need to vary his epithets or to use a proper number of them in a given stretch of verse. To answer that question we must again have recourse to the audience's indifference to the fixed epithet. They quickly learned not to look for any particularized meaning. They were so familiar with the fact that the noun–epithet combination is no more than a heroic mode of expressing a noun that all they expected to find in the epithet was an element ennobling the style; from this point of view our explanation of the similarity of meaning shown by several epithets is valid, since the epithet expresses above all the heroic character of a person or thing. And so the audience became indifferent to which fixed epithet the poet used in a given line. This indifference is the complement of the indifference he felt for the use or the omission of the fixed epithet. Though Homer's listener had no concern for that variety of expression which we require in our modern styles, he did expect a character or object frequently mentioned to have a certain number of epithets. But after a while, when he had heard a certain number of them he paid them no more attention. It was inevitable that he would hear a certain number of them, since a noun occurring with any frequency will appear in different grammatical cases and in combination with different expressions, thereby giving rise to the use of epithets of different metrical values, which is to say, to different fixed epithets. The necessities of versification themselves provoke that variety of epithets which is required, it could be said, by the inattention of the audience.

MILMAN PARRY

The Traditional Poetic
Language of Oral Poetry

In a society where there is no reading
and writing, the poet, as we know from the study of such peoples in our
own time, always makes his verse out of formulas. He can do it in no other
way. Not having the device of pen and paper which, as he composed, would
hold his partly formed thought in safe-keeping while his unhampered mind
ranged where it would after other ideas and other words, he makes his
verses by choosing from a vast number of fixed phrases which he has heard
in the poems of other poets. Each one of these phrases does this: it expresses
a given idea in words which fit into a given length of the verse. Each one
of these fixed phrases, or formulas, is an extraordinary creation in itself. It
gives the words which are best suited for the expression of the idea, and
is made up of just those parts of speech which, in the place which it is to
fill in the verse, will accord with the formulas which go before and after
to make the sentence and the verse. Each formula is thus made in view of
the other formulas with which it is to be joined; and the formulas taken
all together make up a diction which is the material for a completely unified
technique of verse-making. Finally, the formulas of an oral poetry are not
each one of them without likeness to any other; in that case the technique
would be far too unwieldy. They fall into smaller groups of phrases which
have between them a likeness of idea and words, and these in turn fall into

groups which have a larger pattern in common, until the whole diction is schematized in such a way that the poet, habituated to the scheme, hits without effort, as he composes, upon the type of formula and the particular formula which, at any point in his poem, he needs to carry on his verse and his sentence.

A single man or even a whole group of men who set out in the most careful way could not make even a beginning at such an oral diction. It must be the work of many poets over many generations. When one singer (for such is the name these oral poets most often give themselves) has hit upon a phrase which is pleasing and easily used, other singers will hear it, and then, when faced at the same point in the line with the need of expressing the same idea, they will recall it and use it. If the phrase is so good poetically and so useful metrically that it becomes in time the one best way to express a certain idea in a given length of the verse, and as such is passed on from one generation of poets to another, it has won a place for itself in the oral diction as a formula. But if it does not suit in every way, or if a better way of fitting the idea to the verse and the sentence is found, it is straightway forgotten, or lives only for a short time, since with each new poet and with each new generation of poets it must undergo the twofold test of being found pleasing and useful. In time the needed number of such phrases is made up: each idea to be expressed in the poetry has its formula for each metrical need, and the poet, who would not think of trying to express ideas outside the traditional field of thought of the poetry, can make his verses easily by means of a diction which time has proved to be the best.

Actually, of course, this birth of a diction is beyond observation, and unless it can really be shown that a people reverting from written to oral poetry created anew a formulaic diction we must suppose that it took place in a very distant past, since the poetry of an unlettered race has as much claim to age as have any of its other institutions. But if the birth of a formulaic diction is only to be described theoretically, we can see in living oral poetries how such a diction is passed on from one age to another, and how it gradually changes.

The young poet learns from some older singer not simply the general style of the poetry, but the whole formulaic diction. This he does by hearing and remembering many poems, until the diction has become for him the habitual mode of poetic thought. He knows no other style, and he is ever kept from quitting the traditional diction and using phrases of his own make because he could not find any as pleasing or as useful as the old ones, and moreover, since he is composing by word of mouth, he must go on without stopping from one phrase to the next. Since his poetry has being only in the course of his singing, and is not fixed on paper where it can show itself to him verse by verse, he never thinks of it critically phrase by phrase, but only faces the problem of its style when he is actually under the stress of singing. Thus whatever change the single poet makes in the traditional diction is slight, perhaps the change of an old formula, or the making of a new one on the pattern of an old, or the fusing of old formulas, or a new way of putting them together. An oral style is thus highly conservative; yet the causes for change are there, and sooner or later must come into play.

These causes for change have nothing to do with any wish on the part of the single poet for what is new or striking in style. They exist above the poets, and are two: the never-ceasing change in all spoken language, and the association between peoples of a single language but of different dialects.

As the spoken language changes, the traditional diction of an oral poetry likewise changes so long as there is no need of giving up any of the formulas. For example, a change in the sound of a vowel or consonant which calls for no change in the metrical value of a word soon makes its way into the poetic language: the singer naturally pronounces the word as he usually does, and there is not the least thing to keep him from doing so. But when a change in the form of a word must also change its metrical value it is far otherwise, for the poet, if he then wished to keep up with the spoken language, would have to put up with a phrase which was metrically false, or give it up altogether and make himself a new one. But neither of these two choices is at all pleasing. The rhythm must be kept fairly regular, and the oral verse-making makes it very hard for him to find new words; it is even doubtful if with all the good will and time in the world he could do so in any great number of cases. Each formula, as it was said above, is the long-proven choice of a long line of singers, and it is not possible that a phrase which is useful in oral composition could be made in any other way than by a singer who, making his verses through his sense of the scheme of the formulaic diction, created, in the stress of the moment, a new phrase more or less like an older one. For otherwise the new phrase would not fit into the scheme of the diction, and since it could be used only with an effort it would not be used at all. Finally the change in the spoken language would very likely be such that a phrase to express the same idea in words of the same metrical pattern would be out of the question. The new phrase must be shorter or longer, or begin or end differently. Then the formulas to which it would be joined must also be changed, and so on. Thus by no wilful choice, but by the constraint of his technique of verse-making, the singer keeps the formula though its language has become archaic.

As it happens, this archaic language does not at all displease him. His style is thus lifted above the commonplace of daily speech and made distant and wondrous. But though the old words and forms are thus desirable, they are never wilfully sought after. When the formula can be changed it sooner or later will be, and the cleavage between the old and the new in the style depends on whether it is easy or hard to change the formula. An oral diction may thus in time become very archaic, since even though a word has been lost altogether from the spoken language its context in the poetry will teach the poet and his public its meaning. In the case of words which are not a needed part of the thought, such as the ornamental epithets, the meaning of the word may even be lost altogether. In time, however, a point must be reached in the case of each formula where its meaning, needed for the thought, is lost, and here an even heavier constraint than ease of verse-making comes into play: the formula must be given up cost what it may, and the singers must do the best they can to find another one to take its place. Thus the language of oral poetry changes as a whole neither faster nor slower than the spoken language, but in its parts it changes readily when no loss of formulas is called for, belatedly when there must be such a loss, so that the traditional diction has in it words and forms of everyday use side by side with others that belong to earlier stages of the language. The number of new words and old words varies, of course, from one oral poetry to another as different factors have force: a complex verse-form, a fondness for tales of an heroic past rather than of the present, and the practice of poetry by a class of professional singers all tend toward a greater conservatism, whereas a short verse without enjambement, a change in the way of living of a people, and the lack of a class whose gain it is to keep the best poetry of the past all allow a quicker change. But the principle of change and conservatism of language is the same in all cases.

I have written so far, in telling of how the language of oral poetry comes to be archaic, as if the formula were the unit of diction, and such it is in the end. But in practice the oral poet by no means limits his borrowing to the single formula; rather he uses whole passages which he has heard. This is, indeed, his whole art: to make a poem like the poems he has heard. I know only too well that this is sure to suggest the thought of plagiarism to those not familiar with oral poetry, but it must be understood above all that plagiarism is not possible in traditional literature. One oral poet is better than another not because he has by himself found a more striking way of expressing his own thought but because he has been better able to make use of the tradition. He strives not to create a new ideal in poetry but to achieve that which everyone knows to be the best. This is true even of the poetry which may tell of happenings of the singer's own day: the event may be new, but it will be told in the traditional way on the pattern of passages from other poems, and in more or less the same phrases as were used in those passages, so that the only difference between the poem made about the present and that which tells of the past is that the former will be made from the memory of a larger number of different poems. For if the tale is old, and, as is usually the case, regarded as more or less true, the singer may tell it just about as he heard it.

Yet no graver mistake could be made than to think the art of the singer calls only for memory. Those who have sought to record oral poetry in lands where it still lives have straightway found that the same poem, that is to say, a poem on the same subject, could be sung badly or well, and that the people carefully set apart the poor singers from the good. Still the fame of such a singer comes not from quitting the tradition but from putting it to the best use. The poorer singer will repeat a poem with the loss of its most pleasing lines or its most dramatic moments, but the good singer will keep what is striking, and even add, on the pattern of other poems, lines which he knows will please, and new incidents, or give a fuller tale with many such borrowings. He may even have heard the same tale told by a singer living at a distance who inherited from a different tradition; then he will fuse the poems, using the best in each. Thus the highest sort of oral verse-making achieves the new by the best and most varied and perhaps the fullest use of the old. This is the meaning of what Telemachus says:

> Men acclaim that song the most
> which has come round newest of all to those who hear it.
> (*Odyssey* 1.351–2)

It is the same in all thriving oral poetries. The good singer wins his fame by his ease and versatility in handling a tradition which he knows more thoroughly than anyone else and of which his talent shows him the highest use, but his poetry remains throughout the sum of longer and shorter passages which he has heard.

The formula thus is by no means the unit of the singer's poetry, but it nevertheless ever tends to become so, for no singer ever tells the same tale twice in the same words. His poem will always follow the same general pattern, but this verse or that will be left out, or replaced by another verse or part of a verse, and he will leave out and add whole passages as the time and the mood of his hearers calls for a fuller or a briefer telling of a tale or of a given part of a tale. Thus the oral poem even in the mouth of the same singer is ever in a state of change; and it is the same when his poetry is sung by others. His great name and the fame of his verse may urge those who have learned from him to a more careful and more faithful use of memory than that which they would show for the poetry of a lesser singer. But the memory of the hearer depends after all on his being habituated to the diction as a whole, rather than on the learning of the poem word by word, so that he too must change and add and leave out verses and parts of verses, and this process will go on until all that is left of the poem are its single formulas and shorter passages which are the final units in the traditional diction. It should be added here that an oral poetry practiced by guilds of singers with masters and apprentices would tend to a more faithful keeping of poems which had won fame, and that one singer might win such a name that his disciples would find their profit in keeping his poetry as nearly without change as they could; but then they are no longer singers but rhapsodes, their task is not that of creation but only of memory, and they are merely keeping from age to age the verse which was first composed by a singer who made his poetry, in the way that we have seen, by an ever varying use of what he had sung and heard others sing.

MILMAN PARRY

The Traditional Metaphor
in Homer

Aristotle tells in his *Poetics* of the
kinds of words which make for a poetic diction, then he adds: "It is a great
thing to make a fitting use of each one of these devices [i.e., of poetic
word-forms], as well as of compounds and glosses, but the greatest thing of
all is being metaphorical. This alone can be gotten from no one else, and
is the sign of born talent, since to use metaphors well is to have a sense
for likenesses. Compounds best suit the dithyramb, glosses heroic verse,
and metaphors iambic verse. In heroic verse, finally, all the devices which
I have named are useful. . . ." Further on he says: "The heroic meter is
the steadiest and the fullest, so that it is the readiest to take glosses and
metaphors." Now if we take the term "heroic," as we usually do, as meaning
most of all the *Iliad* and *Odyssey*, Aristotle has said in so many words that
Homer's metaphors will show us as nothing else in his style can just why
he is great. What, then, are we to make of it when modern scholars tell
us that the metaphor has only a small place in Homer, and that it is usually
put to no striking use? That it was Aristotle who was mistaken is clear,
but we must learn why he thus fell into error. In doing so we shall find we
have to deal with that principle of criticism on which at the present time,
more than on any others, depends the true understanding of Homeric
poetry.

From *The Making of Homeric Verse: The Collected Papers of Milman Parry*, edited by Adam
Parry. Copyright © 1971 by Oxford University Press. Translations by Richmond Lattimore
from *The Iliad*, Chicago: The University of Chicago Press, 1951 and Albert Cook from *The
Odyssey*, New York: W. W. Norton, 1974.

Aristotle's statement does not hold for all Greek heroic poetry because he had in mind as he wrote not so much Homer as the epics of his own age. We may even be sure he was thinking of the two chief epic poets of the fifth century, Choerilus and Antimachus. We know how much Plato liked the verse of Antimachus, and how he defended him against the vogue which Choerilus was having. Aristotle often quotes both of them and does so in a way which shows he took for granted a very common knowledge of their work. In one place he says briefly: "In the way Homer does, not Choerilus," and in the *Rhetoric* he quotes only from the first line of a passage in Antimachus, though it is only in the following lines that the artifice of which he is treating is illustrated. Now the two poets had very bad names for their use of metaphor. Proclus must be giving a critical commonplace when he says: "If the grand manner has anything artificial about it, it becomes very forced and bombastic. The fault usually lies in the use of metaphor, as in the case of Antimachus." Choerilus on his side had called stones "the bones of the earth," and rivers "the arteries of the earth," and though it must be partly through chance, his few fragments show a straining of metaphor far beyond anything to be found in what we have of Antimachus. In his *Perseid* a noble Persian, brought low in defeat, is forced to drink from a broken clay cup: "Here in my hands, all my fortune, is the shard of a cup broken in twain, a timber from a shipwreck of banqueters, such as oft the gale of Dionysus doth cast up on the coast of pride." This, indeed, is what one might look for after his prologue, which Aristotle quotes: "Happy the man who in those times was skilled in song and comrade of the Muses, when the meadow was unmowed. Now, when all has been allotted and the arts have their outcomes, we are left last in the race, and though we gaze everywhither there is no chariot newly yoked to which we may win." One sees straightway that the very thing might be done for Choerilus which was done by a critic of modern poetry who made a study of the metaphors of Guillaume Apollinaire, the French symbolist poet, because he could find in them the essence of the poet's thought. But what is true of Choerilus and Antimachus, and of Aristotle's friend Aeschrion who called the new moon, "heaven's fair new letter," and of modern verse, is not true of Homer.

It is not that metaphors are lacking in Homer, or that when taken by themselves they are not striking enough. The rhetoricians usually took their examples from the *Iliad* and *Odyssey*. Aristotle has the highest praise for Homer's metaphors "from living to lifeless," such as that in which he says of Sisyphus' punishment, "back to the bottom rolled the shameless stone," or speaks of spears which, having fallen short, "stood in the ground, yearning to sate themselves on flesh." Demetrius dwells at length on "the ruinous battle quivered with spears," and Byzantine writers are still quoting "unquenchable laughter," "shepherd of the people," and "the seed of fire." When thus weighed alone, however, these phrases are not at all what they are in their place in the poems. There the way they are used and their use over and over have given them a sense which is utterly lost when they are torn from the poetry. They are fixed metaphors. . . .

[Very great] in reading Homer is the need of . . . understanding that what a diction loses through common use it gains in the kind of charm which suits the times, for the diction of the *Iliad* and *Odyssey*, being altogether traditional, is fixed to a point of which English poetry can give us only a faint notion, and is filled with phrases emptier of meaning than any in Pope or Falconer. I have written elsewhere about the traditional diction of the Homeric poems, but there is no need here of giving the results of other studies. The metaphor, being typical, will give us knowledge enough of the diction as a whole.

When one has set aside the phrases in which the metaphor is not real, being only the tangible term used for the intangible thing, as in "he roused up a plague," "to ward off the bane"; or a poetic shift of the parts of speech, as in "unhappy woes," "violent warfare," there are left only some twenty-five metaphors in the six hundred and eleven lines of the first *Iliad*. This is a small enough number in itself, but in reality the place of the metaphor is far more limited than the mere number would show, because only two of these metaphors bear on more than the single word. In the other cases it lies either in an epithet or on a word which merely takes the place of the *kyrion onoma*, the "regular word," with what force of metaphor we must see.

The "watr'y way" of English verse doubtless goes back in some way or other to Homer's *hygra keleutha*, which is one of the two cases in the first book where the metaphor goes beyond the single word; the loss of meaning in the phrases, however, is of course due in each case to the way it has been used in each of the two languages. Were *hygra keleutha* found only once in the Greek epic we might perhaps give the phrase all its force, and the English use would have no bearing on it, but by the time one has read the *Iliad* and *Odyssey* one has met the same phrase four more times, always with "sail over," and once indeed the same whole verse of the first *Iliad*. Moreover, one then finds the verse *Odyssey* 3.71 = *Odyssey* 9.252 without change in the Homeric *Hymn to Apollo*, so that not only does the use over and over of the metaphor wear out its force, but the use with it of other words which are always the same, and which always bring back the phrase with the same rhythm at the same place in the verse, act strongly in making it habitual: Homer's formulaic diction is in this much like the chant of ritual. But if the phrase can thus lose its meaning for us, how much more must it have lost for the Greeks who lived when epic poetry flourished; for we know from Thucydides that the verse was used "everywhere in the same way by the old poets." Nor is this all. The reader has likewise found seven times in Homer and once in the *Hymns hygrē*, "wet," used all by itself for the sea; and itself is used as often in its metaphorical as in its real meaning: Homer also calls the sea "the fishy ways," "the misty ways," and speaks of "the speedy ways of the winds." By this time the reader would think of the meaning of the metaphor only if he stopped and tried to.

The metaphors which lie in the fixed epithets are of the same sort, and there is no need of going so fully into the background of their thought in the diction. Going on with the metaphors of the first *Iliad*, "winged words" is used by Homer one hundred and twenty-three times; "rosy-fingered dawn," twenty-seven times; "bronze-shirted Achaeans," twenty-four times; "silver-footed Thetis," thirteen times; "ox-eyed Hera," eleven times; "swift-faring ships," eleven times. "Fleet ships" is used four more times in the first book and a hundred times altogether. "Laughter unquenchable" is found only three times, and the phrase has been much admired in English chiefly because of the English words, but the phrase could not have had such vividness for Homer, who uses "unquenchable" over and over for the shouting of men, and also speaks of "might unquenchable" and "fame unquenchable." "Nourishing Phthia," where the idea of the metaphor is that of men tending beasts at pasture, is not found outside the first book of the *Iliad*, but the same metaphor is found sixteen times in "the nourishing earth" and in "nourishing Achaea."

It is clear to anyone reading the *Iliad* and *Odyssey* that these epithets are used by the poet largely for the help they give him in making his verses. Pope pointed out the same thing in the poetry of his own time, but where the English poets would from time to time pause and pick out an elegant epithet to fill out their couplet, having a large choice of such words and usually making the choice more or less in view of the thought at that point, Homer had usually only one epithet which he used, one might say, without thinking, and he had moreover for any noun that he used at all often a whole set of such epithets, each one made to fulfil a different metrical need. This technique of Homer's epithets can be analyzed into whole systems, as I have shown elsewhere. Here it will be enough to give a few examples from the phrases we have just studied. Homer, to simplify his verse-making, has a system of verses which expresses the idea such and such a person said, answered, asked, and so on, giving also the tone of voice when the poet wishes, or some other detail. One special line of this type which is needed is that in which the character who is to speak has been the subject of the last verses so that the use of his name in the line would be clumsy. The one verse that will do this is "he uttered winged words and addressed her." Homer has this one line for this one frequent need, and its use always brings in "winged words." Likewise, the formulaic line which expresses the idea "at dawn" always brings in the epithet "rosy-fingered." The metrical purpose of the other phrases could likewise be shown. Now the bearing of the practice on the meaning of the metaphor is clear: a phrase which is used because it is helpful is not being used because of its meaning.

There remain thirteen metaphors from the first *Iliad:* all but one of them bear only on the single word, which is thus no more than a word used in the place of some words which would have more usually been used. Pope's use of the word "crowned" for "topped" . . . was such a word. Here too the word is generally used by Homer alone often enough to wear out even for a modern reader the force of the metaphor. "Heads" for "peaks," a ship "running," a wave "howling," a god "standing over" a city, the "crowning" of bowls with wine, "a wall against war," "clothed in shame-lessness," even the curious and untranslatable *echet' empephuuia*, have all lost their meaning. "He shall swallow his wrath," "to pour out wealth," "a ravening king," and "thou shalt rend thy heart" may, for a while, keep the force of their metaphor because they are not found elsewhere in Homer. But because there is nothing outside the word to show the reader that Homer had the notion of the metaphor in his mind, and because he soon ceases in reading Homer to seek for any active force in such single words, they too finally become for him simply epic words with no more meaning than the usual term would have.

The last metaphor of the first book is that which praises the speech of Nestor: "from his tongue flowed voice sweeter than honey." Here, there can be no doubt, the metaphor was meant to be felt, but even here there is nothing which one could wish to take as the work of Homer's own new thought. First, the metaphor lies only in the words "sweeter than honey" since "flow" is used too often elsewhere of speech to carry here the idea of "flowing honey." Then the same idea is found twice in the *Theogony.* And finally the same metaphor is used again by Homer, this time, and here, as it happens, the following line shows clearly how little Homer felt its force,

unless one should wish to make Homer mix metaphors with all the ruthlessness of an Elizabethan. The metaphor is of anger:

> Sweeter than trickling honey
> it waxes in the breasts of men like smoke.
>
> (*Iliad* 18.109–10)

So even the one active metaphor of the first *Iliad*—and the rest of Homer
is in no way different—fails to do what Aristotle said the metaphor must
do—that is, show why Homer was like no other poet.

At least, it fails to do so in the way that Aristotle meant, for really
these metaphors that have been emptied of their meaning do show just
what the natural talent of Homer was: it was a talent that worked not in
the new but in the traditional. A careless reader of the foregoing pages
may have thought that each one of the fixed metaphors which had lost its
force was so much to be counted against Homer, but the example of fixed
diction in English poetry should have shown him that what the words and
phrases lost in meaning they had gained in kind of charm which pleased
the poet and his hearers. As the fixed diction of the Augustan age can only
be understood as the expression of a whole way of life which we may call
the proper, so Homer's traditional diction is the work of a way of life which
we may call the heroic, if one will give that word all the meaning it had
for the men of Homer's time. It is a term which can only be understood
in the measure that one can think and feel as they did, for the heroic was
to them no more or less than the statement of all that they would be or
would do if they could. To give form to this heroic cast of thought they
had the old tales that had come down in time, and they had a rhythm in
which to tell them, and words and phrases with which to tell them. The
making of this diction was due to countless poets and to many generations
who in time had found the heroic word and phrase for every thought, and
every word in it was holy and sweet and wondrous, and no one would think
of changing it wilfully. The Muses it was truly who gave those poets voices
sweeter than honey. And those parts of the diction which did not carry
the story itself, since their meaning was not needed for understanding, lost
that meaning, but became, as it were, a familiar music of which the mind
is pleasantly aware, but which it knows so well that it makes no effort to
follow it. Indeed, poetry thus approaches music most closely when the
words have rather a mood than a meaning. Nor should one think that since
the meaning is largely lost it ceases to matter if the meaning is good. Though
the meaning be felt rather than understood it is there, as it matters whether
music idly heard be bad or good. Of such a kind is the charm of the fixed
metaphor in Homer. It is an incantation of the heroic.

Aristotle did not understand this. Between the final vanishing of the old oral poetry and his own time two hundred years or more had already passed, and, thinking of Homer as he thought of the epic poetry of his own age, he failed to see that the metaphor was one thing for Antimachus and another for Homer. Modern critics, on the other hand, whose study was more careful, have found that Homer used the metaphor quite otherwise than Aristotle thought, and we ourselves have seen how utterly right they are, so that we are forced to choose between Aristotle's view of the nature of metaphor, in which case we must condemn Homer as mere copier, and the view that a traditional poet is good not because of the new that he brings into verse but because he knows how to make use of the traditional. If we do this we have found a charm far beyond any which can be found by men who wilfully wish to read Homer as they would any poetry of their own day. Indeed, the Greeks were not the men to carry the historical method of criticism to any such point. For that there had to come a new world which did not know the old by birthright but which, seeking rules of art for itself in times past reasoned much about that art, and more and more closely. In literary criticism generally this was the growth of the historical spirit. In Homeric criticism it was first the growing scorn for Homer's art in the sixteenth and seventeenth and eighteenth centuries in Italy, France, and England; then the period of Wolf and his followers who, however much they may have failed to grasp the meaning of what they did find, left no doubt that the *Iliad* and *Odyssey* were not such poems as we would ever write, or as Virgil and Dante and Milton wrote; and lastly of our own days in which, through a study of the oral poetries of peoples outside our own civilization, we have grasped the idea of traditional poetry. There is not a verse in Homer that does not become clearer and greater when we have understood that he too was a traditional poet. This way lies all true criticism and liking of his poems.

RACHEL BESPALOFF

Priam and Achilles
Break Bread

W̲e remember the scene on which the
Iliad ends: Priam has come to Achilles to reclaim his son's body. Prone at
the feet of the victor, he assumes a majesty that does not derive from his
office. By a new investiture, the king of Ilion has become "the king of
suppliants." From now on, this majesty is inviolable; in the calm that bathes
total disaster, it rises above injury and attains to saintliness. "Have some
awe of the gods, Achilles, and, remembering your own father, take pity
on me. I am far more pitiable than he, for I have endured what no other
mortal on earth has, to put to my mouth the hand of a man who has killed
my sons." This speech is quite without vehemence; self-respect gives the
words the exact weight of truth. In insisting on his right to pity, the
vanquished is not bowing down to destiny in the person of the man he is
entreating. The unheard-of ordeal he inflicts on himself, equal to the love
that sustains him, has nothing base about it. Here, however, occurs an
exceptional deviation from the laws of the mechanism of violence; this is
the only case in the *Iliad* where supplication sobers the man to whom it is
addressed instead of exasperating him. Suddenly it becomes plain that
Achilles is just as much Achilles' victim as Priam's sons were. At the sight
of the old king, to whom he has left nothing but the royalty of misfortune,
the conqueror is struck dumb; he seems to come to himself and be cured
of his frenzy. The old man's words arouse in him "the desire to mourn for

Translated by Mary McCarthy. From *On the Iliad*. Copyright © 1947 by The Bollingen
Foundation. Harper & Bros.

his father." The killer is a man again, burdened with childhood and death. "He took the old man's hand and gently pushed him away. Both remembered. . . ." Here, I think, comes one of the most beautiful silences in the *Iliad*—one of those absolute silences in which the din of the Trojan War, the vociferations of men and gods, and the rumblings of the Cosmos, are engulfed. The Becoming of the universe hangs suspended in this impalpable element whose duration is an instant and forever.

If Priam today were to think of entreating Achilles, he would find Achilles no longer there. Outrage, bent on destruction, does not stop with the body or the soul. It insinuates itself into the very consciousness that the vanquished has of himself. It makes the victim ugly in his own eyes. It even dirties the pity one can feel for him. Humiliation, poisoned by the lie that the fact of force is wrapped in, has never before so eroded the inwardness of existence. Certainly the pact between force and fraud is as old as humanity. But at least it used to be possible to distinguish between the two. Achilles, even in his most inconsequential actions, refuses to let the two be confused. He eludes, to some extent, the definition Péguy gives of the man to whom supplications are addressed: ". . . a man who has what they call a fine position . . . one of the strong ones of the earth . . . a happy man, a man who appears to be and who *is* happy." One of the strong ones of the earth Achilles certainly is; yet he is far from being a happy man, in spite of all his prizes and rewards. Unlike Agamemnon, so clever at turning the grudges of his dangerous ally to his own advantage, he is not a chief of state; he is no fox, like Odysseus, patron saint of those wily traders whose audacity made Greece into a world. Nor is he one of those harsh Achaian lords whose strength is measured numerically by the herds and land they possess. Achilles has conquered, but he will not exploit his victories. It is Odysseus who will level Ilion, guardian of the routes to Asia and the barbarian seas. With Achilles, cruelty is not a technique, still less a method, but a sort of paroxysm of irritation in pursuit and counterstroke. It seems to be his only means of renewing the illusion of omnipotence which supplies him with his reason for living. The perfect conformity of his nature to his vocation of destroyer makes him the least free person there is; but it gives him in return a bodily freedom which is in itself a magnificent spectacle. One does not have to lower oneself to admire this "great proud soul" that is its own prisoner in a sovereign body. But if Priam admires Achilles, Homer does not tell us that he honors him. We do not see him in any way subjugated by the prestige of the hero, though misfortune has made him bow to him. He would certainly not set him as an example for his people or his sons.

During this strange pause arranged for him by destiny on the extreme edge of suffering, Priam delights in Achilles' beauty—the beauty of force. The soul, delivered from the bondage of events, substitutes the order of contemplation for the order of passion; it is a moment of sacred truce. Under the influence of grief, the atrocious reality had hardened into something stony; now it melts, becomes fluid and fleeting. Hatred is disconcerted and relents. The two adversaries can exchange looks without seeing each other as targets, as objects which there is merit in destroying. Thanks to this detachment, private life, the love of the gods and of earthly beauty, the frail and obstinate will of whatever defies death to flower and bear fruit—all those things that rage had trampled down—are reborn and breathe again. "Come now, sit upon a seat, and let sorrows rest in our minds, in spite of our pain. Chill grief is profitless," Achilles advises. At this moment, he is overwhelmed by compassion, though still remorseless. He lifts up the prostrate old man, comforts him, praises his courage, and never for a moment repents the evil he has done him and will continue to do him. Priam's job is to resign himself and endure his fate. Achilles himself is "an unhappy son doomed to die before his time," in exile. All men live in affliction: there is no other basis for true equality. Homer was anxious to have precisely the conqueror recall this fact to the conquered. To save the suppliant's honor, but also to rid himself of a troublesome responsibility, Achilles ducks behind fatality. Priam receives in silence the lesson read him by his son's murderer. He does not protest against such scandalous behavior. This "wisdom" does not shock and anger him, as it did Job. "How long wilt Thou afflict my soul and oppress me with Thy sermons?" Unlike Job, he does not have the resource of pleading his cause before God. Job can blame God who has despoiled him and who refuses him justice. "The Almighty is living who fills my soul with bitterness." But Priam remains silent when Achilles tenders him these counsels of resignation. Why get angry, justify oneself, come to one's own defense? Encircled by a stony fatality, he must turn to stone himself, like Niobe. Christianity was nurtured on Job's lament. It may owe more than we think to Priam's silence.

Achilles mistrusts himself. He is afraid that he will break this truce with one of his habitual outbursts. Consequently, he is careful not to give that side of his nature any pretext. "Priam must not see his son. At the sight of his son, in his grief of heart he might not be able to control his wrath, and Achilles, then, might be angered and kill him, thus violating Zeus's command." That is what he wants to avoid. Cautioned by Thetis, he consents to return to Priam his son's corpse. "From the countless ransoms provided for Hector's head," he detaches two pieces of linen, also a well-woven tunic. And when his female captives have washed the body of his enemy and anointed it with oil, "and have thrown over it, besides the tunic, a beautiful piece of linen, then Achilles himself lifts it and sets it upon a bier which his comrades with him lift onto the well-polished chariot." When this is done, he must weep again, and then apologize to Patroclus for putting an end to the reprisals—he promises him a fair share of the ransom offered for the murderer's body. His scruples put to rest, he calms himself, tells Priam that his son has been returned, and invites him to share his meal. "Let us think about eating, noble old man; later on you may lament your dear son, bringing him back to Ilion; he will get many tears from you." Priam does not refuse this meal, these funeral meats between life and death, this intermission of peace and communion between war and war. Homer never leaves out anything that shows how the body reacts to the changes of the soul. He knows the hunger of a man hollow by affliction—the body must take its just revenge on the exhausted soul before the soul can extort new tears from it. This nocturnal meal is no dream-meal, removed from the life of the flesh; it is a celebration of the things that surpass and sanctify the body's existence. "When they have banished thirst and appetite," Achilles and his guest relax and forget, or at least want to forget, the inexpiable. "Priam marvels at Achilles and finds him beautiful." Achilles, for his part, marvels at Priam and is struck by his noble appearance.

Here again beauty holds out for the sufferer a possibility of redemption. These pauses in the flux of Becoming, where beauty achieves translucence in the eternal, are not "beautiful moments" without moorings, having no ties to reality. They do not stand beyond time that beats out the furious rhythm of action. When Helen climbs the ramparts of Troy or when Priam enters Achilles' tent, these places become premises of truth, where *forgetfulness of an offense* in the contemplation of the eternal is made possible (pardon for an offense being unknown to the ancient world). Thus we find Homer already expressing, with a fullness unequalled by the philosophers, an intuition of the identity of truth and beauty that fructifies Greek thought.

Holding himself a little withdrawn, standing, as it were, at the crossroads between the tragic and the contemplative order, Priam appears in the epic like the poet's delegate, the incarnation of Homeric wisdom (we do not realize that he dominates the poem until we have finished reading it). He typifies the watcher of tragedy, the man who sees it all, more completely and more truly than Zeus on Mount Ida because he is also a sufferer in the drama he is witnessing. Thanks to him, the prestige of weakness triumphs momentarily over the prestige of force. When he admires the enemy who is crushing him and justifies the stranger whose presence is the ruin of his city, the old king gives absolution to life in its totality. In this minute of ecstatic lucidity, the haggard world recomposes its features, and the horror of what is to come is abolished in suffering hearts. It is useless to go beyond this. For Priam, the future is the burning of Troy, and for Achilles, it is Paris' arrow. Job will regain through faith all the treasures of the real world, but what Priam is about to recover is only Hector's corpse. Yet out of this encounter on the borders of night comes a dawn of joy, unknown to joy, that reconciles life to itself. Niobe awakes and stretches her petrified limbs.

Achilles does not stop with carrying out the gods' orders. He goes farther and promises Priam to suspend the battle and hold the army in check until Hector's funeral is over. Then, with tenderness and respect, with that infinite delicacy that is the adjunct of true force, "he takes the old man by the wrist, lest he should fear in his mind."

This, then, is Achilles, more like Alexander or the great Condé than like the barbarians he descends from. His courtliness alone, apparent in the grace of his welcome, betrays a man of high lineage in whom brutality threatens an already high-wrought civilization. We must not forget that this disillusioned conqueror has a passion for music. Odysseus finds him at his *cythara* when he comes with his embassy to try to mollify him, the "beautiful, curiously wrought *cythara*" that he seized for his own use from the spoils of a city he destroyed. "His heart delighted in touching it and he was singing the exploits of heroes." We must not forget about this song. Friendship and music are Achilles' only deliverance. But is it deliverance that he really wants? The glory he has chosen in preference to a long life is the immortality of omnipotence, not the immortality of the soul. It would be possible to see in Achilles the Dionysiac strain, a passion for destruction growing out of a hatred for the destructibility of all things; and in Hector, the Apollonian part, the will toward preservation growing out of love for human achievements in their vulnerability. It would be possible, except for the fact that Homer's characters are infinitely more complex than we suspect if we let the concentration and voluntary abbreviation of the classic style lead us astray.

Close study of the poem's composition is an endless labor. Clarity multiplies the enigmas; the precision of the strokes emphasizes the evasiveness of life. Beneath the marvellous unity of the form, the ambiguity of the real comes to life again. The great symmetries of Becoming are respected and kept in focus throughout, but they only reveal more distinctly the presence of something incommensurable. Things that seem as if they ought to defy, by their very nature, plastic sculptural treatment—the furtive, the fleeting, the teeming of possibilities, the mirror play of contrasts—get incorporated into these statues somehow, by some miraculous process, and the calm of the statues is not for an instant disturbed. Homer's heroes appear to us in relief, as actors on the tragic scene; at the same time, however, they wear the halo of mortal existences. "To be a classic," says Nietzsche, "one must have *all* the gifts and *all* the needs, but one must force them all under the same yoke." And it might be Homer to whom Nietzsche is referring when he asserts that the greatness of the classic artist is measured by "the infallible sureness with which chaos obeys and takes form at the sound of his voice, at the necessity his hand expresses in a series of forms."

MAURICE BLANCHOT

The Song of the Sirens:
Encountering the Imaginary

The Sirens: evidently they really sang, but in a way that was not satisfying, that only implied in which direction lay the true sources of the song, the true happiness of the song. Nevertheless, through their imperfect songs, songs which were only a song still to come, they guided the sailor towards that space where singing would really begin. They were therefore not deceiving him; they were really leading him to his goal. But what happened when he reached that place? What was that place? It was a place where the only thing left was to disappear, because in this region of source and origin, music itself had disappeared more completely than in any other place in the world; it was like a sea into which the living would sink with their ears closed and where the Sirens, too, even they, as proof of their good will, would one day have to disappear.

What sort of song was the Sirens' song? What was its defect? Why did this defect make it so powerful? The answer some people have always given is that it was an inhuman song—no doubt a natural noise (what other kind is there?), but one that remained in the margins of nature; in any case, it was foreign to man, and very low, awakening in him that extreme delight in falling which he cannot satisfy in the normal conditions of his life. But, others say, there was something even stranger in the enchantment: it caused the Sirens merely to reproduce the ordinary singing of mankind, and because the Sirens, who were only animals—very beautiful

Translated by Lydia Davis. From *The Gaze of Orpheus*. Copyright © 1981 by Lydia Davis. Station Hill.

animals because they reflected womanly beauty—could sing the way men sing, their song became so extraordinary that it created in anyone who heard it a suspicion that all human singing was really inhuman. Was it despair, then, that killed men moved to passion by their own singing? That despair verged upon rapture. There was something marvellous about the song: it actually existed, it was ordinary and at the same time secret, a simple, everyday song which they were suddenly forced to recognize, sung in an unreal way by strange powers, powers which were, in a word, imaginary; it was a song from the abyss and once heard it opened an abyss in every utterance and powerfully enticed whoever heard it to disappear into that abyss.

Remember that this song was sung to sailors, men prepared to take risks and fearless in their impulses, and it was a form of navigation too: it was a distance, and what it revealed was the possibility of traveling that distance, of making the song into a movement towards the song and of making this movement into the expression of the greatest desire. Strange navigation, and what was its goal? It has always been possible to believe that those who approached it were not able to do more than approach it, that they died from impatience, from having said too soon: "Here it is; here is where I will drop anchor." Others have claimed that, on the contrary, it was too late: the goal had always been overshot; the enchantment held out an enigmatic promise and through this promise exposed men to the danger of being unfaithful to themselves, unfaithful to their human song and even to the essence of song, by awakening in them hope and the desire for a marvellous beyond, and that beyond was only a desert, as though the region where music originated was the only place completely without music, a sterile dry place where silence, like noise, burned all access to the song in anyone who had once had command of it. Does this mean that there was something evil in the invitation which issued from the depths? Were the Sirens nothing more than unreal voices, as custom would have us believe, unreal voices which were not supposed to be heard, a deception intended to seduce, and which could only be resisted by disloyal or cunning people?

Men have always made a rather ignoble effort to discredit the Sirens by accusing them flatly of lying: they were liars when they sang, frauds when they sighed, fictions when they were touched—nonexistent in every way; and the good sense of Ulysses was enough to do away with this puerile nonexistence.

It is true, Ulysses did overcome them, but how did he do it? Ulysses—the stubbornness and caution of Ulysses, the treachery by which he took pleasure in the spectacle of the Sirens without risking anything and without accepting the consequences; this cowardly, mediocre and tran-quil pleasure, this moderate pleasure, appropriate to a Greek of the period of decadence who never deserved to be the hero of the *Iliad*; this happy and confident cowardice, rooted in a privilege which set him apart from the common condition, the others having no right to such elite happiness but only to the pleasure of seeing their leader writhe ludicrously, grimacing with ecstasy in empty space, but also a right to the satisfaction of gaining mastery over their master (no doubt this was the lesson they learned, this was for them the true song of the Sirens): Ulysses' attitude, the amazing deafness of a man who is deaf because he can hear, was enough to fill the Sirens with a despair which until then had been felt only by men, and this despair turned them into real and beautiful girls, just this once real and worthy of their promise, and therefore capable of vanishing into the truth and depth of their song.

Even once the Sirens had been overcome by the power of tech-nology, which will always claim to trifle in safety with unreal (inspired) powers, Ulysses was still not free of them. They enticed him to a place which he did not want to fall into and, hidden in the heart of *The Odyssey*, which had become their tomb, they drew him—and many others—into that happy, unhappy voyage which is the voyage of the tale—of a song which is no longer immediate, but is narrated, and because of this made to seem harmless, an ode which has turned into an episode.

THE SECRET LAW OF THE TALE

This is not an allegory. A very obscure struggle takes place between every tale and the encounter with the Sirens, that enigmatic song which is powerful because of its insufficiency. A struggle in which Ulysses' pru-dence—whatever degree he has of truth, of mystification, of obstinate ability not to play the game of the gods—has always been exercised and perfected. What we call the novel was born of this struggle. What lies in the foreground of the novel is the previous voyage, the voyage which takes Ulysses to the moment of the encounter. This voyage is a completely human story, it takes place within the framework of human time, it is bound up with men's passions; it actually takes place and is rich enough and varied enough to consume all the narrator's strength and attention. Once the tale has become a novel, far from appearing poorer it takes on all the richness and breadth of an exploration, one which sometimes embraces the immensity of the voyage and sometimes confines itself to a small patch of space on the deck and occasionally descends into the depths of the ship where no one ever knew what the hope of the sea was. The rule the sailors must obey is this:

no allusion can be made to a goal or a destination. And with good reason, surely. No one can sail away with the deliberate intention of reaching the Isle of Capri, no one can set his course for it, and if anyone decides to go there he will still proceed only by chance, by some chance to which he is linked by an understanding difficult to penetrate. The rule is therefore silence, discretion, forgetfulness.

We must recognize that a certain preordained modesty, a desire not to have any pretensions and not to lead to anything, would be enough to make many novels irreproachable books and to make the genre of the novel the most attractive of genres, the one which, in its discretion and its cheerful nothingness, takes upon itself the task of forgetting what others degrade by calling it the essential. Diversion is its profound song. To keep changing direction, to move on in an apparently random way, avoiding all goals, with an uneasy motion that is transformed into a happy sort of distraction—this has been its primary and most secure justification. It is no small thing to make a game of human time and out of that game to create a free occupation, one stripped of all immediate interest and usefulness, essentially superficial and yet in its surface movement capable of absorbing all being. But clearly, if the novel fails to play this role today, it is because technics has transformed men's time and their ways of amusing themselves.

The tale begins at a point where the novel does not go, though in its refusals and its rich neglect it is leading towards it. Heroically, pretentiously, the tale is the tale of one single episode, that in which Ulysses encounters the inadequate and enticing song of the Sirens. Except for this great, naive pretension, apparently nothing has changed, and because of its form the tale seems to continue to fulfill its ordinary vocation as a narrative. For example, *Aurélia* is presented as the simple account of a meeting, and so is *Une Saison en Enfer,* and so is *Nadja.* Something has happened, something which someone has experienced who tells about it afterwards, in the same way that Ulysses needed to experience the event and survive it in order to become Homer, who told about it. Of course the tale is usually about an exceptional event, one which eludes the forms of everyday time and the world of the usual sort of truth, perhaps any truth. This is why it so insistently rejects everything which could connect it with the frivolity of a fiction (the novel, on the other hand, contains only what is believable and familiar and yet is very anxious to pass for fiction). In the *Gorgias,* Plato says "Listen to a beautiful tale. Now you will think it is a fable, but I believe it is a tale. I will tell you what I am going to tell you as a true thing." What he told was the story of the Last Judgment.

Yet if we regard the tale as the true telling of an exceptional event which has taken place and which someone is trying to report, then we have not even come close to sensing the true nature of the tale. The tale is not the narration of an event, but that event itself, the approach to that event, the place where that event is made to happen—an event which is yet to come and through whose power of attraction the tale can hope to come into being, too.

This is a very delicate relationship, undoubtedly a kind of extravagance, but it is the secret law of the tale. The tale is a movement towards a point, a point which is not only unknown, obscure, foreign, but such that apart from this movement it does not seem to have any sort of real prior existence, and yet it is so imperious that the tale derives its power of attraction only from this point, so that it cannot even "begin" before reaching it—and yet only the tale and the unpredictable movement of the tale create the space where the point becomes real, powerful, and alluring.

WHEN ULYSSES BECOMES HOMER

What would happen if instead of being two distinct people Ulysses and Homer comfortably shared their roles, and were one and the same presence? If the tale Homer told were simply Ulysses' movement within the space opened up for him by the Song of the Sirens? If Homer's capacity to narrate were limited by how far he went as Ulysses—a Ulysses free of all impediments, though tied down—towards the place where the power to speak and to narrate was apparently promised to him as long as he disappeared there?

This is one of the strange things about the tale, or shall we say one of its pretensions. It only "narrates" itself, and in the same moment that this narration comes into being it creates what it is narrating; it cannot exist as a narration unless it creates what is happening in that narration, because then it contains the point or the plane where the reality "described" by the story can keep uniting with its reality as a tale, can secure this reality and be secured by it.

But isn't this a rather naive madness? In one sense, yes. That is why there are no tales, and that is why there is no lack of tales.

To listen to the Song of the Sirens is to cease to be Ulysses and become Homer, but only in Homer's story does the real encounter take place, where Ulysses becomes the one who enters into a relationship with the force of the elements and the voice of the abyss.

This seems obscure, it is like the embarrassment the first man would have felt if, in order to be created, he himself had had to pronounce in a completely human way the divine *Fiat lux* that would actually cause his eyes to open.

Actually, this way of presenting things simplifies them a great deal—which is why it produces these artificial or theoretical complications. Of course it is true that only in Melville's book does Ahab meet Moby Dick; yet it is also true that only this encounter allows Melville to write the book, it is such an imposing encounter, so enormous, so special that it goes beyond all the levels on which it takes place, all the moments in time where we attempt to situate it, and seems to be happening long before the book begins, but it is of such a nature that it also could not happen more than once, in the future of the work and in that sea which is what the work will be, having become an ocean on its own scale.

Ahab and the whale are engaged in a drama, what we can call a metaphysical drama, using the word loosely, and the Sirens and Ulysses are engaged in the same struggle. Each wants to be everything, wants to be the absolute world, which would make it impossible for him to coexist with the other absolute world, and yet the greatest desire of each is for this coexistence and this encounter. To bring Ahab and the whale, the Sirens and Ulysses together in one space—this is the secret wish which turns Ulysses into Homer and Ahab into Melville, and makes the world that results from this union into the greatest, most terrible, and most beautiful of all possible worlds: a book, alas, only a book.

Of Ahab and Ulysses, the one with the greater will to power is not the more liberated. Ulysses has the kind of deliberate stubbornness which leads to universal domination: his trick is to seem to limit his power; in a cold and calculating way he finds out what he can still do, faced with the other power. He will be everything, if he can maintain a limit, if he can preserve that interval between the real and the imaginary which is just what the Song of the Sirens invites him to cross. The result is a sort of victory for him, a dark disaster for Ahab. We cannot deny that Ulysses understood something of what Ahab saw, but he stood fast within that understanding, while Ahab became lost in the image. In other words, one resisted the metamorphosis while the other entered it and disappeared inside it. After the test, Ulysses is just as he had been before, and the world is poorer, perhaps, but firmer and more sure. Ahab is no longer, and for Melville himself the world keeps threatening to sink into that worldless space towards which the fascination of one single image draws him.

THE METAMORPHOSIS

The tale is bound up with the metamorphosis alluded to by Ulysses and Ahab. The action that the tale causes to take place in the present is that of metamorphosis on all the levels it can attain. If for the sake of convenience—because this statement cannot be exact—we say that what makes the novel move forward is everyday, collective or personal time, or more precisely, the desire to urge time to speak, then the tale moves forward through that *other* time, it makes that other voyage, which is the passage from the real song to the imaginary song, the movement which causes the real song to become imaginary little by little, though all at once (and this "little by little, though all at once" is the very time of the metamorphosis), to become an enigmatic song always at a distance, designating this distance as a space to be crossed and designating the place to which it leads as the point where singing will cease to be a lure.

The tale wants to cross this space, and what moves it is the transformation demanded by the empty fullness of this space, a transformation which takes place in all directions and no doubt powerfully transforms the writer but transforms the tale itself no less and everything at stake in the tale, where in a sense nothing happens except this very crossing. . . .

All the ambiguity arises from the ambiguity of time which comes into play here and which allows us to say and to feel that the fascinating image of the experience is present at a certain moment, even though this presence does not belong to any present, and even destroys the present which it seems to enter. It is true, Ulysses was really sailing, and one day, on a certain date, he encountered the enigmatic song. And so he can say: now—this is happening now. But what happened now? The presence of a song which was still to be sung. And what did he touch in the presence? Not the occurence of an encounter which had become present, but the overture of the infinite movement which is the encounter itself, always at a distance from the place where it asserts itself and the moment when it asserts itself, because it is this very distance, this imaginary distance, in which absence is realized, and only at the end of this distance does the event begin to take place, at a point where the proper truth of the encounter comes into being and where, in any case, the words which speak it would originate.

Always still to come, always in the past already, always present—beginning so abruptly that it takes your breath away—and yet unfurling itself like the eternal return and renewal—"Ah," says Goethe, "*in another age you were my sister or my wife*"—this is the nature of the event for which the tale is the approach. This event upsets relations in time, and yet affirms time, the particular way time happens, the tale's own time which enters the narrator's duration in such a way as to transform it, and the time of the metamorphoses where the different temporal ecstasies coincide in an imaginary simultaneity and in the form of the space which art is trying to create.

MAX HORKHEIMER,
THEODOR W. ADORNO

The Concept of Enlightenment

The entanglement of myth, domination, and labor is preserved in one of the Homeric narratives. Book XII of the *Odyssey* tells of the encounter with the Sirens. Their allurement is that of losing oneself in the past. But the hero to whom the temptation is offered has reached maturity through suffering. Throughout the many mortal perils he has had to endure, the unity of his own life, the identity of the individual, has been confirmed for him. The regions of time part for him as do water, earth, and air. For him, the flood of that-which-was has retreated from the rock of the present, and the future lies cloudy on the horizon. What Odysseus left behind him entered into the nether world; for the self is still so close to prehistoric myth, from whose womb it tore itself, that its very own experienced past becomes mythic prehistory. And it seeks to encounter that myth through the fixed order of time. The threefold schema is intended to free the present moment from the power of the past by referring that power behind the absolute barrier of the unrepeatable and placing it at the disposal of the present as practicable knowledge. The compulsion to rescue what is gone as what is living instead of using it as the material of progress was appeased only in art, to which history itself appertains as a presentation of past life. So long as art declines to pass as cognition and is thus separated from practice, social practice tolerates it as it tolerates pleasure. But the Sirens' song has not yet been rendered powerless by reduction to the condition of art. They know "everything that ever happened on this so fruitful earth," including the events in which Odysseus himself took part, "all those

---

things that Argos' sons and the Trojans suffered by the will of the gods on the plains of Troy." While they directly evoke the recent past, with the irresistible promise of pleasure as which their song is heard, they threaten the patriarchal order which renders to each man his life only in return for his full measure of time. Whoever falls for their trickery must perish, whereas only perpetual presence of mind forces an existence from nature. Even though the Sirens know all that has happened, they demand the future as the price of that knowledge, and the promise of the happy return is the deception with which the past ensnares the one who longs for it. Odysseus is warned by Circe, that divinity of reversion to the animal, whom he resisted and who therefore gives him strength to resist other powers of disintegration. But the allurement of the Sirens remains superior; no one who hears their song can escape. Men had to do fearful things to themselves before the self, the identical, purposive, and virile nature of man, was formed, and something of that recurs in every childhood. The strain of holding the I together adheres to the I in all stages; and the temptation to lose it has always been there with the blind determination to maintain it. The narcotic intoxication which permits the atonement of deathlike sleep for the euphoria in which the self is suspended, is one of the oldest social arrangements which mediate between self-preservation and self-destruction—an attempt of the self to survive itself. The dread of losing the self and of abrogating together with the self the barrier between oneself and other life, the fear of death and destruction, is intimately associated with a promise of happiness which threatened civilization in every moment. Its road was that of obedience and labor, over which fulfillment shines forth perpetually—but only as illusive appearance, as devitalized beauty. The mind of Odysseus, inimical both to his own death and to his own happiness, is aware of this. He knows only two possible ways to escape. One of them he prescribes for his men. He plugs their ears with wax, and they must row with all their strength. Whoever would survive must not hear the temptation of that which is unrepeatable, and he is able to survive only by being unable to hear it. Society has always made provision for that. The laborers must be fresh and concentrate as they look ahead, and must ignore whatever lies to one side. They must doggedly sublimate in additional effort the drive that impels to diversion. And so they become practical.—The other possibility Odysseus, the seigneur who allows the others to labor for themselves, reserves to himself. He listens, but while bound impotently to the mast; the greater the temptation the more he has his bonds tightened—just as later the burghers would deny themselves happiness all the more doggedly as it drew closer to them with the growth of their own power. What Odysseus hears is without consequence for him; he is able only to nod his head as a sign to be set free from his bonds; but it is too late; his men, who do not listen, know only the song's danger but nothing of its beauty, and leave him at the mast in order to save him and themselves. They reproduce the oppressor's life together with their own, and the oppressor is no longer able to escape his social role. The bonds with which he has irremediably tied himself to practice, also keep the Sirens away from practice: their temptation is neutralized and becomes a mere object of contemplation—becomes art. The prisoner is present at a concert, an inactive eavesdropper like later concertgoers, and his spirited call for liberation fades like applause. Thus the enjoyment of art and manual labor break apart as the world of prehistory is left behind. The epic already contains the appropriate theory. The cultural material is in exact correlation to work done according to command; and both are grounded in the inescapable compulsion to social domination of nature.

Measures such as those taken on Odysseus' ship in regard to the Sirens form presentient allegory of the dialectic of enlightenment. Just as the capacity of representation is the measure of domination, and domination is the most powerful thing that can be represented in most performances, so the capacity of representation is the vehicle of progress and regression at one and the same time. Under the given conditions, exemption from work—not only among the unemployed but even at the other end of the social scale—also means disablement. The rulers experience existence, with which they need no longer concern themselves, only as a substratum, and hence wholly ossify into the condition of the commanding self. Primitive man experienced the natural thing merely as the evasive object of desire. "But the master, who has interposed the servant between it and himself, in this way relates himself only to the dependence of the thing and enjoys it pure; however, he leaves the aspect of [its] independence to the servant, who works upon it." Odysseus is represented in labor. Just as he cannot yield to the temptation to self-abandonment, so, as proprietor, he finally renounces even participation in labor, and ultimately even its management, whereas his men—despite their closeness to things—cannot enjoy their labor because it is performed under pressure, in desperation, with senses stopped by force. The servant remains enslaved in body and soul; the master regresses. No authority has yet been able to escape paying this price, and the apparent cyclical nature of the advance of history is partly explained by this debilitation, the equivalent of power. Mankind, whose versatility and knowledge become differentiated with the division of labor, is at the same time forced back to anthropologically more primitive stages, for with the technical easing of life the persistence of domination brings about a fixation of the instincts by means of heavier repression. Imagination atrophies. The disaster is not merely that individuals might remain behind society or its material production. Where the evolution of the machine has already turned into that of the machinery of domination (so that technical and social tendencies, always interwoven, converge in the total schematization of men), untruth is not represented merely by the outdistanced. As against that, adaptation to the power of progress involves the progress of power, and each time anew brings about those degenerations which show not unsuccessful but successful progress to be its contrary. The curse of irresistible progress is irresistible regression.

This regression is not restricted to the experience of the sensuous world bound up with the circumambient animate, but at the same time affects the self-dominant intellect, which separates from sensuous experience in order to subjugate it. The unification of intellectual functions by means of which domination over the senses is achieved, the resignation of thought to the rise of unanimity, means the impoverishment of thought and of experience: the separation of both areas leaves both impaired. The restriction of thought to organization and administration, practiced by rulers from the cunning Odysseus to the naïve managing directors of today, necessarily implies the restriction which comes upon the great as soon as it is no longer merely a question of manipulating the small. Hence the spirit becomes the very apparatus of domination and self-domination which bourgeois thought has always mistakenly supposed it to be. The stopped ears which the pliable proletarians have retained ever since the time of myth have no advantage over the immobility of the master. The over-maturity of society lives by the immaturity of the dominated. The more complicated and precise the social, economic, and scientific apparatus with whose service the production system has long harmonized the body, the more impoverished the experiences which it can offer. The elimination of qualities, their conversion into functions, is translated from science by means of rationalized modes of labor to the experiential world of nations, and tends to approximate it once more to that of the amphibians. The regression of the masses today is their inability to hear the unheard-of with their own ears, to touch the unapprehended with their own hands—the new form of delusion which deposes every conquered mythic form. Through the mediation of the total society which embraces all relations and emotions, men are once again made to be that against which the evolutionary law of society, the principle of self, had turned: mere species beings, exactly like one another through isolation in the forcibly united collectivity. The oarsmen, who cannot speak to one another, are each of them yoked in the same rhythm as the modern worker in the factory, movie theater, and collective. The actual working conditions in society compel conformism—not the conscious influences which also made the suppressed men dumb and separated them from truth. The impotence of the worker is not merely a stratagem of the rulers, but the logical consequence of the industrial society into which the ancient Fate—in the very course of the effort to escape it—has finally changed.

But this logical necessity is not conclusive. It remains tied to domination, as both its reflection and its tool. Therefore its truth is no less questionable than its evidence is irrefutable.

SIMONE WEIL

"The Iliad," or the Poem of Force

The true hero, the true subject, the center of the *Iliad* is force. Force employed by man, force that enslaves man, force before which man's flesh shrinks away. In this work, at all times, the human spirit is shown as modified by its relations with force, as swept away, blinded, by the very force it imagined it could handle, as deformed by the weight of the force it submits to. For those dreamers who considered that force, thanks to progress, would soon be a thing of the past, the *Iliad* could appear as an historical document; for others, whose powers of recognition are more acute and who perceive force, today as yesterday, at the very center of human history, the *Iliad* is the purest and the loveliest of mirrors.

To define force—it is that x that turns anybody who is subjected to it into a *thing*. Exercised to the limit, it turns man into a thing in the most literal sense: it makes a corpse out of him. Somebody was here, and the next minute there is nobody here at all; this is a spectacle the *Iliad* never wearies of showing us:

> . . . the horses
> Rattled the empty chariots through the files of battle,
> Longing for their noble drivers. But they on the ground
> Lay, dearer to the vultures than to their wives.

The hero becomes a *thing* dragged behind a chariot in the dust:

Translated by Mary McCarthy. From *The Iliad, or The Poem of Force*. Copyright © 1945 by Dwight Macdonald. Pendle Hill.

> All around, his black hair
> Was spread; in the dust his whole head lay,
> That once-charming head; now Zeus had let his enemies
> Defile it on his native soil.

The bitterness of such a spectacle is offered us absolutely undiluted. No comforting fiction intervenes; no consoling prospect of immortality; and on the hero's head no washed-out halo of patriotism descends.

> His soul, fleeing his limbs, passed to Hades,
> Mourning its fate, forsaking its youth and its vigor.

Still more poignant—so painful is the contrast—is the sudden evocation, as quickly rubbed out, of another world: the faraway, precarious, touching world of peace, of the family, the world in which each man counts more than anything else to those about him.

> She ordered her bright-haired maids in the palace
> To place on the fire a large tripod, preparing
> A hot bath for Hector, returning from battle.
> Foolish woman! Already he lay, far from hot baths,
> Slain by grey-eyed Athena, who guided Achilles' arm.

Far from hot baths he was indeed, poor man. And not he alone. Nearly all the *Iliad* takes place far from hot baths. Nearly all of human life, then and now, takes place far from hot baths.

Here we see force in its grossest and most summary form—the force that kills. How much more varied in its processes, how much more surprising in its effects is the other force, the force that does *not* kill, i.e., that does not kill just yet. It will surely kill, it will possibly kill, or perhaps it merely hangs, poised and ready, over the head of the creature it *can* kill, at any moment, which is to say at every moment. In whatever aspect, its effect is the same: it turns a man into a stone. From its first property (the ability to turn a human being into a thing by the simple method of killing him) flows another, quite prodigious too in its own way, the ability to turn a human being into a thing while he is still alive. He is alive; he has a soul; and yet—he is a thing. An extraordinary entity this—a thing that has a soul. And as for the soul, what an extraordinary house it finds itself in! Who can say what it costs it, moment by moment, to accommodate itself to this residence, how much writhing and bending, folding and pleating are required of it? It was not made to live inside a thing; if it does so, under pressure of necessity, there is not a single element of its nature to which violence is not done.

A man stands disarmed and naked with a weapon pointing at him; this person becomes a corpse before anybody or anything touches him. Just a minute ago, he was thinking, acting, hoping:

> Motionless, he pondered. And the other drew near,
> Terrified, anxious to touch his knees, hoping in his heart
> To escape evil death and black destiny . . .
> With one hand he clasped, suppliant, his knees,
> While the other clung to the sharp spear, not letting go . . .

Soon, however, he grasps the fact that the weapon which is pointing at him will not be diverted; and now, still breathing, he is simply matter; still thinking, he can think no longer:

> Thus spoke the brilliant son of Priam
> In begging words. But he heard a harsh reply:
> He spoke. And the other's knees and heart failed him.
> Dropping his spear, he knelt down, holding out his arms.
> Achilles, drawing his sharp sword, struck
> Through the neck and breastbone. The two-edged sword
> Sunk home its full length. The other, face down,
> Lay still, and the black blood ran out, wetting the ground.

If a stranger, completely disabled, disarmed, strengthless, throws himself on the mercy of a warrior, he is not, by this very act, condemned to death; but a moment of impatience on the warrior's part will suffice to relieve him of his life. In any case, his flesh has lost that very important property which in the laboratory distinguishes living flesh from dead—the galvanic response. If you give a frog's leg an electric shock, it twitches. If you confront a human being with the touch or sight of something horrible or terrifying, this bundle of muscles, nerves, and flesh likewise twitches. Alone of all living things, the suppliant we have just described neither quivers nor trembles. He has lost the right to do so. As his lips advance to touch the object that is for him of all things most charged with horror, they do not draw back on his teeth—they cannot:

> No one saw great Priam enter. He stopped,
> Clasped the knees of Achilles, kissed his hands,
> Those terrible man-killing hands that had slaughtered so many of his
> sons.

The sight of a human being pushed to such an extreme of suffering chills us like the sight of a dead body:

> As when harsh misfortune strikes a man if in his own country
> He has killed a man, and arrives at last at someone else's door,

The door of a rich man; a shudder seizes those who see him.
So Achilles shuddered to see divine Priam;
The others shuddered too, looking one at the other.

But this feeling lasts only a moment. Soon the very presence of the suffering
creature is forgotten:

He spoke. The other, remembering his own father, longed to weep;
Taking the old man's arm, he pushed him away.
Both were remembering. Thinking of Hector, killer of men,
Priam wept, abased at the feet of Achilles.
But Achilles wept, now for his father,
Now for Patroclus. And their sobs resounded through the house.

It was not insensibility that made Achilles with a single movement of his
hand push away the old man who had been clinging to his knees; Priam's
words, recalling his own old father, had moved him to tears. It was merely
a question of his being as free in his attitudes and movements as if, clasping
his knees, there were not a suppliant but an inert object. Anybody who is
in our vicinity exercises a certain power over us by his very presence, and
a power that belongs to him alone, that is, the power of halting, repressing,
modifying each movement that our body sketches out. If we step aside for
a passer-by on the road, it is not the same thing as stepping aside to avoid
a billboard; alone in our rooms, we get up, walk about, sit down again
quite differently from the way we do when we have a visitor. But this
indefinable influence that the presence of another human being has on us
is not exercised by men whom a moment of impatience can deprive of life,
who can die before even thought has a chance to pass sentence on them.
In their presence, people move about as if they were not there; they, on
their side, running the risk of being reduced to nothing in a single instant,
imitate nothingness in their own persons. Pushed, they fall. Fallen, they
lie where they are, unless chance gives somebody the idea of raising them
up again. But supposing that at long last they have been picked up, honored
with cordial remarks, they still do not venture to take this resurrection
seriously; they dare not express a wish lest an irritated voice return them
forever to silence:

He spoke; the old man trembled and obeyed.

At least a suppliant, once his prayer is answered, becomes a human
being again, like everybody else. But there are other, more unfortunate
creatures who have become things for the rest of their lives. Their days
hold no pastimes, no free spaces, no room in them for any impulse of their
own. It is not that their life is harder than other men's nor that they occupy

a lower place in the social hierarchy; no, they are another human species, a compromise between a man and a corpse. The idea of a person's being a thing is a logical contradiction. Yet what is impossible in logic becomes true in life, and the contradiction lodged within the soul tears it to shreds. This thing is constantly aspiring to be a man or a woman, and never achieving it—here, surely, is death but death strung out over a whole lifetime; here, surely is life, but life that death congeals before abolishing.

This strange fate awaits the virgin, the priest's daughter:

> I will not give her up. Sooner shall old age come upon her
> In our house in Argos, far from her native land,
> Tending the loom and sharing my bed.

It awaits the young wife, the young mother, the prince's bride:

> And perhaps one day, in Argos, you will weave cloth for another,
> And the Messeian or Hyperian water you will fetch,
> Much against your will, yielding to a harsh necessity.

It awaits the baby, heir to the royal scepter:

> Soon they will be carried off in the hollow ships,
> I with them. And you, my child, will either go with me,
> To a land where you will work at wretched tasks,
> Laboring for a pitiless master. . . .

In the mother's eyes, such a fate is, for her child, as terrible as death; the husband would rather die than see his wife reduced to it; all the plagues of heaven are invoked by the father against the army that subjects his daughter to it. Yet the victims themselves are beyond all this. Curses, feelings of rebellion, comparisons, reflections on the future and the past, are obliterated from the mind of the captive; and memory itself barely lingers on. Fidelity to his city and his dead is not the slave's privilege.

And what does it take to make the slave weep? The misfortune of his master, his oppressor, despoiler, pillager, of the man who laid waste his town and killed his dear ones under his very eyes. This man suffers or dies; *then* the slave's tears come. And really why not? This is for him the only occasion on which tears are permitted, are, indeed, required. A slave will always cry whenever he can do so with impunity—his situation keeps tears on tap for him.

> She spoke, weeping, and the women groaned,
> Using the pretext of Patroclus to bewail their own torments.

Since the slave has no license to express anything except what is pleasing to his master, it follows that the only emotion that can touch or enliven him a little, that can reach him in the desolation of his life, is the emotion of love for his master. There is no place else to send the gift of love; all other outlets are barred, just as, with the horse in harness, bit, shafts, reins bar every way but one. And if, by some miracle, in the slave's breast a hope is born, the hope of becoming, some day, through somebody's influence, *someone* once again, how far won't these captives go to show love and thankfulness, even though these emotions are addressed to the very men who should, considering the very recent past, still reek with horror for them:

> My husband, to whom my father and respected mother gave me,
> I saw before the city transfixed by the sharp bronze.
> My three brothers, children, with me, of a single mother,
> So dear to me! They all met their fatal day.
> But you did not allow me to weep, when swift Achilles
> Slaughtered my husband and laid waste the city of Mynes.
> You promised me that I would be taken by divine Achilles,
> For his legitimate wife, that he would carry me away in his ships,
> To Pythia, where our marriage would be celebrated among the
>   Myrmidons,
> So without respite I mourn for you, you who have always been gentle.

To lose more than the slave does is impossible, for he loses his whole inner life. A fragment of it he may get back if he sees the possibility of changing his fate, but this is his only hope. Such is the empire of force, as extensive as the empire of nature. Nature, too, when vital needs are at stake, can erase the whole inner life, even the grief of a mother:

> But the thought of eating came to her, when she was tired of tears.

Force, in the hands of another, exercises over the soul the same tyranny that extreme hunger does; for it possesses, and *in perpetuo*, the power of life and death. Its rule, moreover, is as cold and hard as the rule of inert matter. The man who knows himself weaker than another is more alone in the heart of a city than a man lost in the desert.

> Two casks are placed before Zeus's doorsill,
> Containing the gifts he gives, the bad in one, the good in the other . . .
> The man to whom he gives baneful gifts, he exposes to outrage;
> A frightful need drives across the divine earth;
> He is a wanderer, and gets no respect from gods or men.

Force is as pitiless to the man who possesses it, or thinks he does, as it is to its victims; the second it crushes, the first it intoxicates. The truth is, nobody really possesses it. The human race is not divided up, in the *Iliad,* into conquered persons, slaves, suppliants, on the one hand, and conquerors and chiefs on the other. In this poem there is not a single man who does not at one time or another have to bow his neck to force. The common soldier in the *Iliad* is free and has the right to bear arms; nevertheless he is subject to the indignity of orders and abuse:

> But whenever he came upon a commoner shouting out,
> He struck him with his scepter and spoke sharply:
> "Good for nothing! Be still and listen to your betters,
> You are weak and cowardly and unwarlike,
> You count for nothing, neither in battle nor in council."

Thersites pays dear for the perfectly reasonable comments he makes, comments not at all different, moreover, from those made by Achilles:

> He hit him with his scepter on back and shoulders,
> So that he doubled over, and a great tear welled up,
> And a bloody welt appeared on his back
> Under the golden scepter. Frightened, he sat down,
> Wiping away his tears, bewildered and in pain.
> Troubled though they were, the others laughed long at him.

Achilles himself, that proud hero, the undefeated, is shown us at the outset of the poem, weeping with humiliation and helpless grief—the woman he wanted for his bride has been taken from under his nose, and he has not dared to oppose it:

> . . . But Achilles
> Weeping, sat apart from his companions,
> By the white-capped waves, staring over the boundless ocean.

What has happened is that Agamemnon has deliberately humiliated Achilles, to show that he himself is the master:

> . . . So you will learn
> That I am greater than you, and anyone else will hesitate
> To treat me as an equal and set himself against me.

But a few days pass and now the supreme commander is weeping in his turn. He must humble himself, he must plead, and have, moreover, the added misery of doing it all in vain.

In the same way, there is not a single one of the combatants who is spared the shameful experience of fear. The heroes quake like everybody else. It only needs a challenge from Hector to throw the whole Greek force into consternation—except for Achilles and his men, and they did not happen to be present:

He spoke and all grew still and held their peace,
Ashamed to refuse, afraid to accept.

But once Ajax comes forward and offers himself, fear quickly changes sides:

A shudder of terror ran through the Trojans, making their limbs weak;
And Hector himself felt his heart leap in his breast.
But he no longer had the right to tremble, or to run away. . . .

Two days later, it is Ajax's turn to be terrified:

Zeus the father on high, makes fear rise in Ajax.
He stops, overcome, puts behind him his buckler made of seven hides,
Trembles, looks at the crowd around, like a wild beast. . . .

Even to Achilles the moment comes; he too must shake and stammer with fear, though it is a river that has this effect on him, not a man. But, with the exception of Achilles, every man in the *Iliad* tastes a moment of defeat in battle. Victory is less a matter of valor than of blind destiny, which is symbolized in the poem by Zeus's golden scales:

Then Zeus the father took his golden scales,
In them he put the two fates of death that cuts down all men,
One for the Trojans, tamers of horses, one for the bronze-sheathed
  Greeks.
He seized the scales by the middle; it was the fatal day of Greece that
  sank.

By its very blindness, destiny establishes a kind of justice. Blind also is she who decrees to warriors punishment in kind. He that takes the sword, will perish by the sword. The *Iliad* formulated the principle long before the Gospels did, and in almost the same terms:

Ares is just, and kills those who kill.

Perhaps all men, by the very act of being born, are destined to suffer violence; yet this is a truth to which circumstance shuts men's eyes. The strong are, as a matter of fact, never absolutely strong, nor are the weak absolutely weak, but neither is aware of this. They have in common a refusal to believe that they both belong to the same species: the weak see no relation between themselves and the strong, and vice versa. The man who is the possessor of force seems to walk through a non-resistant element; in the human substance that surrounds him nothing has the power to interpose, between the impulse and the act, the tiny interval that is reflection. Where there is no room for reflection, there is none either for justice or prudence. Hence we see men in arms behaving harshly and madly.

We see their sword bury itself in the breast of a disarmed enemy who is in the very act of pleading at their knees. We see them triumph over a dying man by describing to him the outrages his corpse will endure. We see Achilles cut the throats of twelve Trojan boys on the funeral pyre of Patroclus as naturally as we cut flowers for a grave. These men, wielding power, have no suspicion of the fact that the consequences of their deeds will at length come home to them—they too will bow the neck in their turn. If you can make an old man fall silent, tremble, obey, with a single word of your own, why should it occur to you that the curses of this old man, who is after all a priest, will have their own importance in the gods' eyes? Why should you refrain from taking Achilles' girl away from him if you know that neither he nor she can do anything but obey you? Achilles rejoices over the sight of the Greeks fleeing in misery and confusion. What could possibly suggest to him that this rout, which will last exactly as long as he wants it to and end when his mood indicates it, that this very rout will be the cause of his friend's death, and, for that matter, of his own? Thus it happens that those who have force on loan from fate count on it too much and are destroyed.

But at the time their own destruction seems impossible to them. For they do not see that the force in their possession is only a limited quantity; nor do they see their relations with other human beings as a kind of balance between unequal amounts of force. Since other people do not impose on their movements that halt, that interval of hesitation, wherein lies all our consideration for our brothers in humanity, they conclude that destiny has given complete license to them, and none at all to their inferiors. And at this point they exceed the measure of the force that is actually at their disposal. Inevitably they exceed it, since they are not aware that it is limited. And now we see them committed irretrievably to chance; suddenly things cease to obey them. Sometimes chance is kind to them, sometimes cruel. But in any case there they are, exposed, open to misfortune; gone is the armor of power that formerly protected their naked souls; nothing, no shield, stands between them and tears.

This retribution, which has a geometrical rigor, which operates automatically to penalize the abuse of force, was the main subject of Greek thought. It is the soul of the epic. Under the name of Nemesis, it functions as the mainspring of Aeschylus's tragedies. To the Pythagoreans, to Socrates and Plato, it was the jumping-off point of speculation upon the nature of man and the universe. Wherever Hellenism has penetrated, we find the idea of it familiar. In Oriental countries which are steeped in Buddhism, it is perhaps this Greek idea that has lived on under the name of Kharma.

The Occident, however, has lost it, and no longer even has a word to express it in any of its languages: conceptions of limit, measure, equilibrium, which ought to determine the conduct of life are, in the West, restricted to a servile function in the vocabulary of technics. We are only geometricians of matter; the Greeks were, first of all, geometricians in their apprenticeship to virtue.

The progress of the war in the *Iliad* is simply a continual game of seesaw. The victor of the moment feels himself invincible, even though, only a few hours before, he may have experienced defeat; he forgets to treat victory as a transitory thing. At the end of the first day of combat described in the *Iliad,* the victorious Greeks were in a position to obtain the object of all their efforts, i.e., Helen and her riches—assuming of course, as Homer did, that the Greeks had reason to believe that Helen was in Troy. Actually, the Egyptian priests, who ought to have known, affirmed later on to Herodotus that she was in Egypt. In any case, that evening the Greeks are no longer interested in her or her possessions:

> "For the present, let us not accept the riches of Paris;
> Nor Helen; everybody sees, even the most ignorant,
> That Troy stands on the verge of ruin."
> He spoke, and all the Achaeans acclaimed him.

What they want is, in fact, everything. For booty, all the riches of Troy; for their bonfires, all the palaces, temples, houses; for slaves, all the women and children; for corpses, all the men. They forget one detail, that *everything* is not within their power, for they are not in Troy. Perhaps they will be there tomorrow; perhaps not. Hector, the same day, makes the same mistake:

> For I know well in my entrails and in my hearts,
> A day will come when Holy Troy will perish,
> And Priam, and the nation of Priam of the good lance.
> But I think less of the grief that is in store for the Trojans,
> And of Hecuba herself, and of Priam the king,
> And of my brothers, so numerous and so brave,
> Who will fall in the dust under the blows of the enemy,
> Than of you that day when a Greek in his bronze breastplate
> Will drag you away weeping and deprive you of your liberty.
>
> But as for me, may I be dead, and may the earth have covered me
> Before I hear you cry out or see you dragged away!

At this moment what would he not give to turn aside those horrors which he believes to be inevitable? But at this moment nothing he *could* give would be of any use. The next day but one, however, the Greeks have run away miserably, and Agamemnon himself is in favor of putting to the sea again. And now Hector, by making a very few concessions, could readily secure the enemy's departure; yet now he is even unwilling to let them go empty-handed:

> Set fires everywhere and let the brightness mount the skies
> Lest in the night the long-haired Greeks,
> Escaping, sail over the broad back of ocean . . .
> Let each of them take home a wound to heal
> . . . thus others will fear
> To bring dolorous war to the Trojans, tamers of horses.

His wish is granted; the Greeks stay; and the next day they reduce Hector and his men to a pitiable condition:

> As for them—they fled across the plain like cattle
> Whom a lion hunts before him in the dark midnight . . .
> Thus the mighty Agamemnon, son of Atreus, pursued them,
> Steadily killing the hindmost; and still they fled.

In the course of the afternoon, Hector regains the ascendancy, withdraws again, then puts the Greeks to flight, then is repulsed by Patroclus, who has come in with his fresh troops. Patroclus, pressing his advantage, ends by finding himself exposed, wounded and without armor, to the sword of Hector. And finally that evening the victorious Hector hears the prudent counsel of Polydamas and repudiates it sharply:

> Now that wily Kronos's son has given me
> Glory at the ships; now that I have driven the Greeks to the sea,
> Do not offer, fool, such counsels to the people.
> No Trojan will listen to you; nor would I permit it . . .
> So Hector spoke, and the Trojans acclaimed him. . . .

The next day Hector is lost. Achilles has harried him across the field and is about to kill him. He has always been the stronger of the two in combat; how much the more so now, after several weeks of rest, ardent for vengeance and victory, against an exhausted enemy? And Hector stands alone, before the walls of Troy, absolutely alone, alone to wait for death and to steady his soul to face it:

> Alas, were I to slip through the gate, behind the rampart,
> Polydamas at once would heap dishonor on me . . .
> And now that through my recklessness I have destroyed my people,
> I fear the Trojans and the long-robed Trojan women,
> I fear to hear from some one far less brave than I:
> "Hector, trusting his own strength too far, has ruined his people." . . .

> Suppose I were to down my bossed shield,
> My massive helmet, and, leaning my spear against the wall,
> Should go to meet renowned Achilles? . . .
> But why spin out these fancies? Why such dreams?
> I would not reach him, nor would he pity me,
> Or respect me. He would kill me like a woman
> If I came naked thus . . .

Not a jot of the grief and ignominy that fall to the unfortunate is Hector spared. Alone, stripped of the prestige of force, he discovers that the courage that kept him from taking to the shelter of the walls is not enough to save him from flight:

> Seeing him, Hector began to tremble. He had not the heart
> To stay . . .
> . . . It is not for a ewe nor the skin of an ox,
> That they are striving, not these ordinary rewards of the race;
> It is for a life that they run, the life of Hector, tamer of horses.

Wounded to death, he enhances his conqueror's triumph by vain supplications:

> I implore you, by your soul, by your knees, by your parents. . . .

But the auditors of the *Iliad* knew that the death of Hector would be but a brief joy to Achilles, and the death of Achilles but a brief joy to the Trojans, and the destruction of Troy but a brief joy to the Achaeans.

Thus violence obliterates anybody who feels its touch. It comes to seem just as external to its employer as to its victim. And from this springs the idea of a destiny before which executioner and victim stand equally innocent, before which conquered and conqueror are brothers in the same distress. The conquered brings misfortune to the conqueror, and vice versa:

> A single son, short-lived, was born to him.
> Neglected by me, he grows old—for far from home
> I camp before Troy, injuring you and your sons.

A moderate use of force, which alone would enable man to escape being enmeshed in its machinery, would require superhuman virtue, which is as rare as dignity in weakness. Moreover, moderation itself is not without its perils, since prestige, from which force derives at least three quarters of its strength, rests principally upon that marvelous indifference that the strong feel toward the weak, an indifference so contagious that it infects the very people who are the objects of it. Yet ordinarily excess is not arrived at through prudence or politic considerations. On the contrary, man dashes to it as to an irresistible temptation. The voice of reason is occasionally heard in the mouths of the characters in the *Iliad*. Thersites' speeches are reasonable to the highest degree; so are the speeches of the angry Achilles:

> Nothing is worth my life, not all the goods
> They say the well-built city of Ilium contains. . . .
> A man can capture steers and fatted sheep
> But, once gone, the soul cannot be captured back.

But words of reason drop into the void. If they come from an inferior, he is punished and shuts up; if from a chief, his actions betray them. And failing everything else, there is always a god handy to advise him to be unreasonable. In the end, the very idea of wanting to escape the role fate has allotted one—the business of killing and dying—disappears from the mind:

> We to whom Zeus
> Has assigned suffering, from youth to old age,
> Suffering in grievous wars, till we perish to the last man.

Already these warriors, like Craonne's so much later, felt themselves to be "condemned men." . . .

Such is the nature of force. Its power of converting a man into a thing is a double one, and in its application double-edged. To the same degree, though in different fashions, those who use it and those who endure it are turned to stone. This property of force achieves its maximum effectiveness during the clash of arms, in battle, when the tide of the day has turned, and everything is rushing toward a decision. It is not the planning man, the man of strategy, the man acting on the resolution taken, who wins or loses a battle; battles are fought and decided by men deprived of these faculties, men who have undergone a transformation, who have dropped either to the level of inert matter, which is pure passivity, or to the level of blind force, which is pure momentum. Herein lies the last secret of war, a secret revealed by the *Iliad* in its similes, which liken the warriors either to fire, flood, wind, wild beasts, or God knows what blind cause of disaster, or else to frightened animals, trees, water, sand, to anything in nature that is set into motion by the violence of external forces. Greeks and Trojans, from one day to the next, sometimes even from one hour to the next, experience, turn and turn about, one or the other of these transmutations:

> As when a lion, murderous, springs among the cattle
> Which by thousands are grazing over some vast marshy field. . . .
> And their flanks heave with terror; even so the Achaians
> Scattered in panic before Hector and Zeus, the great father.

> As when a ravening fire breaks out deep in a bushy wood
> And the wheeling wind scatters sparks far and wide,
> And trees, root and branch, topple over in flames;
> So Atreus' son, Agamemnon, roared through the ranks
> Of the Trojans in flight. . . .

The art of war is simply the art of producing such transformations, and its equipment, its processes, even the casualties it inflicts on the enemy, are only means directed toward this end—its true object is the warrior's soul. Yet these transformations are always a mystery; the gods are their authors, the gods who kindle men's imagination. But however caused, this petri-factive quality of force, two-fold always, is essential to its nature; and a soul which has entered the province of force will not escape this except by a miracle. Such miracles are rare and of brief duration.

The wantonness of the conqueror that knows no respect for any creature or thing that is at its mercy or is imagined to be so, the despair of the soldier that drives him on to destruction, the obliteration of the slave or the conquered man, the wholesale slaughter—all these elements combine in the *Iliad* to make a picture of uniform horror, of which force is the sole hero. A monotonous desolation would result were it not for those few luminous moments, scattered here and there throughout the poem, those brief, celestial moments in which man possesses his soul. The soul that awakes then, to live for an instant only and be lost almost at once in force's vast kingdom, awakes pure and whole; it contains no am-biguities, nothing complicated or turbid; it has no room for anything but courage and love. Sometimes it is in the course of inner deliberations that a man finds his soul: he meets it, like Hector before Troy, as he tries to face destiny on his own terms, without the help of gods or men. At other times, it is in a moment of love that men discover their souls—and there is hardly any form of pure love known to humanity of which the *Iliad* does not treat. The tradition of hospitality persists, even through several gen-erations, to dispel the blindness of combat.

> Thus I am for you a beloved guest in the breast of Argos . . .
> Let us turn our lances away from each other, even in battle.

The love of the son for the parents, of father for son, of mother for son, is continually described, in a manner as touching as it is curt:

> Thetis answered, shedding tears,
> "You were born to me for a short life, my child, as you say . . ."

Even brotherly love:

My three brothers whom the same mother bore for me,
So dear. . . .

Conjugal love, condemned to sorrow, is of an astonishing purity. Imaging the humiliations of slavery which await a beloved wife, the husband passes over the one indignity which even in anticipation would stain their tenderness. What could be simpler than the words spoken by his wife to the man about to die?

. . . Better for me
Losing you, to go under the earth. No other comfort
Will remain, when you have encountered your death-heavy fate,
Only grief, only sorrow. . . .

Not less touching are the words expressed to a dead husband:

Dear husband, you died young, and left me your widow
Alone in the palace. Our child is still tiny,
The child you and I, crossed by fate, had together.
I think he will never grow up . . .
For not in your bed did you die, holding my hand
And speaking to me prudent words which forever
Night and day, as I weep, might live in my memory.

The most beautiful friendship of all, the friendship between comrades-at-arms, is the final theme of The Epic:

. . . But Achilles
Wept, dreaming of the beloved comrade; sleep, all-prevailing,
Would not take him; he turned over again and again.

But the purest triumph of love, the crowning grace of war, is the friendship that floods the hearts of mortal enemies. Before it a murdered son or a murdered friend no longer cries out for vengeance. Before it—even more miraculous—the distance between benefactor and suppliant, between victor and vanquished, shrinks to nothing:

But when thirst and hunger had been appeased,
Then Dardanian Priam fell to admiring Achilles.
How tall he was, and handsome; he had the face of a god;
And in his turn Dardanian Priam was admired by Achilles,
Who watched his handsome face and listened to his words.
And when they were satisfied with contemplation of each other . . .

These moments of grace are rare in the Iliad, but they are enough to make us feel with sharp regret what it is that violence has killed and will kill again.

However, such a heaping-up of violent deeds would have a frigid effect, were it not for the note of incurable bitterness that continually makes itself heard, though often only a single word marks its presence, often a mere stroke of the verse, or a run-on line. It is in this that the *Iliad* is absolutely unique, in this bitterness that proceeds from tenderness and that spreads over the whole human race, impartial as sunlight. Never does the tone lose its coloring of bitterness; yet never does the bitterness drop into lamentation. Justice and love, which have hardly any place in this study of extremes and of unjust acts of violence, nevertheless bathe the work in their light without ever becoming noticeable themselves, except as a kind of accent. Nothing precious is scorned, whether or not death is its destiny; everyone's unhappiness is laid bare without dissimulation or disdain; no man is set above or below the condition common to all men; whatever is destroyed is regretted. Victors and vanquished are brought equally near us; under the same head, both are seen as counterparts of the poet, and the listener as well. If there is any difference, it is that the enemy's misfortunes are possibly more sharply felt.

> So he fell there, put to sleep in the sleep of bronze,
> Unhappy man, far from his wife, defending his own people. . . .

And what accents echo the fate of the lad Achilles sold at Lemnos!

> Eleven days he rejoiced his heart among those he loved,
> Returning from Lemnos; the twelfth day, once more,
> God delivered him into the hands of Achilles,
> To him who had to send him, unwilling, to Hades.

And the fate of Euphorbus, who saw only a single day of war.

> Blood soaked his hair, the hair like to the Graces' . . .

When Hector is lamented:

> . . . guardian of chaste wives and little children. . . .

In these few words, chastity appears, dirtied by force, and childhood, de-livered to the sword. The fountain at the gates of Troy becomes an object of poignant nostalgia when Hector runs by, seeking to elude his doom:

> Close by there stood the great stone tanks,
> Handsomely built, where silk-gleaming garments
> Were washed clean by Troy's lovely daughters and housewives
> In the old days of peace, long ago, when the Greeks had not come.
> Past these did they run their race, pursued and pursuer.

The whole of the *Iliad* lies under the shadow of the greatest calamity the human race can experience—the destruction of a city. This calamity could not tear more at the heart had the poet been born in Troy. But the tone is not different when the Achaeans are dying, far from home.

Insofar as this other life, the life of the living, seems calm and full, the brief evocations of the world of peace are felt as pain:

> With the break of dawn and the rising of the day,
> On both sides arrows flew, men fell.
> But at the very hour that the woodcutter goes home to fix his meal
> In the mountain valleys when his arms have had enough
> Of hacking great trees, and disgust rises in his heart,
> And the desire for sweet food seizes his entrails,
> At that hour, by their valor, the Danaans broke the front.

Whatever is not war, whatever war destroys or threatens, the *Iliad* wraps in poetry; the realities of war, never. No reticence veils the step from life to death:

> Then his teeth flew out; from two sides,
> Blood came to his eyes; the blood that from lips and nostrils
> He was spilling, open-mouthed; death enveloped him in its black cloud.

The cold brutality of the deeds of war is left undisguised; neither victors nor vanquished are admired, scorned, or hated. Almost always, fate and the gods decide the changing lot of battle. Within the limits fixed by fate, the gods determine with sovereign authority victory and defeat. It is always they who provoke those fits of madness, those treacheries, which are forever blocking peace; war is their true business; their only motives, caprice and malice. As for the warriors, victors or vanquished, those comparisons which liken them to beasts or things can inspire neither admiration nor contempt, but only regret that men are capable of being so transformed.

E. R. DODDS

Agamemnon's Apology

The recesses of feeling, the darker, blinder strata of character, are the only places in the world in which we catch real fact in the making.

—WILLIAM JAMES

I shall begin by considering a particular aspect of Homeric religion. To some classical scholars the Homeric poems will seem a bad place to look for any sort of religious experience. "The truth is," says Professor Mazon in a recent book, "that there was never a poem less religious than the *Iliad*." This may be thought a little sweeping; but it reflects an opinion which seems to be widely accepted. Professor Murray thinks that the so-called Homeric religion "was not really religion at all"; for in his view "the real worship of Greece before the fourth century almost never attached itself to those luminous Olympian forms." Similarly Dr. Bowra observes that "this complete anthropomorphic system has *of course* no relation to real religion or to morality. These gods are a delightful, gay invention of poets."

Of course—if the expression "real religion" means the kind of thing that enlightened Europeans or Americans of to-day recognize as being religion. But if we restrict the meaning of the word in this way, are we not in danger of undervaluing, or even of overlooking altogether, certain types of experience which we no longer interpret in a religious sense, but which may nevertheless in their time have been quite heavily charged with religious significance? My purpose in the present chapter is not to quarrel with the distinguished scholars I have quoted over their use of terms, but to call attention to one kind of experience in Homer which is *prima facie* religious and to examine its psychology.

Let us start from that experience of divine temptation or infatuation (*atē*) which led Agamemnon to compensate himself for the loss of his own mistress by robbing Achilles of his. "Not I," he declared afterwards, "not I was the cause of this act, but Zeus and my portion and the Erinys who walks in darkness: they it was who in the assembly put wild *atē* in my understanding, on that day when I arbitrarily took Achilles' prize from him. So what could I do? Deity will always have its way." By impatient modern readers these words of Agamemnon's have sometimes been dismissed as a weak excuse or evasion of responsibility. But not, I think, by those who read carefully. An evasion of responsibility in the juridical sense the words certainly are not; for at the end of his speech Agamemnon offers compensation precisely on this ground—"But since I was blinded by *atē* and Zeus took away my understanding, I am willing to make my peace and give abundant compensation." Had he acted of his own volition, he could not so easily admit himself in the wrong; as it is, he will pay for his acts. Juridically, his position would be the same in either case; for early Greek justice cared nothing for intent—it was the act that mattered. Nor is he dishonestly inventing a moral alibi; for the victim of his action takes the same view of it as he does. "Father Zeus, great indeed are the *atai* thou givest to men. Else the son of Atreus would never have persisted in rousing the *thūmos* in my chest, nor obstinately taken the girl against my will." You may think that Achilles is here politely accepting a fiction, in order to save the High King's face? But no: for already in Book 1, when Achilles is explaining the situation to Thetis, he speaks of Agamemnon's behaviour as his *atē*; and in Book 9 he exclaims, "Let the son of Atreus go to his doom and not disturb me, for Zeus the counsellor took away his understanding." It is Achilles' view of the matter as much as Agamemnon's; and in the famous words which introduce the story of the Wrath—"The plan of Zeus was fulfilled"—we have a strong hint that it is also the poet's view.

If this were the only incident which Homer's characters interpreted in this peculiar way, we might hesitate as to the poet's motive: we might guess, for example, that he wished to avoid alienating the hearers' sympathy too completely from Agamemnon, or again that he was trying to impart a deeper significance to the rather undignified quarrel of the two chiefs by representing it as a step in the fulfilment of a divine plan. But these explanations do not apply to other passages where "the gods" or "some god" or Zeus are said to have momentarily "taken away" or "destroyed" or "ensorcelled" a human being's understanding. Either of them might indeed be applied to the case of Helen, who ends a deeply moving and evidently sincere speech by saying that Zeus has laid on her and Alexandros an evil doom, "that we may be hereafter a theme of song for men to come." But when we are simply told that Zeus "ensorcelled the mind of the Achaeans," so that they fought badly, no consideration of persons comes into play; still less in the general statement that "the gods can make the most sensible man senseless and bring the feeble-minded to good sense." And what, for example, of Glaucus, whose understanding Zeus took away, so that he did what Greeks almost never do—accepted a bad bargain, by swopping gold armour for bronze? Or what of Automedon, whose folly in attempting to double the parts of charioteer and spearman led a friend to ask him "which of the gods had put an unprofitable plan in his breast and taken away his excellent understanding?" These two cases clearly have no connection with any deeper divine purpose; nor can there be any question of retaining the hearers' sympathy, since no moral slur is involved.

At this point, however, the reader may naturally ask whether we are dealing with anything more than a *façon de parler*. Does the poet mean anything more than that Glaucus was a fool to make the bargain he did? Did Automedon's friend mean anything more than "What the dickens prompted you to behave like that?" Perhaps not. The hexameter formulae which were the stock-in-trade of the old poets lent themselves easily to the sort of semasiological degeneration which ends by creating a *façon de parler*. And we may note that neither the Glaucus episode nor the futile *aristeia* of Automedon is integral to the plot even of an "expanded" *Iliad*: they may well be additions by a later hand. Our aim, however, is to understand the original experience which lies at the root of such stereotyped formulae—for even a *façon de parler* must have an origin. It may help us to do so if we look a little more closely at the nature of *atē* and of the agencies to which Agamemnon ascribes it, and then glance at some other sorts of statement which the epic poets make about the sources of human behaviour.

There are a number of passages in Homer in which unwise and unaccountable conduct is attributed to *atē*, or described by the cognate verb *aasasthai*, without explicit reference to divine intervention. But *atē* in Homer is not itself a personal agent: the two passages which speak of *atē* in personal terms, *Il*. 9.505ff. and 19.91ff., are transparent pieces of allegory. Nor does the word ever, at any rate in the *Iliad*, mean objective disaster, as it so commonly does in tragedy. Always, or practically always, *atē* is a state of mind—a temporary clouding or bewildering of the normal consciousness. It is, in fact, a partial and temporary insanity; and, like all insanity, it is ascribed, not to physiological or psychological causes, but to an external "daemonic" agency. In the *Odyssey*, it is true, excessive consumption of wine is said to cause *atē*; the implication, however, is probably not that *atē* can be produced "naturally" but rather that wine has something supernatural or daemonic about it. Apart from this special case, the agents productive of *atē*, where they are specified, seem always to be supernatural beings, so we may class all instances of nonalcoholic *atē* in Homer under the head of what I propose to call "psychic intervention."

If we review them, we shall observe that *atē* is by no means necessarily either a synonym for, or a result of, wickedness. The assertion of Liddell and Scott that *atē* is "mostly sent as the punishment of guilty rashness" is quite untrue of Homer. The *atē* (here a sort of stunned bewilderment) which overtook Patroclus after Apollo had struck him might possibly be claimed as an instance, since Patroclus had rashly routed the Trojans *hyper aisan*; but earlier in the scene this rashness is itself ascribed to the will of Zeus and characterised by the verb *aasthē*. Again, the *atē* of one Agastrophus in straying too far from his chariot, and so getting himself killed, is not a "punishment" for rashness; the rashness is itself the *atē*, or a result of the *atē*, and it involves no discernible moral guilt—it is just an unaccountable error, like the bad bargain which Glaucus made. Again, Odysseus was neither guilty nor rash when he took a nap at an unfortunate moment, thus giving his companions a chance to slaughter the tabooed oxen. It was what we should call an accident; but for Homer, as for early thought in general, there is no such thing as accident—Odysseus knows that his nap was sent by the gods *eis atēn*, "to fool him." Such passages suggest that *atē* had originally no connection with guilt. The notion of *atē* as a punishment seems to be either a late development in Ionia or a late importation from outside: the only place in Homer where it is explicitly asserted is the unique *Litai* passage in *Iliad* 9, which suggests that it may possibly be a Mainland idea, taken over along with the Meleager story from an epic composed in the mother country.

A word next about the agencies to which *atē* is ascribed. Agamemnon cites, not one such agency, but three: Zeus and *moira* and the Erinys who walks in darkness (or, according to another and perhaps older reading, the Erinys who sucks blood). Of these, Zeus is the mythological agent whom the poet conceives as the prime mover in the affair: "the plan of Zeus was fulfilled." It is perhaps significant that (unless we make Apollo responsible for the *atē* of Patroclus) Zeus is the only individual Olympian who is credited with causing *atē* in the *Iliad* (hence *atē* is allegorically described as his eldest daughter). *Moira*, I think, is brought in because people spoke of any unaccountable personal disaster as part of their "portion" or "lot," meaning simply that they cannot understand why it happened, but since it has happened, evidently "it had to be." People still speak in that way, more especially of death, for which *mira* has in fact become a synonym in modern Greek, like *moros* in classical Greek. I am sure it is quite wrong to write *Moira* with a capital "M" here, as if it signified either a personal goddess who dictates to Zeus or a Cosmic Destiny like the Hellenistic *Heimarmenē*. As goddesses, *Moirai* are always plural, both in cult and in early literature, and with one doubtful exception they do not figure at all in the *Iliad*. The most we can say is that by treating his "portion" as an agent—by making it *do* something—Agamemnon is taking a first step towards personification. Again, by blaming his *moira* Agamemnon no more declares himself a systematic determinist than does the modern Greek peasant when he uses similar language. To ask whether Homer's people are determinists or libertarians is a fantastic anachronism: the question has never occurred to them, and if it were put to them it would be very difficult to make them understand what it meant. What they do recognize is the distinction between normal actions and actions performed in a state of *atē*. Actions of the latter sort they can trace indifferently either to their *moira* or to the will of a god, according as they look at the matter from a subjective or an objective point of view. In the same way Patroclus attributes his death directly to the immediate agent, the man Euphorbus, and indirectly to the mythological agent, Apollo, but from a subjective standpoint to his bad *moira*. It is, as the psychologists say, "overdetermined."

On this analogy, the Erinys should be the immediate agent in Agamemnon's case. That she should figure at all in this context may well surprise those who think of an Erinys as essentially a spirit of vengeance, still more those who believe, with Rohde, that the Erinyes were originally the vengeful dead. But the passage does not stand alone. We read also in the *Odyssey* of "the heavy *atē* which the hard-hitting goddess Erinys laid on the understanding of Melampus." In neither place is there any question of revenge or punishment. The explanation is perhaps that the Erinys is the personal agent who ensures the fulfilment of a *moira*. That is why the Erinyes cut short the speech of Achilles' horses: it is not "according to *moira*" for horses to talk. That is why they would punish the sun, according to Heraclitus, if the sun should "transgress his measures" by exceeding the task assigned to him. Most probably, I think, the moral function of the Erinyes as ministers of vengeance derives from this primitive task of enforcing a *moira* which was at first morally neutral, or rather, contained by implication both an "ought" and a "must" which early thought did not clearly distinguish. So in Homer we find them enforcing the claims to status which arise from family or social relationship and are felt to be part of a person's *moira*: a parent, an elder brother, even a beggar, has something due to him as such, and can invoke "his" Erinyes to protect it. So too they are called upon to witness oaths; for the oath creates an assignment, a *moira*. The connection of Erinys with *moira* is still attested by Aeschylus, though the *moirai* have now become quasi-personal; and the Erinyes are still for Aeschylus dispensers of *atē*, although both they and it have been moralised. It rather looks as if the complex *moira*-Erinys-*atē* had deep roots, and might well be older than the ascription of *atē* to the agency of Zeus. In that connection it is worth recalling that Erinys and *aisa* (which is synonymous with *moira*) go back to what is perhaps the oldest known form of Hellenic speech, the Arcado-Cypriot dialect.

Here, for the present, let us leave *atē* and its associates, and consider briefly another kind of "psychic intervention" which is no less frequent in Homer, namely, the communication of power from god to man. In the *Iliad*, the typical case is the communication of *mĕnos* during a battle, as when Athena puts a triple portion of *menos* into the chest of her protégé Diomede, or Apollo puts *menos* into the *thumos* of the wounded Glaucus. This *menos* is not primarily physical strength; nor is it a permanent organ of mental life like *thymos* or *nŏŏs*. Rather it is, like *atē*, a state of mind. When a man feels *menos* in his chest, or "thrusting up pungently into his nostrils," he is conscious of a mysterious access of energy; the life in him is strong, and he is filled with a new confidence and eagerness. The connection of *menos* with the sphere of volition comes out clearly in the related words *menoinan*, "to be eager," and *dysmenēs*, "wishing ill." It is significant that often, though not always, a communication of *menos* comes as a response to prayer. But it is something much more spontaneous and instinctive than what we call "resolution"; animals can have it, and it is used by analogy to describe the devouring energy of fire. In man it is the vital energy, the "spunk," which is not always there at call, but comes and goes mysteriously and (as we should say) capriciously. But to Homer it is not caprice: it is the act of a god, who "increases or diminishes at will a man's *arĕtē* (that is to say, his potency as a fighter)." Sometimes, indeed, the *menos* can be roused by verbal exhortation; at other times its onset can only be explained by saying that a god has "breathed it into" the hero, or "put it in his chest," or, as we read in one place, transmitted it by contact, through a staff.

I think we should not dismiss these statements as "poetic invention" or "divine machinery." No doubt the particular instances are often invented by the poet for the convenience of his plot; and certainly the psychic intervention is sometimes linked with a physical one, or with a scene on Olympus. But we can be pretty sure that the underlying idea was not invented by any poet, and that it is older than the conception of anthropomorphic gods physically and visibly taking part in a battle. The temporary possession of a heightened *menos* is, like *atē*, an abnormal state which demands a supernormal explanation. Homer's men can recognise its onset, which is marked by a peculiar sensation in the limbs. "My feet beneath and hands above feel eager," says one recipient of the power: that is because, as the poet tells us, the god has made them nimble. This sensation, which is here shared by a second recipient, confirms for them the divine origin of the *menos*. It is an abnormal experience. And men in a condition of divinely heightened *menos* behave to some extent abnormally. They can perform the most difficult feats with ease: that is a traditional mark of divine power. They can even, like Diomede, fight with impunity against gods— an action which to men in their normal state is excessively dangerous. They are in fact for the time being rather more, or perhaps rather less, than human. Men who have received a communication of *menos* are several times compared to ravening lions; but the most striking description of the state is in Book 15, where Hector goes berserk, he foams at the mouth, and his eyes glow. From such cases it is only a step to the idea of actual possession (*daimonan*); but it is a step which Homer does not take. He does say of Hector that after he had put on Achilles' armour "Ares entered into him and his limbs were filled with courage and strength"; but Ares here is hardly more than a synonym for the martial spirit, and the communication of power is produced by the will of Zeus, assisted perhaps by the divine armour. Gods do of course for purposes of disguise assume the shape and appearance of individual human beings; but that is a different belief. Gods may appear at times in human form, men may share at times in the divine attribute of power, but in Homer there is nevertheless no real blurring of the sharp line which separates humanity from deity.

In the *Odyssey*, which is less exclusively concerned with fighting, the communication of power takes other forms. The poet of the "Telemachy" imitates the *Iliad* by making Athena put *menos* into Telemachus; but here the *menos* is the *moral* courage which will enable the boy to face the overbearing suitors. That is literary adaptation. Older and more authentic is the repeated claim that minstrels derive their creative power from God. "I am self-taught," says Phemius; "it was a god who implanted all sorts of lays in my mind." The two parts of his statement are not felt as contradictory: he means, I think, that he has not memorised the lays of other minstrels, but is a creative poet who relies on the hexameter phrases welling up spontaneously as he needs them out of some unknown and uncontrollable depth; he sings "out of the gods," as the best minstrels always do. . . .

But the most characteristic feature of the *Odyssey* is the way in which its personages ascribe all sorts of mental (as well as physical) events to the intervention of a nameless and indeterminate daemon or "god" or "gods." These vaguely conceived beings can inspire courage at a crisis or take away a man's understanding, just as gods do in the *Iliad*. But they are also credited with a wide range of what may be called loosely "monitions." Whenever someone has a particularly brilliant or a particularly foolish idea; when he suddenly recognises another person's identity or sees in a flash the meaning of an omen; when he remembers what he might well have forgotten or forgets what he should have remembered, he or someone else will see in it, if we are to take the words literally, a psychic intervention by one of these anonymous supernatural beings. Doubtless they do not always expect to be taken literally: Odysseus, for example, is hardly serious in ascribing to the machinations of a daemon the fact that he went out without his cloak on a cold night. But we are not dealing simply with an "epic convention." For it is the poet's characters who talk like this, and not the poet: his own convention is quite other—he operates, like the author of the *Iliad*, with clear-cut anthropomorphic gods such as Athena and Poseidon, not with anonymous daemons. If he has made his characters employ a different convention, he has presumably done so because that is how people did in fact talk: he is being "realistic."

And indeed that is how we should expect people to talk who believed (or whose ancestors had believed) in daily and hourly monitions. The recognition, the insight, the memory, the brilliant or perverse idea, have this in common, that they come suddenly, as we say, "into a man's head." Often he is conscious of no observation or reasoning which has led up to them. But in that case, how can he call them "his"? A moment ago they were not in his mind; now they are there. Something has put them there, and that something is other than himself. More than this he does not know. So he speaks of it noncommittally as "the gods" or "some god," or more often (especially when its prompting has turned out to be bad) as a daemon. And by analogy he applies the same explanation to the ideas and actions of other people when he finds them difficult to understand or out of character. A good example is Antinous' speech in *Odyssey* 2, where, after praising Penelope's exceptional intelligence and propriety, he goes on to say that her idea of refusing to remarry is not at all proper, and concludes that "the gods are putting it into her chest." Similarly, when Telemachus for the first time speaks out boldly against the suitors, Antinous infers, not without irony, that "the gods are teaching him to talk big." His teacher is in fact Athena, as the poet and the reader know; but Antinous is not to know that, so he says "the gods."

A similar distinction between what the speaker knows and what the poet knows may be observed in some places in the *Iliad*. When Teucer's bowstring breaks, he cries out with a shudder of fear that a daemon is thwarting him; but it was in fact Zeus who broke it, as the poet has just told us. It has been suggested that in such passages the poet's point of view is the older: that he still makes use of the "Mycenaean" divine machinery, while his characters ignore it and use vaguer language like the poet's Ionian contemporaries, who (it is asserted) were losing their faith in the old anthropomorphic gods. In my view, as we shall see in a moment, this is almost an exact reversal of the real relationship. And it is anyhow clear that Teucer's vagueness has nothing to do with scepticism: it is the simple result of ignorance. By using the word *daemon* he "expresses the fact that a higher power has made something happen," and this fact is all he knows. As Ehnmark has pointed out, similar vague language in reference to the supernatural was commonly used by Greeks at all periods, not out of scepticism, but simply because they could not identify the particular god concerned. It is also commonly used by primitive peoples, whether for the same reason or because they lack the idea of personal gods. That its use by the Greeks is very old is shown by the high antiquity of the adjective *daemŏnios*. That word must originally have meant "acting at the monition of a daemon"; but already in the *Iliad* its primitive sense has so far faded that Zeus can apply it to Hera. A verbal coinage so defaced has clearly been in circulation for a long time.

We have now surveyed, in such a cursory manner as time permits, the commonest types of psychic intervention in Homer. We may sum up the result by saying that all departures from normal human behaviour whose causes are not immediately perceived, whether by the subjects' own consciousness or by the observation of others, are ascribed to a supernatural agency, just as is any departure from the normal behaviour of the weather or the normal behaviour of a bowstring. This finding will not surprise the nonclassical anthropologist: he will at once produce copious parallels from Borneo or Central Africa. But it is surely odd to find this belief, this sense of constant daily dependence on the supernatural, firmly embedded in poems supposedly so "irreligious" as the *Iliad* and the *Odyssey*. And we may also ask ourselves why a people so civilised, clear-headed, and rational as the Ionians did not eliminate from their national epics these links with Borneo and the primitive past, just as they eliminated fear of the dead, fear of pollution, and other primitive terrors which must originally have played a part in the saga. I doubt if the early literature of any other European people—even my own superstitious countrymen, the Irish—postulates supernatural interference in human behaviour with such frequency or over so wide a field.

Nilsson is, I think, the first scholar who has seriously tried to find an explanation of all this in terms of psychology. In a paper published in 1924, which has now become classical, he contended that Homeric heroes are peculiarly subject to rapid and violent changes of mood: they suffer, he says, from mental instability. And he goes on to point out that even to-day a person of this temperament is apt, when his mood changes, to look back with horror on what he has just done, and exclaim, "I didn't really mean to do that!"—from which it is a short step to saying, "It wasn't really I who did it." "His own behaviour," says Nilsson, "has become alien to him. He cannot understand it. It is for him no part of his Ego." This is a perfectly true observation, and its relevance to some of the phenomena we have been considering cannot, I think, be doubted. Nilsson is also, I believe, right in holding that experiences of this sort played a part—along with other elements, such as the Minoan tradition of protecting goddesses—in building up that machinery of *physical* intervention to which Homer resorts so constantly and, to our thinking, often so superfluously. We find it superfluous because the divine machinery seems to us in many cases to do no more than duplicate a natural psychological causation. But ought we not perhaps to say rather that the divine machinery "duplicates" a psychic intervention—that is, presents it in a concrete pictorial form? This was not superfluous; for only in this way could it be made vivid to the imagination of the hearers. The Homeric poets were without the refinements of language which would have been needed to "put across" adequately a purely psychological miracle. What more natural than that they should first supplement, and later replace, an old unexciting threadbare formula like *menos embale thumōi* by making the god appear as a physical presence and exhort his favourite with the spoken word? How much more vivid than a mere inward monition is the famous scene in *Iliad* 1 where Athena plucks Achilles by the hair and warns him not to strike Agamemnon! But she is visible to Achilles alone: "none of the others saw her." That is a plain hint that she is the projection, the pictorial expression, of an inward monition—a monition which Achilles might have described by such a vague phrase as *enepneuse phresi daimōn.* And I suggest that in general the inward monition, or the sudden unaccountable feeling of power, or the sudden unaccountable loss of judgement, is the germ out of which the divine machinery developed.

One result of transposing the event from the interior to the external world is that the vagueness is eliminated: the indeterminate daemon has to be made concrete as some particular personal god. In *Iliad* 1 he becomes Athena, the goddess of good counsel. But that was a matter for the poet's choice. And through a multitude of such choices the poets must gradually have built up the personalities of their gods, "distinguishing," as Herodotus says, "their offices and skills, and fixing their physical appearance." The poets did not, of course, invent the gods (nor does Herodotus say so): Athena, for example, had been, as we now have reason to believe, a Minoan house-goddess. But the poets bestowed upon them personality—and thereby, as Nilsson says, made it impossible for Greece to lapse into the magical type of religion which prevailed among her Oriental neighbours.

Some, however, may be disposed to challenge the assertion on which, for Nilsson, all this construction rests. *Are* Homer's people exceptionally unstable, as compared with the characters in other early epics? The evidence adduced by Nilsson is rather slight. They come to blows on small provocation; but so do Norse and Irish heroes. Hector on one occasion goes berserk; but Norse heroes do so much oftener. Homeric men weep in a more uninhibited manner than Swedes or Englishmen; but so do all the Mediterranean peoples to this day. We may grant that Agamemnon and Achilles are passionate, excitable men (the story requires that they should be). But are not Odysseus and Ajax in their several ways proverbial types of steady endurance, as is Penelope of female constancy? Yet these stable characters are not more exempt than others from psychic intervention. I should hesitate on the whole to press this point of Nilsson's, and should prefer instead to connect Homeric man's belief in psychic intervention with two other peculiarities which do unquestionably belong to the culture described by Homer.

The first is a negative peculiarity: Homeric man has no unified concept of what we call "soul" or "personality" (a fact to whose implications Bruno Snell has lately called particular attention). It is well known that Homer appears to credit man with a *psyche* only after death, or when he is in the act of fainting or dying or is threatened with death: the only recorded function of the *psyche* in relation to the living man is to leave him. Nor has Homer any other word for the living personality. The *thymos* may once have been a primitive "breath-soul" or "life-soul"; but in Homer it is neither the soul nor (as in Plato) a "part of the soul." It may be defined, roughly and generally, as the organ of feeling. But it enjoys an independence which the word "organ" does not suggest to us, influenced as we are by the later concepts of "organism" and "organic unity." A man's *thymos* tells him that he must now eat or drink or slay an enemy, it advises him on his course of action, it puts words into his mouth. He can converse with it, or with his "heart" or his "belly," almost as man to man. Sometimes he scolds these detached entities; usually he takes their advice, but he may also reject it and act, as Zeus does on one occasion, "without the consent of his *thymos.*" In the latter case, we should say, like Plato, that the man had controlled *himself.* But for Homeric man the *thymos* tends not to be felt as part of the self: it commonly appears as an independent inner voice. A man may even hear two such voices, as when Odysseus "plans in his *thymos*" to kill the Cyclops forthwith, but a second voice (*heteros thymos*) restrains him. This habit of (as we should say) "objectifying emotional drives," treating them as not-self, must have opened the door wide to the religious idea of psychic intervention, which is often said to operate, not directly on the man himself, but on his *thymos* or on its physical seat, his chest or midriff. We see the connection very clearly in Diomede's remark that Achilles will fight "when the *thymos* in his chest tells him to and a god rouses him" (overdetermination again).

A second peculiarity, which seems to be closely related to the first, must have worked in the same direction. This is the habit of explaining character or behaviour in terms of knowledge. The most familiar instance is the very wide use of the verb *oida*, "I know," with a neuter plural object to express not only the possession of technical skill but also what we should call moral character or personal feelings: Achilles "knows wild things, like a lion," Polyphemus "knows lawless things," Nestor and Agamemnon "know friendly things to each other." This is not merely a Homeric "idiom": a similar transposition of feeling into intellectual terms is implied when we are told that Achilles has "a merciless *understanding,*" or that the Trojans "*remembered* flight and *forgot* resistance." This intellectualist approach to the explanation of behaviour set a lasting stamp on the Greek mind: the so-called Socratic paradoxes, that "virtue is knowledge," and that "no one does wrong on purpose," were no novelties, but an explicit generalised formulation of what had long been an ingrained habit of thought. Such a habit of thought must have encouraged the belief in psychic intervention. If character is knowledge, what is not knowledge is not part of the character, but comes to a man from outside. When he acts in a manner contrary to the system of conscious dispositions which he is said to "know," his action is not properly his own, but has been dictated to him. In other words, unsystematised, nonrational impulses, and the acts resulting from them, tend to be excluded from the self and ascribed to an alien origin.

Evidently this is especially likely to happen when the acts in question are such as to cause acute shame to their author. We know how in our own society unbearable feelings of guilt are got rid of by "projecting" them in phantasy on to someone else. And we may guess that the notion of *atē* served a similar purpose for Homeric man by enabling him in all good faith to project on to an external power his unbearable feelings of shame. I say "shame" and not "guilt," for certain American anthropologists have lately taught us to distinguish "shame-cultures" from "guilt-cultures," and the society described by Homer clearly falls into the former class. Homeric man's highest good is not the enjoyment of a quiet conscience, but the enjoyment of *timē*, public esteem: "Why should I fight," asks Achilles, "if the good fighter receives no more *timē* than the bad?" And the strongest moral force which Homeric man knows is not the fear of god, but respect for public opinion, *aidōs: aideomai Trōas* says Hector at the crisis of his fate, and goes with open eyes to his death. The situation to which the notion of *atē* is a response arose not merely from the impulsiveness of Homeric man, but from the tension between individual impulse and the pressure of social conformity characteristic of a shame-culture. In such a society, any-thing which exposes a man to the contempt or ridicule of his fellows, which causes him to "lose face," is felt as unbearable. That perhaps explains how not only cases of moral failure, like Agamemnon's loss of self-control, but such things as the bad bargain of Glaucus, or Automedon's disregard of proper tactics, came to be "projected" on to a divine agency. On the other hand, it was the gradually growing sense of guilt, characteristic of a later age, which transformed *atē* into a punishment, the Erinyes into ministers of vengeance, and Zeus into an embodiment of cosmic justice. . . .

What I have thus far tried to do is to show, by examining one particular type of religious experience, that behind the term "Homeric religion" there lies something more than an artificial machinery of serio-comic gods and goddesses, and that we shall do it less than justice if we dismiss it as an agreeable interlude of lighthearted buffoonery between the presumed profundities of an Aegean Earth-religion about which we know little, and those of an "early Orphic movement" about which we know even less.

ERICH AUERBACH

Odysseus' Scar

Readers of the *Odyssey* will remember the well-prepared and touching scene in book 19, when Odysseus has at last come home, the scene in which the old housekeeper Euryclea, who had been his nurse, recognizes him by a scar on his thigh. The stranger has won Penelope's good will; at his request she tells the housekeeper to wash his feet, which, in all old stories, is the first duty of hospitality toward a tired traveler. Euryclea busies herself fetching water and mixing cold with hot, meanwhile speaking sadly of her absent master, who is probably of the same age as the guest, and who perhaps, like the guest, is even now wandering somewhere, a stranger; and she remarks how astonishingly like him the guest looks. Meanwhile Odysseus, remembering his scar, moves back out of the light; he knows that, despite his efforts to hide his identity, Euryclea will now recognize him, but he wants at least to keep Penelope in ignorance. No sooner has the old woman touched the scar than, in her joyous surprise, she lets Odysseus' foot drop into the basin; the water spills over, she is about to cry out her joy; Odysseus restrains her with whispered threats and endearments; she recovers herself and conceals her emotion. Penelope, whose attention Athena's foresight had diverted from the incident, has observed nothing.

All this is scrupulously externalized and narrated in leisurely fashion. The two women express their feelings in copious direct discourse. Feelings though they are, with only a slight admixture of the most general considerations upon human destiny, the syntactical connection between part and part is perfectly clear, no contour is blurred. There is also room and time for orderly, perfectly well-articulated, uniformly illuminated descriptions of implements, ministrations, and gestures; even in the dramatic moment of recognition, Homer does not omit to tell the reader that it is with his right hand that Odysseus takes the old woman by the throat to keep her from speaking, at the same time that he draws her closer to him with his left. Clearly outlined, brightly and uniformly illuminated, men and things stand out in a realm where everything is visible; and not less clear—wholly expressed, orderly even in their ardor—are the feelings and thoughts of the persons involved.

In my account of the incident I have so far passed over a whole series of verses which interrupt it in the middle. There are more than seventy of these verses—while to the incident itself some forty are devoted before the interruption and some forty after it. The interruption, which comes just at the point when the housekeeper recognizes the scar—that is, at the moment of crisis—describes the origin of the scar, a hunting accident which occurred in Odysseus' boyhood, at a boar hunt, during the time of his visit to his grandfather Autolycus. This first affords an opportunity to inform the reader about Autolycus, his house, the precise degree of the kinship, his character, and, no less exhaustively than touchingly, his behavior after the birth of his grandson; then follows the visit of Odysseus, now grown to be a youth; the exchange of greetings, the banquet with which he is welcomed, sleep and waking, the early start for the hunt, the tracking of the beast, the struggle, Odysseus' being wounded by the boar's tusk, his recovery, his return to Ithaca, his parents' anxious questions—all is narrated, again with such a complete externalization of all the elements of the story and of their interconnections as to leave nothing in obscurity. Not until then does the narrator return to Penelope's chamber, not until then, the digression having run its course, does Euryclea, who had recognized the scar before the digression began, let Odysseus' foot fall back into the basin.

The first thought of a modern reader—that this is a device to increase suspense—is, if not wholly wrong, at least not the essential explanation of this Homeric procedure. For the element of suspense is very slight in the Homeric poems; nothing in their entire style is calculated to keep the reader or hearer breathless. The digressions are not meant to keep the reader in suspense, but rather to relax the tension. And this frequently occurs, as in the passage before us. The broadly narrated, charming, and subtly fashioned story of the hunt, with all its elegance and self-sufficiency, its wealth of idyllic pictures, seeks to win the reader over wholly to itself as long as he is hearing it, to make him forget what had just taken place during the foot-washing. But an episode that will increase suspense by retarding the action must be so constructed that it will not fill the present entirely, will not put the crisis, whose resolution is being awaited, entirely out of the reader's mind, and thereby destroy the mood of suspense; the crisis and the suspense must continue, must remain vibrant in the background. But Homer—and to this we shall have to return later—knows no background. What he narrates is for the time being the only present, and fills both the stage and the reader's mind completely. So it is with the passage before us. When the young Euryclea (vv. 401ff.) sets the infant Odysseus on his grandfather Autolycus' lap after the banquet, the aged Euryclea, who a few lines earlier had touched the wanderer's foot, has entirely vanished from the stage and from the reader's mind.

Goethe and Schiller, who though not referring to this particular episode, exchanged letters in April 1797 on the subject of "the retarding element" in the Homeric poems in general, put it in direct opposition to the element of suspense—the latter word is not used, but is clearly implied when the "retarding" procedure is opposed, as something proper to epic, to tragic procedure (letters of April 19, 21, and 22). The "retarding element," the "going back and forth" by means of episodes, seems to me, too, in the Homeric poems, to be opposed to any tensional and suspensive striving toward a goal, and doubtless Schiller is right in regard to Homer when he says that what he gives us is "simply the quiet existence and operation of things in accordance with their natures"; Homer's goal is "already present in every point of his progress." But both Schiller and Goethe raise Homer's procedure to the level of a law for epic poetry in general, and Schiller's words quoted above are meant to be universally binding upon the epic poet, in contradistinction from the tragic. Yet in both modern and ancient times, there are important epic works which are composed throughout with no "retarding element" in this sense but, on the contrary, with suspense throughout, and which perpetually "rob us of our emotional freedom"—which power Schiller will grant only to the tragic poet. And besides it seems to me undemonstrable and improbable that this procedure of Homeric poetry was directed by aesthetic considerations or even by an aesthetic feeling of the sort postulated by Goethe and Schiller. The effect, to be sure, is precisely that which they describe, and is, furthermore, the actual source of the conception of epic which they themselves hold, and with them all writers decisively influenced by classical antiquity. But the true cause of the impression of "retardation" appears to me to lie elsewhere—namely, in the need of the Homeric style to leave nothing which it mentions half in darkness and unexternalized.

The excursus upon the origin of Odysseus' scar is not basically different from the many passages in which a newly introduced character, or even a newly appearing object or implement, though it be in the thick of a battle, is described as to its nature and origin; or in which, upon the appearance of a god, we are told where he last was, what he was doing there, and by what road he reached the scene; indeed, even the Homeric epithets seem to me in the final analysis to be traceable to the same need for an externalization of phenomena in terms perceptible to the senses. Here is the scar, which comes up in the course of the narrative; and Homer's feeling simply will not permit him to see it appear out of the darkness of an unilluminated past; it must be set in full light, and with it a portion of the hero's boyhood—just as, in the *Iliad*, when the first ship is already burning and the Myrmidons finally arm that they may hasten to help, there is still time not only for the wonderful simile of the wolf, not only for the order of the Myrmidon host, but also for a detailed account of the ancestry of several subordinate leaders (16, vv. 155ff.). To be sure, the aesthetic effect thus produced was soon noticed and thereafter consciously sought; but the more original cause must have lain in the basic impulse of the Homeric style: to represent phenomena in a fully externalized form, visible and palpable in all their parts, and completely fixed in their spatial and temporal relations. Nor do psychological processes receive any other treatment: here too nothing must remain hidden and unexpressed. With the utmost fullness, with an orderliness which even passion does not disturb, Homer's personages vent their inmost hearts in speech; what they do not say to others, they speak in their own minds, so that the reader is informed of it. Much that is terrible takes place in the Homeric poems, but it seldom takes place wordlessly: Polyphemus talks to Odysseus; Odysseus talks to the suitors when he begins to kill them; Hector and Achilles talk at length, before battle and after; and no speech is so filled with anger or scorn that the particles which express logical and grammatical connections are lacking or out of place. This last observation is true, of course, not only of speeches but of the presentation in general. The separate elements of a phenomenon are most clearly placed in relation to one another; a large number of conjunctions, adverbs, particles, and other syntactical tools, all clearly circumscribed and delicately differentiated in meaning, delimit persons, things, and portions of incidents in respect to one another, and at the same time bring them together in a continuous and ever flexible connection; like the separate phenomena themselves, their relationships—their temporal, local, causal, final, consecutive, comparative, concessive, antithetical, and conditional limitations—are brought to light in perfect fullness; so that a continuous rhythmic procession of phenomena passes by, and never is there a form left fragmentary or half-illuminated, never a lacuna, never a gap, never a glimpse of unplumbed depths.

And this procession of phenomena takes place in the foreground—that is, in a local and temporal present which is absolute. One might think that the many interpolations, the frequent moving back and forth, would create a sort of perspective in time and place; but the Homeric style never gives any such impression. The way in which any impression of perspective is avoided can be clearly observed in the procedure for introducing episodes, a syntactical construction with which every reader of Homer is familiar; it is used in the passage we are considering, but can also be found in cases when the episodes are much shorter. To the word scar (v. 393) there is first attached a relative clause ("which once long ago a boar . . ."), which enlarges into a voluminous syntactical parenthesis; into this an independent sentence unexpectedly intrudes (v. 396: "A god himself gave him . . ."), which quietly disentangles itself from syntactical subordination, until, with verse 399, an equally free syntactical treatment of the new content begins a new present which continues unchallenged until, with verse 467 ("The old woman now touched it . . ."), the scene which had been broken off is resumed. To be sure, in the case of such long episodes as the one we are considering, a purely syntactical connection with the principal theme would hardly have been possible; but a connection with it through perspective would have been all the easier had the content been arranged with that end in view; if, that is, the entire story of the scar had been presented as a recollection which awakens in Odysseus' mind at this particular moment. It would have been perfectly easy to do; the story of the scar had only to be inserted two verses earlier, at the first mention of the word scar, where the motifs "Odysseus" and "recollection" where already at hand. But any such subjectivistic-perspectivistic procedure, creating a foreground and background, resulting in the present lying open to the depths of the past, is entirely foreign to the Homeric style; the Homeric style knows only a foreground, only a uniformly illuminated, uniformly objective present. And so the excursus does not begin until two lines later, when Euryclea has discovered the scar—the possibility for a perspectivistic connection no longer exists, and the story of the wound becomes an independent and exclusive present.

The genius of the Homeric style becomes even more apparent when it is compared with an equally ancient and equally epic style from a different world of forms. I shall attempt this comparison with the account of the sacrifice of Isaac, a homogeneous narrative produced by the so-called Elohist. The King James version translates the opening as follows (Genesis 22: 1): "And it came to pass after these things, that God did tempt Abraham, and said to him, Abraham! and he said, Behold, here I am." Even this opening startles us when we come to it from Homer. Where are the two speakers? We are not told. The reader, however, knows that they are not normally to be found together in one place on earth, that one of them, God, in order to speak to Abraham, must come from somewhere, must enter the earthly realm from some unknown heights or depths. Whence does he come, whence does he call to Abraham? We are not told. He does not come, like Zeus or Poseidon, from the Aethiopians, where he has been enjoying a sacrificial feast. Nor are we told anything of his reasons for tempting Abraham so terribly. He has not, like Zeus, discussed them in set speeches with other gods gathered in council; nor have the deliberations in his own heart been presented to us; unexpected and mysterious, he enters the scene from some unknown height or depth and calls: Abraham! It will at once be said that this is to be explained by the particular concept of God which the Jews held and which was wholly different from that of the Greeks. True enough—but this constitutes no objection. For how is the Jewish concept of God to be explained? Even their earlier God of the desert was not fixed in form and content, and was alone; his lack of form, his lack of local habitation, his singleness, was in the end not only maintained but developed even further in competition with the comparatively far more manifest gods of the surrounding Near Eastern world. The concept of God held by the Jews is less a cause than a symptom of their manner of comprehending and representing things.

This becomes still clearer if we now turn to the other person in the dialogue, to Abraham. Where is he? We do not know. He says, indeed: Here I am—but the Hebrew word means only something like "behold me," and in any case is not meant to indicate the actual place where Abraham is, but a moral position in respect to God, who has called to him—Here am I awaiting thy command. Where he is actually, whether in Beersheba or elsewhere, whether indoors or in the open air, is not stated; it does not interest the narrator, the reader is not informed; and what Abraham was doing when God called to him is left in the same obscurity. To realize the difference, consider Hermes' visit to Calypso, for example, where command, journey, arrival and reception of the visitor, situation and occupation of the person visited, are set forth in many verses; and even on occasions when gods appear suddenly and briefly, whether to help one of their favorites or to deceive or destroy some mortal whom they hate, their bodily forms, and usually the manner of their coming and going, are given in detail.

Here, however, God appears without bodily form (yet he "appears"), coming from some unspecified place—we only hear his voice, and that utters nothing but a name, a name without an adjective, without a descriptive epithet for the person spoken to, such as is the rule in every Homeric address; and of Abraham too nothing is made perceptible except the words in which he answers God: *Hinne-ni*, Behold me here—with which, to be sure, a most touching gesture expressive of obedience and readiness is suggested, but it is left to the reader to visualize it. Moreover the two speakers are not on the same level: if we conceive of Abraham in the foreground, where it might be possible to picture him as prostrate or kneeling or bowing with outspread arms or gazing upward, God is not there too: Abraham's words and gestures are directed toward the depths of the picture or upward, but in any case the undetermined, dark place from which the voice comes to him is not in the foreground.

After this opening, God gives his command, and the story itself begins: everyone knows it; it unrolls with no episodes in a few independent sentences whose syntactical connection is of the most rudimentary sort. In this atmosphere it is unthinkable that an implement, a landscape through which the travelers passed, the serving-men, or the ass, should be described, that their origin or descent or material or appearance or usefulness should be set forth in terms of praise; they do not even admit an adjective: they are serving-men, ass, wood, and knife, and nothing else, without an epithet; they are there to serve the end which God has commanded; what in other respects they were, are, or will be, remains in darkness. A journey is made, because God has designated the place where the sacrifice is to be performed; but we are told nothing about the journey except that it took three days, and even that we are told in a mysterious way: Abraham and his followers rose "early in the morning" and "went unto" the place of which God had told him; on the third day he lifted up his eyes and saw the place from afar. That gesture is the only gesture, is indeed the only occurrence during the whole journey, of which we are told; and though its motivation lies in the fact that the place is elevated, its uniqueness still heightens the impression that the journey took place through a vacuum; it is as if, while he traveled on, Abraham had looked neither to the right nor to the left, had suppressed any sign of life in his followers and himself save only their footfalls.

Thus the journey is like a silent progress through the indeterminate and the contingent, a holding of the breath, a process which has no present, which is inserted, like a blank duration, between what has passed and what lies ahead, and which yet is measured: three days! Three such days positively demand the symbolic interpretation which they later received. They began "early in the morning." But at what time on the third day did Abraham lift up his eyes and see his goal? The text says nothing on the subject. Obviously not "late in the evening," for it seems that there was still time enough to climb the mountain and make the sacrifice. So "early in the morning" is given, not as an indication of time, but for the sake of its ethical significance; it is intended to express the resolution, the promptness, the punctual obedience of the sorely tried Abraham. Bitter to him is the early morning in which he saddles his ass, calls his serving-men and his son Isaac, and sets out; but he obeys, he walks on until the third day, then lifts up his eyes and sees the place. Whence he comes, we do not know, but the goal is clearly stated: Jeruel in the land of Moriah. What place this is meant to indicate is not clear—"Moriah" especially may be a later correction of some other word. But in any case the goal was given, and in any case it is a matter of some sacred spot which was to receive a particular consecration by being connected with Abraham's sacrifice. Just as little as "early in the morning" serves as a temporal indication does "Jeruel in the land of Moriah" serve as a geographical indication; and in both cases alike, the complementary indication is not given, for we know as little of the hour at which Abraham lifted up his eyes as we do of the place from which he set forth—Jeruel is significant not so much as the goal of an earthly journey, in its geographical relation to other places, as through its special election, through its relation to God, who designated it as the scene of the act, and therefore it must be named.

In the narrative itself, a third chief character appears: Isaac. While God and Abraham, the serving-men, the ass and the implements are simply named, without mention of any qualities or any other sort of definition, Isaac once receives an appositive; God says, "Take Isaac, thine only son, whom thou lovest." But this is not a characterization of Isaac as a person, apart from his relation to his father and apart from the story; he may be handsome or ugly, intelligent or stupid, tall or short, pleasant or unpleasant—we are not told. Only what we need to know about him as a personage in the action, here and now, is illuminated, so that it may become apparent how terrible Abraham's temptation is, and that God is fully aware of it. By this example of the contrary, we see the significance of the descriptive adjectives and digressions of the Homeric poems; with their indications of the earlier and as it were absolute existence of the persons described, they prevent the reader from concentrating exclusively on a present crisis; even when the most terrible things are occurring, they prevent the establishment of an overwhelming suspense. But here, in the story of

Abraham's sacrifice, the overwhelming suspense is present; what Schiller makes the goal of the tragic poet—to rob us of our emotional freedom, to turn our intellectual and spiritual powers (Schiller says "our activity") in one direction, to concentrate them there—is effected in this Biblical narrative, which certainly deserves the epithet epic.

We find the same contrast if we compare the two uses of direct discourse. The personages speak in the Bible story too; but their speech does not serve, as does speech in Homer, to manifest, to externalize thoughts—on the contrary, it serves to indicate thoughts which remain unexpressed. God gives his command in direct discourse, but he leaves his motives and his purpose unexpressed; Abraham, receiving the command, says nothing and does what he has been told to do. The conversation between Abraham and Isaac on the way to the place of sacrifice is only an interruption of the heavy silence and makes it all the more burdensome. The two of them, Isaac carrying the wood and Abraham with fire and a knife, "went together." Hesitantly, Isaac ventures to ask about the ram, and Abraham gives the well-known answer. Then the text repeats: "So they went both of them together." Everything remains unexpressed.

It would be difficult, then, to imagine styles more contrasted than those of these two equally ancient and equally epic texts. On the one hand, externalized, uniformly illuminated phenomena, at a definite time and in a definite place, connected together without lacunae in a perpetual foreground; thoughts and feelings completely expressed; events taking place in leisurely fashion and with very little of suspense. On the other hand, the externalization of only so much of the phenomena as is necessary for the purpose of the narrative, all else left in obscurity; the decisive points of the narrative alone are emphasized, what lies between is nonexistent; time and place are undefined and call for interpretation; thoughts and feelings remain unexpressed, are only suggested by the silence and the fragmentary speeches; the whole, permeated with the most unrelieved suspense and directed toward a single goal (and to that extent far more of a unity), remains mysterious and "fraught with background."

BRUNO SNELL

Homer's View of Man

W̲e find it difficult to conceive of a
mentality which made no provision for the body as such. Among the early
expressions designating what was later rendered as *sōma* or "body," only
the plurals *guia, melea* [both "limbs"], etc. refer to the physical nature of
the body; for *chrōs* is merely the limit of the body, and *demas* represents
the frame, the structure, and occurs only in the accusative of specification.
As it is, early Greek art actually corroborates our impression that the
physical body of man was comprehended, not as a unit but as an aggregate.
Not until the classical art of the fifth century do we find attempts to depict
the body as an organic unit whose parts are mutually correlated. In the
preceding period the body is a mere construct of independent parts variously
put together. It must not be thought, however, that the pictures of human
beings from the time of Homer are like the primitive drawings to which
our children have accustomed us, though they too simply add limb to limb.
Our children usually represent the human shape as shown in fig. 1, whereas
fig. 2 reproduces the Greek concept as found on the vases of the geometric
period.

Our children first draw a body as the central and most important
part of their design; then they add the head, the arms and the legs. The
geometric figures, on the other hand, lack this central part; they are nothing
but *melea kai guia*, i.e. limbs with strong muscles, separated from each other
by means of exaggerated joints. This difference is of course partially dependent upon the clothes they wore, but even after we have made due
allowance for this the fact remains that the Greeks of this early period seem

Translated by T. G. Rosenmeyer. From *The Discovery of the Mind: The Greek Origins of
European Thought.* Copyright © 1960 by Harper & Row.

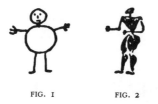

FIG. 1   FIG. 2

to have seen in a strangely "articulated" way. In their eyes the individual limbs are clearly distinguished from each other, and the joints are, for the sake of emphasis, presented as extraordinarily thin, while the fleshy parts are made to bulge just as unrealistically. The early Greek drawing seeks to demonstrate the agility of the human figure, the drawing of the modern child its compactness and unity.

Thus the early Greeks did not, either in their language or in the visual arts, grasp the body as a unit. The phenomenon is the same as with the verbs denoting sight; in the latter, the activity is at first understood in terms of its conspicuous modes, of the various attitudes and sentiments connected with it, and it is a long time before speech begins to address itself to the essential function of this activity. It seems, then, as if language aims progressively to express the essence of an act, but is at first unable to comprehend it because it is a function, and as such neither tangibly apparent nor associated with certain unambiguous emotions. As soon, however, as it is recognized and has received a name, it has come into existence, and the knowledge of its existence quickly becomes common property. Concerning the body, the chain of events may have been somewhat like this: in the early period a speaker, when faced by another person, was apparently satisfied to call out his name: this is Achilles, or to say: this is a man. As a next step, the most conspicuous elements of his appearance are described, namely his limbs as existing side by side; their functional correlation is not apprehended in its full importance until somewhat later. True enough, the function is a concrete fact, but its objective existence does not manifest itself so clearly as the presence of the individual corporeal limbs, and its prior significance escapes even the owner of the limbs himself. With the discovery of this hidden unity, of course, it is at once appreciated as an immediate and self-explanatory truth.

This objective truth, it must be admitted, does not exist for man until it is seen and known and designated by a word; until, thereby, it has become an object of thought. Of course the Homeric man had a body exactly like the later Greeks, but he did not know it *qua* body, but merely as the sum total of his limbs. This is another way of saying that the Homeric Greeks did not yet have a body in the modern sense of the word; body, *sōma*, is a later interpretation of what was originally comprehended as *melē* or *guia,* i.e. as limbs. Again and again Homer speaks of fleet legs, of knees in speedy motion, of sinewy arms; it is in these limbs, immediately evident as they are to his eyes, that he locates the secret of life.

To return now to the intellect and the soul, we find there too the same perspective. Again Homer has no one word to characterize the mind or the soul. *Psyche,* the word for soul in later Greek, has no original connexion with the thinking and feeling soul. For Homer, *psyche* is the force which keeps the human being alive. There is, therefore, a gap in the Homeric vocabulary, comparable to the deficiency in "physical" terminology which we discussed above. As before, the gap is filled with a number of words which do not possess the same centre of gravity as the modern terms, but which cover more or less the same area. For the area of the "soul," the most important words are *psyche, thymos,* and *noos.* Concerning the *psyche* Homer says that it forsakes man at the moment of death, and that it flutters about in Hades; but it is impossible to find out from his words what he considers to be the function of the *psyche* during man's lifetime. There is no lack of theories about the nature of the *psyche* prior to death, but so far from relying on the testimony of the Homeric poems they are based only on conjectures and analogies. One would do well to remember how little Homer says about the *psyche* of the living and of the dying man; for one thing, it leaves its owner when he is dying, or when he loses consciousness; secondly he says that the *psyche* is risked in battle, a battle is fought for it, one wishes to save his *psyche,* and so forth. There is no justification here for assuming two different connotations of *psyche,* for although we shall have occasion to translate it as "life," that is not its true meaning. The *psyche* which is the prize of battle, which is risked, and saved, is identical with the soul which departs from a dying man.

Of this departure, Homer mentions only a few details. The *psyche* leaves through the mouth, it is breathed forth; or again it leaves through a wound, and then flies off to Hades. There it leads a ghostlike existence, as the spectre (*eidōlon*) of the deceased. The word *psyche* is akin to *psychein,* "to breathe," and denotes the breath of life which of course departs through the mouth; the escape from a wound evidently represents a secondary development. This vital breath is, as it were, a semi-concrete organ which exists in a man as long as he lives. As for its location, and its function, Homer passes them over in silence, and that means that we cannot know about them either. It appears as if in Homeric times the term *psyche* chiefly evoked the notion of an eschatological soul; at one point Homer says: he has but one *psyche*, he is mortal (*Il.* 21.569); when, however, he wants to say: "as long as the breath of life remains in a man" he avoids the word and puts it (*Il.* 10.89): "as long as my breath remains in my breast and my knees are in motion." Yet in spite of the mention of breath or respiration, the presence of the verb "remain" suggests that the notion of the *psyche* is also involved, and that therefore Homer has a concept of the "breath of life."

The other two words for the "mind" are *thymos* and *noos*. *Thymos* in Homer is the generator of motion or agitation, while *noos* is the cause of ideas and images. All mental phenomena are in one way or another distributed so as to fall in the sphere of either of the two organs. In several passages death is depicted as a departure of the *thymos*, with the result that scholars have attempted to interpret *thymos* as "soul," rivalling the *psyche*. "The *thymos* left his bones" is a phrase which occurs seven times; "quickly the *thymos* went forth from the limbs" is found twice. If we translate *thymos* as "organ of (e)motion," the matter becomes simple enough. Since this organ, prominently among its functions, determines physical motion, it is plausible enough to say that at the point of death the *thymos* leaves the bones and the *melē*, i.e. the limbs with their muscles. But this hardly implies that the *thymos* continues to exist after death; it merely means: what provided motion for the bones and limbs is now gone.

Other passages in which *thymos* and *psyche* are apparently used without any distinction in meaning are more difficult to explain. *Il.* 22.67 Homer says: "when someone by stroke or throw of the sharp bronze has bereft my *rhethē* of *thymos*." At this point the meaning of *rhethē* must be "limbs"; the concept is the same as in the verse just quoted, viz. that the *thymos* departs from the limbs, and this explanation was already given by the ancients. The difficulty arises when we come to the other passages which contain *rhethē*; *Il.* 16.856 = 22.363: "his *psyche* fled from his *rhethē* and went down to Hades." This is unique, for ordinarily the *psyche* leaves the body through the mouth (*Il.* 9.409) or through a wound (*Il.* 14.518; 16.505), i.e. through an aperture of the body. The expression "from the limbs," besides being considerably less plausible and convincing, also presupposes that the soul has its seat in the limbs, a view which is not met with elsewhere in Homer. Now it so happens that the word *rhethos* remained alive in Aeolic, but not in the sense of "limb"; we take this information from the scholia on the verse cited above, whence we conclude that for Sappho and Alcaeus *rhethos* bore the meaning "face." From the Aeolic poets this meaning of the word was handed on to Sophocles (*Antigone* 529), Euripides (*Heracles* 1204) and

Theocritus (29.16). As the same scholion tells us, Dionysius Thrax already came to the conclusion that in Homer too *rhethos* must refer to the face. Other ancient scholars opposed him by pointing to the circumstance that in Homer the *psyche* sometimes leaves the body through a wound. In any case, the solution offered by Dionysius is too simple, for as has already been stated, in *Il.* 22.68 we read that the *thymos* takes its leave from the *rhethē* and they must be the *melē*, for if our interpretation of *thymos* as (e)motion is right, it may be expected to escape from the limbs but not from the face, let alone the mouth. *Il.* 16.856, on the other hand, concerns the *psyche*, and here we are not surprised that it should fly off through the mouth.

The whole confusion is easily resolved once we take into consideration the age of the various passages. *Il.* 22.68 is undoubtedly very late, probably even, as E. Kapp has pointed out to me, dependent on Tyrtaeus. The author is someone who was not conversant with the Aeolic word *rhethos,* and whose understanding of Homer's language was on the whole no longer perfect. Confronted with such seemingly analogous passages as 13.671: "the *thymos* quickly went forth from his limbs (*melē*)" and 16.856: "his *psyche* escaped from the *rhethē* and went down to Hades," he was quick to equate *psyche* with *thymos* and *melē* with *rhethē,* and by a further analogy with a passage like 5.317 he finally formed his own verse. By the standard of Homer's own usage, these words make no sense at all. There are other indications that the concepts of *thymos* and *psyche* are easily confused: *Il.* 7.131 reads: "his *thymos* escaped from his limbs (*melē*) down to Hades." It has long been noticed that the idea of the *thymos* going down to Hades contradicts the usual Homeric conception. The verse is contaminated from 13.671 f.: "quickly the *thymos* went forth from the limbs (*melē*)" and 3.322: "grant that he dies and goes down to Hades." It is just possible that the contamination is the work of a later poet who did not know the Homeric usage. But it is more likely that it was brought about by a rhapsode who confused several sections of verses in his memory, a common enough occurrence in oral delivery. In that case emendation would seem to be called for, and as it happens another part of a verse from Homer furnishes an easy remedy. In 16.856 (= 22.362) we have a reading which is good and meaningful: "the soul [*psyche*] flew down to Hades from the *rhethē*." From this, 7.131 may be reconstructed: [the *psyche* escaped from the *rhethē* down to Hades]. It is true that there remain a number of passages in which *thymos* is the eschatological soul which flies off at the moment of death; but in each case it is the death of an animal which is so described—the death of a horse (*Il.* 16.469), of a stag (*Od.* 10.163), of a boar (*Od.* 19.454) or of a dove (*Il.* 23.880). I have no doubt that the origin of this usage was as follows: evidently people were averse to ascribing the *psyche*, which a human being loses when he dies, also to an animal. They therefore invented the idea of a *thymos* which leaves the animal when it expires. The idea was suggested by the passages which exhibit the *thymos* leaving the limbs or the bones of a man. Those passages in turn which speak of a *thymos* of animals contributed their share to the confusion between *thymos* and *psyche*. But the phrase "the *thymos* flew off" which occurs four times, i.e. with comparative frequency, is always applied to animals—and, incidentally, to no one more than once. This proves that in the early period the two terms were not yet used interchangeably.

Whereas the contrast between *thymos* and *psyche* is clear and emphatic, the line between *thymos* and *noos* cannot be drawn with the same precision. If, as we have suggested, *thymos* is the mental organ which causes (e)motion, while *noos* is the recipient of images, then *noos* may be said generally to be in charge of intellectual matters, and *thymos* of things emotional. Yet they overlap in many respects. To-day, for instance, we regard the head as the seat of thinking, and the heart as the organ of feeling; but that does not prevent us from saying: he carries thoughts of his beloved in his heart—where the heart becomes the seat of thinking, but the thoughts are oriented towards love; or the reverse: he has nothing in his head but revenge—and here again the meaning is: thoughts of vengeance. But these exceptions are only apparent, for they are easily replaced by equivalent turns of expression: he has vengeance in his heart, etc. The same is true of *thymos* = (e)motion and *noos* = understanding; the exceptions which might be cited by way of argument against these equations are not real. Nevertheless it is only fair to concede that the distinction between *thymos* and *noos* is not as evident as that between *thymos* and *psyche*. Here are a few examples.

Ordinarily the sensation of joy is located in the *thymos*. But *Od.* 8.78 we read: Agammenon rejoiced in his *noos* when Achilles and Odysseus quarrelled with each other for the distinction of being the best man. Agamemnon's delight does not spring from the altercation of the two most valiant heroes—that would be absurd—but from his recollection of Apollo's prophecy that Troy would fall when the best heroes contended with one another. The basis of his joy, therefore, is reflection.

Another instance: generally speaking it is the *thymos* which rouses a man to action. But *Il.* 14.61 f. Nestor says: "Let us take counsel . . . if the *noos* may accomplish anything." In this passage *thymos* would be quite meaningless, for Nestor asks them to consider whether "counsel," i.e. an idea, may achieve anything. Although the *thymos* is customarily the abode of joy, pleasure, love, sympathy, anger and all mental agitation, occasionally we also find knowledge residing in it. *Il.* 2.409, for example, we are told that Menelaus did not have to be summoned to the assembly, for "he knew in his *thymos* that his brother was beset by trouble." He knew it, not because he had been informed, or because his perception was especially acute, but by virtue of his instincts, through brotherly sympathy. Or, in the words of the poet, he knew it through an "emotion." Examples of this sort could be multiplied freely. *Noos* is akin to *noein* which means "to realize," "to see in its true colours"; and often it may simply be translated as "to see." Witness *Il.* 5.590: "She saw (*enoēse*) Hector in the ranks." Frequently it is combined with *idein*, but it stands for a type of seeing which involves not merely visual activity but the mental act which goes with the vision. This puts it close to *gignōskein*. But the latter means "to recognize"; it is properly used of the identification of a man, while *noein* refers more particularly to situations; it means: "to acquire a clear image of something." Hence the significance of *noos*. It is the mind as a recipient of clear images, or, more briefly, the organ of clear images: *Il.* 16.688 "The *noos* of Zeus is ever stronger than that of men." *Noos* is, as it were, the mental eye which exercises an unclouded vision. But given a slight shift which in Greek is easily managed, *noos* may come to denote the function rather than the organ. In its capacity as a permanent function *noos* represents the faculty of having clear ideas, i.e. the power of intelligence: *Il.* 13.730 "To one man the god has given works of war . . . but in the heart of another far-seeing Zeus has placed an excellent *noos*." At this point the meaning "mind" shades off into the notion of "thinking." The two are of course closely related; in our language we employ the term "intelligence" to refer both to the intellect and to its activity or capacity. From here it is only a short step, and *noos* will signify also the individual act, the individual image, or the thought. We read, for instance, that someone thinks a *noos*: *Il.* 9.104 and *Od.* 5.23. Thus the area covered by this term exceeds the competence of our words mind, soul, or intelligence. The same is true also of *thymos*. If it is said that someone feels something in his *thymos*, the reference is to an organ which we may translate as "soul" provided we keep in mind that it is the soul as the seat of (e)motions. But *thymos* may also serve as the name of a function, in which case we render it as "will" or "character"; and where it refers to one single act, the word once more transcends the limitations of our "soul" or "mind." The most obvious example occurs *Od.* 9.302 where Odysseus says: "Another *thymos* held me back"; each individual impulse, therefore, is also a *thymos*.

What bearing does all this have on our investigation of Homer's attitude towards the human mind? At first it might be suspected that *thymos* and *noos* are nothing more than the parts of the soul, such as we know from Plato's psychology. But those parts presuppose a psychic whole of which Homer has no cognizance. *Thymos, noos,* and *psyche* as well are separate organs, each having its own particular function. We say: "to look at a thing with different eyes," without meaning to refer to the organ; the idea that someone provides himself with another set of eyes would hardly arise. Rather, the word "eye" here stands for "function of the eye," "vision," and what we actually mean is "to see with a different view." Homer's "another *thymos*" must be similarly understood. But that is not all: the two passages with *noos* cited above (*Il.* 9.104 and *Od.* 5.23) lead us even further, in a most significant direction. *Noos* as understood in their context no longer refers to the function itself but to the result of the *noein. Noon ameinona noēsei* still lends itself to the translation: "he will devise a better thought." But now thought has ceased to be the activity of thinking, and has become the thing thought. *Touton ebouleusas noon* [you counselled this thought] presents the same situation. It is worth pointing out, however, that *noos,* in the only two Homeric passages where it is to be rendered as "thought," appears as the internal object of *noein* and *bouleuein* [counsel, advise]. The *actio verbi* of *noein,* i.e. the function, obviously remains a decisive factor.

We have intentionally avoided bringing into our inquiry the distinction, on the face of it so pertinent, between "concrete" and "abstract." Actually this distinction is for our purposes open to question, and not nearly so fruitful as the difference between organ and function. It might, for instance, be thought that because the word *athymos* [without *thymos*] is found in one Homeric passage, *thymos* must already have possessed an abstract significance. But if that were so, one would have to admit that "heart" and "head" are abstracts too, for it is entirely feasible to say that someone is heartless, or has lost his head. If I declare that someone has a good brain, and I mean his thinking; or: someone has a soft heart, and I mean his feelings, I use the name of the organ in place of that of the function. "Heartless," "brainless," and *athymos* refer to the lack of a function. The metaphoric use of words for organs, which may be interpreted as abstraction, has its place on the most primitive level of speech, for it is precisely on that level that the organ is regarded, not as dead and concrete, but as participating in its function.

As soon as we attempt to describe the mental concepts of Homer by means of the catchwords "organ" and "function" we are bound to encounter terminological difficulties such as always arise for anyone who wishes to reproduce foreign idioms and peculiarities within the terms of his own tongue. If I say that the *thymos* is a mental organ, that it is the organ of a psychic process, I find myself caught in phrases which contain a contra-diction in terms, for in our eyes the ideas of the soul and of an organ are incompatible. To express myself accurately I should have to say: what we interpret as the soul, Homeric man splits up into three components each of which he defines by the analogy of physical organs. Our transcription of *psyche, noos* and *thymos* as "organs" of life, of perception, and of (e)motion are, therefore, merely in the nature of abbreviations, neither totally accurate nor exhaustive; this could not be otherwise, owing to the circumstance that the concept of the "soul"—and also of the "body," as we have seen—is tied up with the whole character and orientation of a language. This means that in the various languages we are sure to find the most divergent interpretations of these ideas.

According to some the remark that Homer had "not yet" acquired the knowledge of many things lowers his stature. Consequently they have tried to explain the difference between his mentality and ours by the prop-osition that Homer stylized his thinking, that for aesthetic or other reasons he avoided the description of mental processes because such details might have detracted from the grand simplicity of his heroes. Is it conceivable that Homer could deliberately have turned his back upon the notions of "intellect" and "soul"? Such psychological finesse, affecting the most subtle particulars, cannot in all fairness be attributed to the ancient epic poet. What is more, the gaps left by Homer's "ignorance" suddenly fall into a meaningful pattern if they are set off against those of his notions which our modern thinking seems to lack. Deliberate stylization is undoubtedly to be found in Homer, but this is not one of the quarters in which it takes effect. Do we expect Homer to present us with that invention of Goethe's humour, Little Mr. Microcosm? Everything human, and especially every-thing great, is one-sided and confined within limits. The belief in the existence of a universal, uniform human mind is a rationalist prejudice.

Actually there is further evidence for our contention that we are dealing with an early stage of European thought, and not with stylization. That Homer's conception of *thymos, noos* and *psyche* still depended to a large extent on an analogy with the physical organs becomes a matter of absolute certainty if we turn to that era of transition when his conception began to be abandoned. To be sure, the evidence for the use of the words *sōma* and *psyche* during the period extending from Homer to the fifth century is not full enough to allow us to trace the origin of the new meanings "body" and "soul" in every detail. Apparently they were evolved as com-plementary terms, and more likely than not it was *psyche* which first started on its course, perhaps under the influence of notions concerning the immortality of the soul. The word denoting the eschatological soul was put to a new use, to designate the soul as a whole, and the word for corpse came to be employed for the living body; the reason for this must be that the element which provided man during his living days with emotions, perceptions and thoughts was believed to survive in the *psyche*. Presumably people felt that animate man had within him a spiritual or intellectual portion, though they were unable to define this element by one term sufficiently accurate and inclusive. As a matter of fact, this is the state of affairs which we shall meet among the early writers of lyric poetry. And it may be inferred that, because the eschatological *psyche* had been correlated with the *sōma* of the dead, the new *psyche*, the "soul," demanding a body to suit it, caused the term *sōma* to be extended so that it was ultimately used also of the living body. But whatever the details of this evolution, the distinction between body and soul represents a "discovery" which so impressed people's minds that it was thereafter accepted as self-evident, in spite of the fact that the relation between body and soul, and the nature of the soul itself, continued to be the topic of lively speculation.

The first writer to feature the new concept of the soul is Heraclitus. He calls the soul of living man *psyche*; in his view man consists of body and soul, and the soul is endowed with qualities which differ radically from those of the body and the physical organs. We can safely say that these new qualities are irreconcilable with the categories of Homer's thought; he does not even dispose of the linguistic prerequisites to describe what Heraclitus predicates of the soul. The new expressions were fashioned in the period which separates Heraclitus from Homer, that is to say the era of the lyric. Heraclitus says (fr. 45): "You could not find the ends of the soul though you travelled every way, so deep is its *logos*." This notion of the depth or profundity of the soul is not unfamiliar to us; but it involves a dimension which is foreign to a physical organ or its function. To say: someone has a deep hand, or a deep ear, is nonsensical, and when we talk of a deep voice, we mean something entirely different; the adjective there refers to vocal expression, not to the function of the voice. In Heraclitus the image of depth is designed to throw light on the outstanding trait of the soul and its realm: that it has its own dimension, that it is not extended in space. To describe this non-spatial substance we are of course obliged to fall back on a metaphor taken from space relations. But in the last analysis Heraclitus means to assert that the soul, as contrasted with things physical, reaches into infinity. Not Heraclitus but the lyric poets who preceded him were the first to voice this new idea, that intellectual and spiritual matters have "depth." Archaic poetry contains such words as "deep-pondering" and "deep-thinking"; concepts like "deep knowledge," "deep thinking," "deep pondering," as well as "deep pain" are common enough in the archaic period. In these expressions, the symbol of depth always points to the infinity of the intellectual and spiritual, which differentiates it from the physical.

Homeric speech does not yet know this aspect of the word "deep." It is more than an ordinary metaphor; it is almost as if speech were by this means trying to break through its confines, to trespass on a forbidden field of adventure. Nor does Homer show himself conversant with the specifically spiritual facet of "deep knowledge," "deep thinking" and so forth. . . . Quantity, not intensity, is Homer's standard of judgment. *Il.* 24.639 Priam laments the fate of Hector: "I groan and brood over countless griefs." "To demand much," "to exhort much" is a frequent figure, even where the act of demanding or exhorting takes place only once. Our "much" offers a similar ambiguity. Never does Homer, in his descriptions of ideas or emotions, go beyond a purely spatial or quantitative definition; never does he attempt to sound their special, non-physical nature. As far as he is concerned, ideas are conveyed through the *noos*, a mental organ which in turn is analogous to the eye; consequently "to know" is *eidenai* which is related to *idein*, "to see," and in fact originally means "to have seen." The eye, it appears, serves as Homer's model for the absorption of experiences. From this point of view the intensive coincides with the extensive; he who has seen much sufficiently often possesses intensive knowledge.

Nor does the *thymos* provide any scope for the development of a notion of intensity. This organ of (e)motion is, among other things, the seat of pain. In Homer's language, the *thymos* is eaten away or torn asunder by pain; the pain which hits the *thymos* is sharp, or immense, or heavy. The analogies are evident: just as a limb is struck by a pointed weapon or by a heavy stone, just as it may be corroded or torn to pieces, so also the *thymos*. As before, the concept of the spiritual is not divorced from the corporeal, and intensity, the proper dimension of the spiritual, receives no attention. Homer is not even acquainted with intensity in its original sense, as "tension." A tension within the soul has no more reality for him than a tension in the eye would, or a tension in the hand. Here too the predicates of the soul remain completely within the bounds set for physical organs. There are no divided feelings in Homer; not until Sappho are we to read of the bitter-sweet Eros. Homer is unable to say: "half-willing, half-unwilling," instead he says: "he was willing, but his *thymos* was not." This does not reflect a contradiction within one and the same organ, but the contention between a man and one of his organs; we should compare our saying: "my hand desired to reach out, but I withdrew it." Two different things or substances engage in a quarrel with one another. As a result there is in Homer no genuine reflexion, no dialogue of the soul with itself.

Besides being "deep," the *logos* of Heraclitus is also a *koinon*, a "common" thing. It pervades everything, and everything shares in it. Again, Homer has no vocabulary to express a concept of this sort; he cannot say that different beings are of the same spirit, that two men have the same mind, or one and the same soul, any more than he would allow that two men have one eye or one hand between them.

A third quality which Heraclitus assigns to the mental sphere also diverges from any predications which could be made of the physical organs; this means that it must clash with the thought and speech of Homer. Heraclitus says (fr. 115): "The soul has a *logos* which increases itself." Whatever the exact significance of this statement, we gather that Heraclitus ascribes to the *psyche* a *logos* capable of extending and adding to itself of its own accord; the soul is regarded as a sort of base from which certain developments are possible. It would be absurd to attach a similar *logos* to the eye, or the hand. For Homer the mental processes have no such capacity for self-induced expansion. Any augmentation of bodily or spiritual powers is effected from without, above all by the deity. In the 16th book of the *Iliad* Homer recounts how the dying Sarpedon with his last words implored his friend Glaucus to help him; but he too was wounded and could not come. So Glaucus prayed to Apollo to relieve him of his pain and restore to him the strength of his arms. Apollo heard his prayer, soothed his pain, and "cast strength in his *thymos.*" As in many other passages in which Homer refers to the intervention of a god, the event has nothing supernatural, or unnatural, about it. We are free to conjecture that Glaucus heard the dying call of Sarpedon, that it caused him to forget his pain, to collect his strength, and to resume the fighting. It is easy to say that Glaucus pulled himself together, that he recovered his self-control; but Homer says, and thinks, nothing of the sort: they are notions which we read back into the scene. We believe that a man advances from an earlier situation by an act of his own will, through his own power. If Homer, on the other hand, wants to explain the source of an increase in strength, he has no course but to say that the responsibility lies with a god.

The same is true in other cases. Whenever a man accomplishes, or pronounces, more than his previous attitude had led others to expect, Homer connects this, in so far as he tries to supply an explanation, with the interference of a god. It should be noted especially that Homer does not know genuine personal decisions; even where a hero is shown pondering two alternatives the intervention of the gods plays the key role. This divine meddling is, of course, a necessary complement of Homer's notions regarding the human mind and the soul. The *thymos* and the *noos* are so very little different from other physical organs that they cannot very well be looked upon as a genuine source of impulses; Aristotle's "first mover" is hidden from Homer's ken, as is the concept of any vital centre which controls the organic system. Mental and spiritual acts are due to the impact of external factors, and man is the open target of a great many forces which impinge on him, and penetrate his very core. That is the reason why Homer has so much to say about forces, why, in fact, he has so many words for our term "force": *menos, sthenos, biē, kikus, is, kratos, alkē, dynamis.* The meaning of each of these words is precise, concrete, and full of implications; so far from serving as abstract symbols of force, as do the later terms *dynamis* and *exousia* which may be used of no matter what function, Homer's words refer to specific functions and particular provinces of experience. *Menos* is the force in the limbs of a man who is burning to tackle a project. *Alkē* is the defensive force which helps to ward off the enemy. *Sthenos* is the muscular force of the body, but also the forceful sway of the ruler. *Kratos* is supremacy, the superior force. That these forces were at one time invested with religious awe is indicated by certain formulas: Alcinous, for example, is called the "force of Alcinous," compare also *biē Hēraklēeiē* [night of Heracles] and *hierē is Tēlemachoio* [strength of Telemachus]. These idioms are difficult to resolve because they have already by Homer's time become fixed and rigid, nor are we in a position to find out whether *biē* was the original term, or *is* or *menos.* In all probability metrical considerations have played their part in the choice. A proper name such as Telemachus or Alcinous cannot appear in the nominative case at the place which is usually preferred for the citation of proper names, viz. the end of the verse; and so the poet resorts to circumlocution. It has also been observed that adjectival formulas of the type of *biē Hēraklēeiē* occur in connexion with those names which are not members of the Trojan circle; hence it seems fair to conclude that they were adopted from earlier epics. But since they must have been meaningful at one time or another, it has been suggested that among the so-called primitive peoples the king or the priest is often regarded as the possessor of a special magic force which elevates him high above the rest of his fellow tribesmen, and that the formulas which we have cited originally described the leaders as invested with such a force. This is a felicitous suggestion; we would, of course, be mistaken to look for a belief of this sort in our Homeric poems. The very fact that the formulas have become hardened, that metrical patterns now determine their use, prevents us from exploiting them toward a "magic" interpretation of the epic poets. The *Iliad* and the *Odyssey* have a great deal to say about forces, but there is not a scrap of evidence to suggest that there is anything mystic about them; all in all magic and witchcraft have left few traces in the poems, except for some rather atrophied survivals. Homeric man has not yet awakened to the fact that he possesses in his own soul the source of his powers, but neither does he attach the forces to his person by means of magical practices; he receives them as a natural and fitting donation from the gods.

No doubt in the days before Homer magic and sorcery held the field, and even Homer's view of the human soul has its roots in such a "magic" stratum. For it is only too obvious that psychic organs such as the *noos* and the *thymos,* incapable as they are of spontaneous thought or action, are at the mercy of wizardry, and that men who interpret their own mental processes along these lines consider themselves a battleground of arbitrary forces and uncanny powers. This enables us to form some vague opinions about the views which men held concerning themselves and their lives in the pre-Homeric period. The heroes of the *Iliad,* however, no longer feel that they are the playthings of irrational forces; they acknowledge their Olympian gods who constitute a well-ordered and meaningful world. The more the Greeks begin to understand themselves, the more they adopt of this Olympian world and, so to speak, infuse its laws into the human mind. It is true that they continued throughout to preserve a belief in magic, but all those who helped to advance the new era had as little regard for it as Homer, for they pursued the path which Homer had trod. However primitive man's understanding of himself as presented in Homer's speech may appear to us, it also points far into the future: it is the first stage of European thinking.

ADAM PARRY

The Language of Achilles

I wish in this paper to explore some of the implications of the formulaic theory of Greek epic verse. In doing so, I shall take the theory itself largely for granted.

Let us first consider a famous passage from the end of the 8th book of the *Iliad*, the one describing the Trojan watch-fires:

> So with hearts made high these sat night-long by the outworks of battle, and their watchfires blazed numerous about them. As when in the sky the stars about the moon's shining are seen in all their glory, when the air has fallen to stillness, and all the high places of the hills are clear, and the shoulders out-jutting, and the deep ravines, as endless as bright air spills from the heavens and all the stars are seen, to make glad the heart of the shepherd; such in their numbers blazed the watchfires the Trojans were burning between the waters of Xanthos and the ships, before Ilium. A thousand fires were burning in the plain, and beside each one sat fifty men in the flare of the blazing firelight. And standing each beside his chariot, chomping white barley and oats, the horses waited for the dawn to mount to her high place.
>
> (*Iliad* 8.553–65)

These lines could be shown, by an examination of parallel passages, to be almost entirely made up of formulaic elements. That they are so amazingly beautiful is of course the consequence of Homer's art in arranging these formulae. But I wish to speak now of the quality of their beauty. Here is a straight English translation: "And they with high thoughts upon the bridges of war sat all night long, and they had fires burning in great number.

From *Transactions of the American Philological Association*, vol. 87 (1956). Copyright © 1956 by the American Philological Association.

As when in heaven the stars around the splendid moon shine out clear and brilliant, when the upper air is still; and all the lookout places are visible, and the steep promontories, and the mountain dells; and from the heaven downward the infinite air breaks open; and the shepherd is delighted in his heart: so many, between the ships and the streams of Xanthus, were the Trojans burning shining fires before the walls of Ilium. A thousand of them were burning in the plain, and by each one were sitting fifty men, in the light of the blazing fire. And the horses, munching white barley and wheat, stood by the chariots, awaiting the throned Dawn."

The feeling of this passage is that the multitude of Trojan watch-fires is something marvellous and brilliant, that fills the heart with gladness. But this description, we remember, comes at the point in the story when the situation of the Achaeans is for the first time obviously perilous; and it is followed by the 9th book, where Agamemnon in desperation makes his extravagant and vain offer to Achilles, if he will save the army. The imminent disaster of the Achaeans is embodied in these very fires. Yet Homer pauses in the dramatic trajectory of his narrative to represent not the horror of the fires, but their glory. I suggest that this is due precisely to the formulaic language he employs. There is a single best way to describe a multitude of shining fires; there are established phrases, each with its special and economical purpose, to compose such a description. Homer may arrange these with consummate art; but the nature of his craft does not incline him, or even allow, him to change them, or in any way to present the particular dramatic significance of the fires in this situation. Instead, he presents the constant qualities of all such fires.

The formulaic character of Homer's language means that everything in the world is regularly presented as all men (all men within the poem, that is) commonly perceive it. The style of Homer emphasizes constantly the accepted attitude toward each thing in the world, and this makes for a great unity of experience.

Moral standards and the values of life are essentially agreed on by everyone in the *Iliad*. The morality of the hero is set forth by Sarpedon in book 12 (310–28). Sarpedon's speech there to Glaucus is divided into two parts. The first expresses the strictly social aspect of the Homeric prince's life: his subjects pay him honour in palpable forms, and he must make himself worthy of this honour by deeds of valour. The second part expresses a more metaphysical aspect: it is the hero's awareness of the imminence of death that leads him to scorn death in action.

The second part of Sarpedon's speech is by far the more famous: perhaps no passage in the *Iliad* is better known. But the first part is equally important for an understanding of the poem. Its assumption is, first, that honour can be fully embodied in the tangible expressions of it (the best seat at the feast, the fullest cups of wine, the finest cuts of meat, and so forth); for everyone agrees on the meaning of these tangible expressions; and second, that there is a perfect correspondence between individual prowess and social honour. For this too is universally agreed on. I need not add that most of Sarpedon's speech, particularly the first part, is made up of traditional formulae, and that the same thoughts, in the same words, appear in other places in the *Iliad*.

The unity of experience is thus made manifest to us by a common language. Men say the same things about the same things, and so the world to them, from its most concrete to its most metaphysical parts, is one. There is no need, as there is in Plato's day, for a man to "define his terms." And accordingly, speech and reality need not be divided into two opposing realms of experience, as we find them divided in the 5th century by the analytic distinction of *logos* and *ergon*; for the formulaic expressions which all men use are felt to be in perfect accordance with reality, to be an adequate representation of it.

Let us examine this last proposition. The epic heroes live a life of action. Speech, counsel and monologue are seen as a form of action. Phoenix tells in the 9th book of the *Iliad* how he was enjoined to bring up Achilles and *teach him all things*, all things, that is, a hero need know, *to be a speaker of words and a doer of deeds* (9.442–3). Phoenix here makes a practical separation, but no real distinction in kind: the hero must know how to do things—in the accepted manner; and how to talk about things— in the accepted manner. The two are complementary halves of a hero's abilities, and the obverse and reverse of his great purpose: to acquire prestige among his fellows.

Speech is a form of action, and, since the economy of the formulaic style confines speech to accepted patterns which all men assume to be true, there need never be a fundamental distinction between speech and reality; or between thought and reality—for thought and speech are not distinguished; or between appearance and reality—for the language of society is the way society makes things seem.

If such a distinction did openly exist, we should know where to find it: it would be in the character of Odysseus, the hero who by the end of the 5th century has become the type of the Sophist, the man who substitutes an illusory speech for the realities of life. But in Homer, at least in the *Iliad*, Odysseus is a great and honourable warrior. His being a master of words is simply a manifestation of this. What words he speaks are felt as a clear reflection of reality, because, like those of Sarpedon, they are in harmony with the assumptions of all society.

Only in the person of Achilles do we find so much as a hint that appearances may be misleading, and conception, in the form of words, a false and ruinous thing. When he answers Odysseus with his great speech in the 9th book, he says he will speak out exactly what he thinks, and what will come to pass. "I hate that man like the gates of Hell who hides one thing in his heart, and says another," he continues. Achilles' words ostensibly refer to himself: "I will not mince words with you." But the reader feels that they apply with a different force to Odysseus. Odysseus' elaborate and eloquent speech, spoken just before in the naive confidence that Achilles, like himself, will consider the gifts as adequate symbols of honour, becomes a little hollow. Achilles' words here make it seem some-how dishonest at heart, and not in accordance with the essence of the situation.

Achilles' own speech that follows is of another sort. Passionate, confused, continually turning back on itself, it presents his own vision with a dreadful candour. And what this candour is concerned with is, precisely, the awful distance between appearance and reality; between what Achilles expected and what he got; between the truth that society imposes on men and what Achilles has seen to be true for himself.

I will not here discuss Achilles' speech in any detail. But few readers of it, I believe, would disagree that it is about such a cleavage between seeming and being as I have indicated. The disillusionment consequent on Achilles' awareness of this cleavage, the questions his awareness of it gives rise to, and the results of all this in the events of the war, are possibly the real plot of the second half of the *Iliad*.

Achilles is thus the one Homeric hero who does not accept the common language, and feels that it does not correspond to reality. But what is characteristic of the *Iliad*, and makes it unique as a tragedy, is that this otherness of Achilles is nowhere stated in clear and precise terms. Achilles can only say, "There was, after all, no grace in it," or ask questions that cannot really be answered: "But why should the Argives be fight-ing against the Trojans?" or make demands that can never be satisfied: " . . . until he pays back all my heart-rendering grief."

Homer in fact, has no language, no terms, in which to express this kind of basic disillusionment with society and the external world. The reason lies in the nature of epic verse. The poet does not make a language of his own; he draws from a common store of poetic diction. This store is a product of bards and a reflection of society: for epic song had a clear social function. Neither Homer, then, in his own person as narrator, nor the characters he dramatizes, can speak any language other than the one which reflects the assumptions of heroic society, those assumptions so beautifully and so serenely enunciated by Sarpedon in book 12.

Achilles has no language with which to express his disillusionment. Yet he expresses it, and in a remarkable way. He does it by misusing the language he disposes of. He asks questions that cannot be answered and makes demands that cannot be met. He uses conventional expressions where we least expect him to, as when he speaks to Patroclus in book 16 of a hope of being offered material gifts by the Greeks, when we know that he has been offered these gifts and that they are meaningless to him; or as when he says that he has won great glory by slaying Hector, when we know that he is really fighting to avenge his comrade, and that he sees no value in the glory that society can confer. All this is done with wonderful subtlety: most readers feel it when they read the *Iliad*; few understand how the poet is doing it. It is not a sign of artistic weakness: Homer profits by not availing himself of the intellectual terminology of the 5th century. Achilles' tragedy, his final isolation, is that he can in no sense, including that of language (unlike, say, Hamlet), leave the society which has become alien to him. And Homer uses the epic speech a long poetic tradition gave him to transcend the limits of that speech.

CEDRIC H. WHITMAN

Geometric Structure of the "Iliad"

Not only in the associations of images and conceptions of both divine and human agents does the *Iliad* reveal its unity, but also in the matter of external form. It is now time to look at the whole poem as a series of scenes, and observe how these scenes are related to each other. Homeric scenes are analogous to the formulae in that they follow a typology designed to assist the singer; scenes of battle, arming, debate, supplication, lamentation, and jubilant victory bear a formal as well as an ideational resemblance to each other, though in Homer a vast degree of variety and shading has been achieved through the expansion, compression, or modification of the basic motifs. This typology of the scenes in the poetry of Homer and other oral singers has been the subject of excellent studies, and one does well to keep in mind the warning of Parry not to find "falsely subtle meanings in repetitions, as meant to recall an earlier scene where the same words were used." And yet, though such echoes would be present in all singers' efforts, one of the traits of Homer's excellence seems to have been the gift to control these echoes more than other oral poets have done. For the fixed elements of the oral style are fixed only in themselves, and out of context. In context they inevitably change color and tone, and it is by no means implausible, on the face of it, that a skilled singer, the scion of many generations of the tradition, should become aware of the subtleties of shifting context and make some effort to use them. Clearly, not every one could be controlled;

From *Homer and the Heroic Tradition*. Copyright © 1958 by the President and Fellows of Harvard College. Harvard University Press, 1958.

moreover, it must be assumed that, like so many processes of poetic composition, much of this effort must have failed to reach the level of full
consciousness. Yet, insofar as the use of balancing, or echoing, motifs
contributes to the broad structure of the poems, conscious intent is probably
to be assumed, since the design which emerges bears the unmistakable
stamp of the waking intellect. In treating imagery, one had to deal with
association and intuition; here, in the matter of structure, one is confronted
by a schematized pattern, rationally worked out and altogether consistent
with the observed artistic practices of the Geometric Age.

Recently, critics have begun to take account of the artistic role in
Homer of the repetitive elements native to oral technique. Stereotyped
themes and scenes, mere serviceable tools originally, and never more than
that in the hands of a poor singer, become in Homer through varying
context the vehicles of characterization and formal design. Thematic motifs,
such as descriptions of sacrifices, ship-launchings, feasts, funerals, arming,
and combat, are on the whole fixities of the poems, as indeed they were
of the world from which the poems arose, and the recitation of such passages
is as ritualistic, in a way, as were the performances of the acts which they
describe. It is natural and true for a society dominated by the rigidities of
ritual to represent its characteristic function in unchanging formulae, normative and in a way eternal. Yet every such thematic motif may be narrated
in varying degrees of fullness. It is not always easy to say what determines
how far a given one may be developed, though the pace of the scene, and
its purport as a whole would, of course, be governing factors. When
Achilles, for instance, pours a libation and prays to Zeus for the safe return
of Patroclus, the process of libation is described in minute detail, even to
the cleansing of the goblet with sulfur. But this is an extremely solemn and
critical moment in the plot, and it would be absurd to elaborate all the
libations in the epic to the same degree. Again, the scene of the sacrifice
performed at Chrysa by Odysseus on behalf of the Achaeans is one of the
most complete of all descriptions of such a ceremony. Here perhaps more
than mere liturgical solemnity is involved; for the arrival, debarkation, and
return of the ship in which Chryseis is sent back are also lengthily described,
in contrast to the more usual brief versions of such processes. The whole
episode at Chrysa, in fact, has a leisurely air, in contrast to the packed
dramatic scene which has preceded. And the reason probably lies in the
fact that the poet here has to account for the passage of twelve days, until
Zeus returns to Olympus and Thetis can present her plea for Achilles. Gaps
of time are rare in epic and regularly avoided. It requires, therefore, a tour
de force on Homer's part to fill an empty space when nothing particular
happened. Odysseus spent only one day and one night at Chrysa, and the

journey there and back probably did not take more than two more days; but the slow detailed pace of this rather neutral episode falsifies the time sense effectively, and one is prepared to accept without shock thereafter the brief summary of Achilles' inaction, and the resumptive line, "but when the twelfth dawn came," and return to the main action.

Apart from the variations in length, there are the variations in contextual significance. The *Odyssey*, for instance, probably has more descriptions of feasts than any other poem ever written. The traditional lines about feasting, therefore, sometimes may seem a little repetitious. Yet, because it makes a difference who is feasting, why, and at whose expense, the lines take on many different meanings, and cast shade upon shade of significance on the highly central theme of hospitality. Hospitality, itself a moral norm, finds its chief expression in the feast, a social norm, which is in turn represented by a set of fixed lines, a poetic norm. Actually, the "feasting" formulae of Homer are extremely numerous, but they are mere verbal variants and do not in themselves imply differences of action. Yet, who can miss the sharp dramatic contrast between the feast spread by Telemachus for Athena-Mentes and that enjoyed simultaneously at the side of the hall by the suitors, and all in the space of twenty-two lines? Similarly, one cannot fail to experience the effect on Telemachus when he passes from the grim, disorderly banquets of the suitors in Ithaca to the stately entertainment, almost suggestive of the Golden Age, to which he is invited by Nestor on the beach at Pylos, and the later one at the palace, both graced by the presence of Athena herself. Nestor spreads a feast in its fullest moral and social significance; as a symbol of society in order, it is deeply appropriate to the educative intention of *Odyssey* 3, and as such also Nestor appeals to it when, in the Ninth *Iliad*, he instructs Agamemnon amid his chaotic fears to give a feast for the elders, as his simple kingly duty. Far from suggesting revelry on the brink of doom, Nestor proposes a feast as the gateway to rational deliberation, the token of civilized, ordered life on the basis of which sane decisions arise. Yet the formulae of the feasts themselves are all closely similar, recurring numberless times, and not differing essentially even when Circe puts food before her guests. The function of a norm is to regularize; but the effect of experience at large is to refract upon the norm infinite lights and perspectives. Hence the variety of Homer, a variety which could not be so complex and subtle if it did not echo constantly from the normative columns of a ritualistic and formulaic fixity, transforming them into whispering pillars.

The principle or intention underlying such practices is perhaps not precisely a structural one, though it could be so called in that it relates to the continuity and interrelation of the stuff of the poems, and especially to the relation between the elements which are universal in the heroic tradition and those which are peculiar to the poem. Less involved with meaning, but more clearly formal and structural, is the phenomenon now known as ring composition. This framing device, whereby an episode or digression is rounded off by the repetition at the end of the formula with which it began, had its origin undoubtedly in the oral singer's need to bind the parts of his story together for the sake of simple coherence. Like the retrospective summaries of preceding action so characteristic of epic, it took both the poet's and the audience's mind back to a point where the next event was to find its orientation. But it has been ably demonstrated that Homer uses this device not only to serve a practical need, but also as an artistic device to give shape and clarity to the sections of his work, which, composed paratactically and with almost equal detail and emphasis in every part, might otherwise fall into an intolerably unarticulated series. Examples thus may be found of both functional and nonfunctional ring composition, and it is particularly common in the *Odyssey*. The famous scene where Eurycleia recognizes Odysseus by the scar on his knee is an example of the former. Between the discovery of the scar and the old woman's instantaneous gesture of surprise, Homer inserts a seventy-five-line episode about the origin of the scar, returning with perfect ease to the moment in hand by the mere repetition of the single verb, "recognized." The minimal nature of such a repetition perhaps illustrates how little is necessary to achieve the purely practical end. At the opening of the same book, a far more striking example of ring composition serves no practical purpose at all. The episode wherein Odysseus and his son stow away the arms under the guidance of Athena is neither a digression nor in any sense detached from the direct and purposeful march of events; it is an important step in the hero's achievement of vengeance. Yet Homer frames it at the end by the full and identical repetition of the two lines which began it:

> Then in the hall, godlike Odysseus was left alone,
> Pondering with Athena death for the suitors.

Here, of course, the effect is to give an extraordinary finality to the scene which preceded, to make it shine with the enclosed inviolability of a perfect circle, so that, however sequential it may be in the plot, it seems like a thing apart. As a prologue to the slaying of the suitors, and at that a prologue involving the miraculous presence of Athena herself, it stands on a slightly different level from the rest of the narrative and seems to have taken place not quite in time at all, but rather in the timeless sphere of the goddess. But it did not have to, not indeed could it have seemed to, had the poet not so enclosed it in echoing formulae. Somewhat similarly, and from no merely functional reason at all, the shipwreck of Odysseus is enclosed by the repetition of the line where Poseidon shakes his head and mutters to himself, as he hurls the waves at the wanderer.

Such a device as ring composition, especially as developed into an architectonic principle, is wholly consistent with Geometric art. The very name "ring composition" arises because such enclosure by identical or very similar elements produces a circular effect, the acoustical analogue of the visual circle; and circles, especially concentric circles, are prime motifs in Protogeometric art. In later Geometric, this design is not so common, but the idea of the circle is carried out in friezes of warriors or mourners running back into themselves, whose moving aesthetic principle is unbroken continuity, perfect and perpetual motion. One may indeed find a similar circularity penetrating all Homeric poetry, especially the *Iliad*, not merely in scenes, but in the poem as a whole; and again the root of the principle lies in a practical need. Ever since the time of Cicero, if not before, Homer's habit of returning to things previously mentioned in reverse order has been observed, and sometimes compared to the rhetorical figures of hysteron proteron. This device, doubtless of mnemonic purpose to assist the singer to keep in mind what he had said before, is also pregnant with stylistic possibilities; like ring composition, it returns to its point of origin and effects circularity of design, while the inverted elements may also be spread out to include as a centerpiece a whole scene or scenes, as in a frame. Thus hysteron proteron and ring composition, too, suggest not only circularity, but also framing and balance.

Moreover, even as ring composition balances by similarity or identity the idea of inversion in hysteron proteron is simply a form of balance by opposites. Probably all aspects of formal symmetry depend ultimately upon these two categories of similarity and opposition, as Plato seemed to know when in the *Timaeus* he finished off his cosmology with the two spheres of Sameness and Difference, which revolve in opposite directions. A basic and highly refined intuition of these two categories, which are in a sense the a priori ground of all cognition, existed from the first in the classical mind, shaping especially its artistic and philosophic approaches to experience. All peoples of course must possess it, but in the Greeks from Homer on it rose to an extraordinary degree of conscious activity, causing in them a tendency to treat all things in the light of antithesis or identity. Of the two, antithesis seemed to be the more appealing, as perhaps the more dynamic. Sameness is static; antithesis embodies movement around a still point. Hence doubtless arise those myriad and various uses of the antithetical particles, *men* and *de*, "on the one hand," and "on the other," of which the greatest and most accomplished stylists, both in prose and poetry, never seem to tire. They are the hallmark of true Hellenic speech in the classical time, not from mere habit, but because they reflect the deep seated intellectual love of polarities, the outside limits of a thought between which somewhere lies a fulcrum of balance. Much has been said about Greek balance and the golden mean. But the concept is a passive one. The active elements were the two extremes, the *men* and the *de*, between which the mean was felt as a theoretical point. Aristotle devised his whole ethical system by reference to the extremes of behavior, between which, though not always in the exact center, lay the mean point which is virtue. For Homer the framework of identity and antithesis is fundamental. We have already observed its operation, on a profound psychological level, in the matter of the rigid typological scenes shifting meaning and effect under the influence of changing context. It exists also on many other levels, such as for instance, the cultural antitypes of the wild Cyclopes and the overcivilized Phaeacians, who were, not surprisingly, formerly neighbors, since intellectually at least opposites attract each other. It is present also in the confrontation and interplay of the two great themes of the *Odyssey*: the homeward journey, *nostos*, is a fixed idea, an assertion of static singleness, which integrates the hero's personality and unifies his will; the Adventures plunge into the variety of experience in a sea as infinite as it is unpredictable, stretching to the "limits of earth," extremes of difference from the hero himself, and often conceived in antinomic pairs.

The principle of circularity, including concentricity, or framing by balanced similarity and antithesis, is one of the chief dynamic forces underlying the symmetry of Geometric vase design. In the *Iliad*, the old device of hysteron proteron has been expanded into a vast scheme far transcending any mere mnemonic purpose, a scheme purely and even abstractly architectonic. Not only are certain whole books of the poem arranged in self-reversing, or balancing, designs, but the poem as a whole is, in a way, an enormous hysteron proteron, in which books balance books and scenes balance scenes by similarity or antithesis, with the most amazing virtuosity. The very serious question arises, of course, as to whether the audience, listening to an oral presentation of the poem, could possibly have caught the signs of such "fearful symmetry," or whether it would have meant anything to them if they did. Granted that the procedure *abba* is useful in small compass to a singer, and perceptible as a structural unit to the audience, such can hardly be the case when *ba* is separated from *ab* by many thousand lines. Yet two things may be said regarding this point. The human mind is a strange organ, and one which perceives many things without conscious or articulate knowledge of them, and responds to them with emotions necessarily and appropriately vague. An audience hence might feel more symmetry than it could possibly analyze or describe. The second point is that poets sometimes perform feats of virtuosity for their own sakes and without much hope of understanding from their audiences, for one of the minor joys of artistic creation is the secret which the artist buries in his work, the beauty (if such indeed it be) which he has deliberately concealed amid the beauties which he has tried to reveal and express. *Finnegans Wake* and the ciphers and acrostics in late Medieval and Renaissance poetry offer good examples, though an even better one is to be found in the poem which serves as prologue to Dylan Thomas's collected works. This poem, some four pages long, employs perhaps the most imperceptible rhyme-scheme ever invented: the first line rhymes with the last, the second with the second last, and so on until a couplet marks the exact middle. Needless to say, the couplet seems fortuitous to the reader, and the rest of the zealous effort goes by unnoticed, unless it is pointed out by someone who heard it from someone else to whom the author explained it. A poet does such things to please himself, one must suppose. As for Homer, his scheme is at least as evident as Thomas's, and demonstrably serves a more real end. In any case, it should not be dismissed as mere empty virtuosity; for if the oral singer was accustomed to designing scenes, or at least some scenes, by means of hysteron proteron, it is not unnatural that he should seek to give shape to the large epic also in the same way, and especially if he had before him the example of the huge vases of the Dipylon, wherein, with no change of technique, the motifs and proportions of earlier Geometric pottery were expanded and adjusted to monumental dimensions.

There is nothing new in perceiving Geometric design in Homer. His use of polarities as a structural principle has been traced in certain contexts with convincing results. His use of the magic numbers three and nine has been compared, less convincingly, to Geometric circles. Long ago, the *Shield of Achilles* was analyzed as a symmetrically balanced set of opposites, and manifestly a designed balance was intended in the fact that the *Iliad* begins with a quarrel and ends with a reconciliation. The men who are reconciled are not the same as those who quarreled, of course; the poem has its own movement and does not end precisely where it began. The formulaic types, Quarrel and Reconciliation, are employed as balanced opposites, while the contextual difference, with all its implications for the character of the hero, creates the poet's meaning. Less meaningful but more surprising is the grouping of the days involved in the poem's action. So far as elapsed, or narrated, time is concerned, the night embassy to Achilles (with the *Doloneia* [X], if genuine) forms the middle point, flanked on each side by a single day's fighting: namely, the indecisive Interrupted Battle of VIII and the extremely decisive Great Battle of XI to XVIII.242. These are in turn framed by two groups of three days each, in which the action is not only closely unified but also similar. Books II to VII devote one day to fighting (II–VII.282), one to burial of the dead (VII.421–433), and one to the building of the wall (VII.434–482). The corresponding group includes three days, too: the day of Achilles' *aristeia* (XIX–XXIII.58), the funeral of Patroclus (XXIII.109–225), and the Funeral Games (XXIII.226–end). The day groupings of I and XXIV then reverse each other neatly: Book I has first the day of Chryses' appeal, followed by nine days of plague, the day of the council and quarrel, and finally a twelve-day gap till the gods return to Olympus; Book XXIV begins with a twelve-day period during which the gods grow steadily more disgusted with Achilles' excesses, followed by the day on which Iris rouses Priam to go to the Greek camp; nine days are then devoted to gathering wood for Hector's pyre, and on the tenth day he is buried. The scheme of days then looks like this:

Book I												Book XXIV
1–9–1–12 – 1 – 1 – 1 – 1 – EMBASSY – 1 – 1 – 1 – 1 – 12–1– 9–1

| | Fight | Burial | Wall | Inter-rupted Battle | night [Doloneia?] | Great Battle | Fight | Burial | Games |

This can scarcely have made itself felt to a listening audience; and yet, it can hardly be fortuitous. Homer seems to have been playing with abstract form for its own sake, and basing his conception of it on the hysteron proteron scheme. Its mathematical symmetry would appeal to any artist of the Geometric Age. If it seems farfetched for such a pristine time, we must bear in mind that there is absolutely nothing primitive about Homer except some parts of his traditional subject matter. And if it seems pointless and imperceptible from the point of view of the general public of Homer's period, we should also ask how many of Mozart's original audiences appreciated the extraordinary economy of tonality in *Don Giovanni*, or caught the musical puns on horns in *Figaro* and *Così fan tutte*. So too, not all the admirers of *Lohengrin* know that, with the exception of one passage near the end of the first act, the opera is written wholly in 2/4 or 4/4 time, a feature of inner unity of no consequence to the conscious receptivity of the layman, but a token for fellow artists, on the one hand, and an unperceived but effectual device, on the other. Music, indeed, abounds in such abstractions, yet aims at achieving its effect even on those who cannot follow them. To dismiss or judge adversely these technical procedures, however, because they are not readily seen by non-professionals, is to assail art and raise the banners of Philistia. The artist hopes, but does not insist, that his technicalities will be universally admired. He can be understood on many levels, and it is only an added pleasure to be caught red-handed in a secret technical virtuosity.

But the *Iliad's* Geometric form is not confined to the grouping of days. As said above in connection with the confrontation of the Quarrel and the Reconciliation, the *Iliad* presents a vast hysteron proteron of scenes, in which episodes, and even whole books, balance each other through similarity or opposition. In this system, the center is not the Embassy, but the Great Battle, and the responsion of parts is most obvious in the early and late parts of the poem. This fact is not surprising, since the technique is essentially one of framing or enclosing; one might even call attention to the later instinct of the rhetoricians and prose stylists, who paid much attention to the rhythm of the beginnings and ends of sentences, and let the rest be filled in less formally. So too, in Geometric pottery, the greatest tendency toward naturalism, imbalance, and loose design is to be found in the scenes or metopes of funeral or war which sometimes appear toward the center of the vase, while the flanking borders and friezes rely upon the strictest conventionalism and exact symmetry. Furthermore, while the beginning and end of the *Iliad* respond mutually throughout the first nine and the last nine books, certain books form separate systems, either singly, or in groups, within the larger system, wherever a section of the narrative achieves a partial self-completeness. Thus the form of Book I, for instance, is not in itself annular, since its action is introductory rather than rounded; but it forms a circle with Book XXIV. Books III to VII, however, whose content intervenes between the adoption and the activation of Zeus' plan, form a perfectly enclosed Geometric system of balancing scenes, framing the *aristeia* of Diomedes.

When one comes to regard the details, they are sometimes surprisingly precise in pattern. The principal scenes of Book I, for instance, are (1) the rejection of Chryses, with the plague and the funeral pyres; (2) the council of chiefs and the Quarrel; (3) Thetis with Achilles, consoling him and agreeing to take a message to Zeus; (4) Thetis with Zeus, where the latter adopts the hero's cause; (5) the disputatious assembly of the gods, where Hera opposes Zeus. Book XXIV takes up this scheme, but reverses it, beginning with (5) the dispute among the gods, with Hera still leading the opposition, though now in a different sense; (4) Thetis with Zeus, receiving notice that the gods no longer support Achilles in his maltreatment of Hector's corpse; (3) Thetis with Achilles, consoling him and bringing him a message from Zeus; (2) Achilles with Priam, where the magnanimous restitution of Hector's body inverts the selfish seizure of Briseis, and the compassion between technical enemies reverses the hostility between technical allies of Book I; and finally (1) the funeral of Hector in Troy, corresponding, though perhaps vaguely, to the first funerals of the poem in the Greek camp. Two important episodes cause a slight asymmetry: the Chrysa-scene, and the coming of Priam. Both are journeys, both have propitiation as their purpose, though beyond this they have little in common; also, they do not fit the hysteron-proteron scheme; still, the pattern of the first and last books emerges as essentially Geometric.

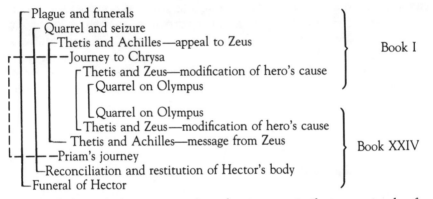

Here the balanced elements involve identity, or similarity, as in the funerals, or the people involved in the scenes; but the antitheses are actually more important. The case of Quarrel—Seizure versus Reconciliation—Restitution is the most striking, but the two scenes between Zeus and Thetis also offer a subtle contrast. In the first, Thetis is a secret suppliant to Zeus, and Hera regards her with a jaundiced eye. In the second, Thetis comes by invitation to Olympus; Athena yields her own seat to her, Hera offers her pleasant words and a goblet of gold, and this time it is Zeus who has the request. Though his words are couched in the form of a command, he is, in a way, appealing to her, for, as he says, he is bound by his promise to her and cannot allow the body of Hector to be stolen. This reversal of positions between Zeus and Thetis deeply underlines the degree to which Achilles has added cubits to his own stature. He now holds the timeless world in the palm of his hand.

The next pair of books does not show an equal elegance of design. Their responsion is more broad and impressionistic, yet both are fundamentally similar in design, and both are Geometric. Book II is in two parts, the Assembly and the Catalogue, both of which deploy for the first time in the poem the host at large. Its spirit is panoramic and epic, rather than dramatic, and it offers a glimpse, rare in heroic poetry, of the feelings of the common soldiery in the persons of Thersites, who is developed with bitter and rather low humor. The Assembly itself falls into two parts of opposing purport, first where the soldiers, misled by Agamemnon, rush to the ships to sail them home, and second where they are brought to heel by Odysseus with hopes of victory, equally misled, and shout vigorously for war at once. It is a disillusioned picture that Homer paints here, of a people deceived and hypnotized like sheep by leaders who are in turn deceived by Zeus. It is, in Jeffers' phrase, the "dance of the dream-led masses down the dark mountain," and the only person who speaks honestly in it is Thersites, the incarnation of the ugly truth. In the perspective of a society driving to its ruin under magnificent but corrupt leadership, truth shows itself in a warped, repulsive form and is silenced by simple violence—a blow from the lordly but greed-ridden and deceiving scepter of the Pelopids. Thus at the center of this broad and brilliant display of the Achaean power stands Thersites, disgraced and weeping, not a little as Achilles also stands, stripped of his shirt as Achilles was stripped of his prize, by the self-willed decisions of the regime.

The two Assemblies are preceded and followed by two private gatherings of the princes, the first in which Agamemnon reveals his dream from Zeus, which is accepted as true by Nestor, and the second in which the king sacrifices a bull to Zeus for the fulfillment of the dream, and Zeus, accepting the sacrifice, refuses the fulfillment. The first part of the book thus falls into the following scenic structure.

Book II [without *Catalogue*]

Deceitful dream sent by Zeus
  Council of Chiefs
    1 Assembly—conscious deception by Agamemnon
      Rush for the ships stemmed by Odysseus and Athena
    2 Assembly—unconscious deception by Odysseus and others
  Council of chiefs
Sacrifice to Zeus, and refusal of the prayer (affirmation of original deception)

Incidentally, the first speech of Agamemnon to the people is an important linking motif, for it is repeated in abbreviated form at the beginning of Book IX. The words which Agamemnon first utters in falsehood, leaning comfortably on his scepter, he repeats in a dark hour in deadly earnest, groaning heavily and weeping "like a spring of dark water," when the truth begins to settle on him.

This first section is then followed by the marshaling, with its six fine similes giving the sense impressions of the host, and the *Catalogue*, giving the factual details of it. The *Catalogue* has been most unjustly despised. In its way, it is just as vivid as the famous similes which introduce it. No love is more deeply imbedded in the Greek soul than the love for places in Greece, with their names, the mountains, valleys, nooks, and rivers of the maternal soil. It is more than patriotic; the *Catalogue*, with its recounting of these place names, their leaders and their legends, has a religious love about it; it is a kind of hymnic invocation. When read aloud, its clear and easy stride seems resistless and inexhaustible, like the movement of any army on the march, and each contingent as it goes by is splendid with the retrospect of home, the continuous surprise of the familiar. At the close of each entry, a stock line gives the number of ships attending the leader, and these lines, varying a little, but all echoing each other, have the incantational validity of a refrain. In antiquity, a hymn to a god recounted his deeds; the hymn to an army recounts its constituents. The whole is balladlike and brilliantly descriptive, freighted, like everything in Homer, with history and tradition, and touched with foreshadowings of the future. A hundred years or so later, Sappho listed an army as one of the things most beautiful in the world, and here we get some idea of what she meant. If the first half of Book II gives an inner view of ugly truth and uglier deceit, the *Catalogue* is a simple vision of the Achaean panorama, seen from without indeed, but seen with clear precise sensibility, and utter mastery of the traditional and formal material.

The twenty-third book again, and for the last time, offers a panorama of the army, and again, its structure is bipartite: *Funeral* and *Games*. Like Book II, it involves a motivating dream, but unlike Agamemnon's dream, that of Achilles is true; that is, the shade of Patroclus appearing in his sleep urges him to do what indeed he should and must do—bury the dead. The pyre scene which follows is in outline the usual formula of such rituals, but enormously inflated with detail, and adorned with symbols of Achilles' devotion, culminating in the offering of the lock of hair, and of his savagery, in the immolation of the captives. It terminates with Achilles again falling asleep exhausted; the gathering and burial of the bones is briefly told, perhaps to balance the scene of the dragging of Hector which opened the book; and then follow the *Games*, linear in design, like the *Catalogue*, with one event following another as the contingents of the army had. Structurally, therefore, it is closely analogous to Book II, though with no reversal of order:

Book XXIII [without *Games*]

to II (dream)

┌ Dragging of Hector and boast of no burial for him ————————↑
│ ┌Achilles asleep—dream of Patroclus ————————————┘
│ [Funeral
│ └Achilles asleep
└ Gathering and burial of bones

So much for the externals, which are here less brilliant than elsewhere. In its import, however, the twenty-third book corresponds to and reverses the second book with peculiar subtlety. If the latter had shown the Achaean society deceived and disordered, dreaming of glories that were not to be, and mastered by either violence or fraud, this spirit is quite reversed in the *Games*, where for the last time all the main characters are passed in review. Musterings for war and festival are in themselves social polarities. Agamemnon, wounded and still smarting with humiliation, is somewhat *hors de combat*; Achilles is the center of the Achaean scene. In contrast to what Thersites had said of Agamemnon's greed for booty, Achilles is the most lavish of prize-givers and, in pointed contrast to Agamemnon's former behavior, he awards the king a gratuitous prize. This is aristocratic society in order, where magnanimity and *noblesse oblige* operate as they should, and men's true abilities appear. Moreover, where Book II harked back to the portents at Aulis, the panorama of the *Games* foreshadows the future in certain details, and draws into the scheme of the *Iliad* hints of the traditional events later told in the *Little Iliad*, *The Sack of Troy*, and the *Returns*.

The Judgment of the Arms is suggested by the wrestling match of Odysseus and Ajax; Diomedes' safe passage home can almost be foreseen in his easy success in the chariot race. The fate of the brave, but illegitimate, Teucer, who was driven away by his father when he returned without Ajax, seems implied when he is worsted in the archery contest by a lesser man, and comes off second best. Particularly interesting is the slip and fall of Ajax of Locris in the dung of the sacrificed oxen. Athena pushed him, she who later, for his rape of Cassandra, was to blast him with lightning on his return home. The Achaeans all "laugh sweetly at him," the same formula in which they had laughed at the discomfiture of Thersites. These two episodes find their function in the accent they place on two contrasted views of the social order. In the world misled by kings deceived by Zeus and their own self-conceptions, the people laugh at the wrong thing—the vulgar but accurate speaker of the truth. In the world ordered by the law of magnanimity, and *areté*, they laugh rightly at the indignity suffered by one who is outwardly a prince, but inwardly, as Homer never is weary of showing, a ruffian and a boor.

Thus in a way, Book XXIII offers a true panorama, and one illustrative of the characters of all, where Book II gave a picture at its best external in the *Catalogue*, and at its worst deceptive in the *Assembly*, where authority overrides the truth. Book II is dominated by Agamemnon and Odysseus, a syndicate designed to choose means and achieve ends; Book XXIII is dominated by Achilles and the shade of Patroclus, already an archetypal friendship, an end in itself, and a landmark of being. . . .

The ninth and the sixteenth books of the *Iliad* are so obviously linked to each other as focal points of the main narrative that it is unnecessary to point out how the latter completes and in a way reverses the former. Achilles' rejection of the embassy, or at least of Agamemnon's offer, is here answered by his yielding to Patroclus. Yet in a sense he had yielded to Ajax also when, in contrast to his former threat to go home, he stated that he would fight when the battle reached his ships. His further modification of his stand here continues to express the force of Achilles' sense of humanity, but also brings into final conflict the two irreconcilables which are rending his will. This conflict is felt and discussed in Book IX; in XVI it must be acted out, partly because the real urgency is now greater, but chiefly because the human demand comes home to Achilles much more closely. Perhaps the most beautiful and clearly significant repetition of a motif in the whole *Iliad* is the one of the "dark-watered spring" which occurs at the beginning of both IX and XVI. When it first occurs, it is Agamemnon who weeps like a dark watered spring when he cries failure and proposes abandonment of the war. His words are identical, though in abbreviated form, with those in which he had made the same proposal in Book II, but then speciously, himself deceived by Zeus. Now it is Patroclus who weeps like the dark spring in Achilles' presence, and the image, now weighted with its former associations and future implications, does more than link the two books together. It also reflects Achilles' torn emotions, his sense of grief, to which wrath has now given place. In Book IX, even to Ajax, he had said that his heart swelled with rage when he remembered the insult. To Patroclus, he calls his feeling "pain," and confesses that he cannot maintain ceaseless rage. Accented by the repeated simile, the altered context gleams the more dramatically, and there is a close union between Achilles' mood and the ears of Patroclus.

Both IX and XVI are approximately of tripartite construction, though in the latter case, the traditional features of a battle scene lend themselves less readily to Geometric balance than does a series of speeches.

Book IX is quite orderly, with its councils at the beginning and end, and the *Embassy* proper in the middle. Agamemnon's first speech is a link, as already noted, to Book II, and falls outside the design. Diomedes' brave retort to him, a paradigm of the simple valor which had been found wanting in the preceding day's fight, is echoed by that hero's restatement of his own value and intentions at the very end of the book. For the rest, the council speeches do not balance precisely, since three by Nestor and one by Agamemnon are answered by only one each of Agamemnon and Odysseus. The symmetry, however, makes itself felt. The *Embassy* proper is extremely formal, both in atmosphere and design. At the center lies the speech of Phoenix, the pattern of *sophrosyne*, to which is opposed, before and after, two speeches of Achilles which eloquently, if with some confusion and indirection, express the absolutism of his position, and his search for its appropriate expression. Phoenix is the only one of the envoys who understands the real and dangerous inner forces in Achilles, and these three speeches, the core of the *Embassy*, are the only ones relating to those forces. The appeals of Odysseus and Ajax are diametrically opposed, the one based on gain (*kerdos*) and self-interest, the other on humanity, the claims of others, and *aidōs*. Achilles' answer to Ajax, with its partial acquiescence and at least theoretical approval of the claims of *aidōs*, is typical of his whole reception of the envoys, whom upon arrival he receives with all the formalities proper to the occasion, and, what is more, with real friendship. The reception of the envoys, therefore, and the answer to Ajax have the common denominator, friendship, which, though set aside by the superior claims of absolute honor for the moment, becomes in Book XVI a force no longer to be denied. The following pattern emerges.

Book IX

- Simile of the dark-watered spring ———————————→ to II
- Agamemnon's proposal to give up ———————————
- Diomedes' speech—simple heroism
- Speeches of Nestor (3) and of Agamemnon
- Achilles singing the glories of men, and his reception of the envoys—*aidōs, friendship*   to XVI
- Odysseus' appeal—*self-interest* (*kerdos*)
- Achilles—the heroic soul—honor *vs.* life
- Phoenix—the heroic soul—*sophrosyne*
- Achilles—the heroic soul—absolute standard
- Ajax' appeal—*claims of others* (*aidōs*)
- Achilles' answer to Ajax—partial acquiescence—*aidōs, friendship*
- Speeches of Agamemnon and Odysseus
- Diomedes' speech—simple heroism

The design of Book XVI is somewhat simpler, but again with three main parts: the first extending to the departure of Patroclus, the second through the Sarpedon episode, and the last from Apollo's first opposition to the death of Patroclus. The centerpiece is the fight with Sarpedon, flanked by two scenes on Olympus having to do with the burial of the Lycian prince. The whole piece is enclosed by two scenes of general melee, the first by the ships and in the plain, the second where Patroclus tries to ascend the walls of Troy. Here Apollo intervenes, and Patroclus' star begins to set as the god first urges Hector on him and then attacks him in person. The last part may not seem very analogous to the first, yet both are full of heavy foreshadowing, and both emphasize powerfully the defection of Achilles. The scene which Homer has inserted between Achilles' speech and the arming of the Myrmidons, the scene of Ajax battered but still struggling faithfully, can only be intended to accent the desperate straits to which Achilles' retirement has reduced his friends. The death of Patroclus is, of course, the nadir of this defection, the point at which it becomes impossible even for Achilles himself to remain inactive. In a sense, there-fore, Ajax' desperate hour prepares for that of Patroclus. Prophetic fore-shadowings also frame the book, both in Patroclus' own speech, where Homer abandons his anonymity long enough to remark that he was begging for his own doom, and in the prayer of Achilles for his safety, which Zeus rejects. These foreshadowings of course come to fulfillment in the final scenes, but not without a recurrence of prophetic motifs, as the dying Patroclus warns Hector of the vengeance of Achilles. Hector's lighthearted reply is, in keeping with his present delusion of victory, a kind of inversion of prophecy. The main scenes of XVI fall into the pattern shown below.

Book XVI

```
                                                              to IX
            "Dark-watered spring" simile  — — — — — — — — — — —↑
   ⌈ Patroclus' appeal and Achilles' answer              (foreshadowing)⌉
   ⎨   Desperate plight of Ajax (defection of Achilles)                 ⎬
   ⌊ Arming of Myrmidons and prayer for Patroclus        (foreshadowing)⌋
      ⌜Fight at ships and on plain (to 393)
         ⌜Olympus—Zeus agrees to bury Sarpedon
         ⎮  Sarpedon episode
         ⌞Olympus—Zeus sends Apollo to bury Sarpedon
      ⌞Fight at the wall                           (foreshadowing, l. 693)
   ⌠ Apollo's opposition—pushing back Patroclus and encouraging Hector
   ⎨   Fight with Cebriones
   ⎮     Death of Patroclus (defection of Achilles)
   ⌡ Prophetic exchange with Hector                     (foreshadowing)
```

So by this series of frames we are brought to the five books of the Great Battle which is the center of the *Iliad*. These battle scenes do not, apparently, fall into any particular system of balances; the hysteron-proteron technique makes its appearance in passages of small compass, but these seem to imply no attempt to spread the device into a principle of large design. In treating battle scenes, Homer relies on the unity of tone in the formulae themselves; the echoes are less planned, more chaotic thus, more suitable to the confusion of war. Yet even here, there is a touch of framing: the battle begins with the shout of Eris, and ends with the shout of Achilles. Moreover the placement of Patroclus' scenes offers the possibility that these also were intentionally drawn toward the extremities of the battle: Patroclus might have been sent out by Achilles at any point, but actually he is sent fairly near the battle's beginning; and he does not return until near the end—strange behavior for a man who was expected to hurry. But aside from these touches, the battle goes simply through its necessary phases, none of which provides sufficient contrast to balance another amid the general similarity of mood, except the Beguiling of Zeus, which forms a single relieving interlude.

The patterned regularity of the nine opening books and the nine closing ones might be pressed in more minute detail; but the object here has not been such detail; it has rather been to demonstrate how the native oral devices of hysteron proteron and ring composition, involving the balance of similarities and opposites, have been enlarged to provide concentric design for an enormously expanded heroic poem. Two special points must be noted. First, it will be recognized that this analysis of the *Iliad* assumes that the books of the poem, as we have them, existed in Homer's own time. As a rule, they are regarded as the arbitrary divisions of the Alexandrine scholars, but there is no reason to retain this view. They are clearly the natural divisions of the poem, and most of them have very marked beginnings and ends, even when the narrative is continuous between them. Also, it has been recently estimated that these books average about the number of lines which it is possible for a singer to perform on a single occasion. It is reasonable therefore to assume that the poem was conceived in terms of the books as we have them, and that the canonical division is not late. Secondly, the problematical Book X obviously does not belong to the Geometric structure as analyzed here, and this fact perhaps should be taken as an indication of its later insertion in the poem. Neither part of the battle, nor of the elaborate rings which enclose the battle, the *Doloneia* corresponds to nothing formally, and leads to nothing dramatically. It is the one part of the *Iliad* which can be omitted with no damage to the poem at all; the rest is from every point of view profoundly organic. On the other hand, the *Doloneia's* lack of any place in the Geometric pattern, though it creates a strong supposition, hardly seems sufficient proof for unauthenticity. Inconcinnities exist in the design in any case, even though none are so glaring as this would be; and in the last analysis the *Iliad*, coming from a tradition where parataxis, both in sentence and in scenic structure, was the rule, need not have departed from it so completely as to exclude all inorganic material. Moreover, Book X bears some significant resemblances to the rest of the *Iliad*, notably in its conception of the relationship between characters, such as Agamemnon and Menelaus, and in the continuation of the fire image. And yet, where everything else is so finely organized, this one episode does introduce a false note, a less mature procedure, with peculiar disregard for a symmetry which must have cost the poet some pains. Though the matter is hardly clear, it seems perhaps best to accept the dictum of the Townley *Scholia*, that this book was added later, perhaps even by Pisistratus.

For the rest, the scenic structure, when laid out entire in a chart, offers an extraordinary analogue to the rhythm and balance of the Dipylon vases. In the simple grouping of books, omitting X, one finds the relation-ship 2 : 5 : 2 : 5 : 2 : 5 : 2, a relationship frequently found also in the alternations of narrow and wide elements in Geometric ware. Within this basic rhythm, if the details seem enormously complex, so are the works of the Dipylon, and their ornamentation depends similarly upon the deploy-ment of traditional motifs in accordance with the first ripe development of the Hellenic sense of form. The underlying psychology of that sense in this early period has already been discussed, and it could only have been such a psychology, and such a conception of what form is, that led Homer to design the *Iliad* as he did, and to seek in his own materials of oral com-position the means to impose order, suitable to a monumental work, on the loose parataxis of the heroic tradition. It is the spirit of the Geometric Age which is at work here, and the form which it produced would have been all but impossible in any other time.

THOMAS GREENE

Form and Craft in the "Odyssey"

The important question about Calypso's garden is whether it is artificial. The opening lines of its description seem to imply that the "copse" is wild. But allusion is later made to the four springs "ingeniously contrived" to water their respective plots, and the parsley and violets studding the lawn seem to be there by design. This may lead us to wonder about the transitional detail: the grapevine which enwreathes the cave's entrance. May not this also represent deliberate training? Doubtless one is not meant to wonder too precisely, but rather to enjoy. This, indeed, is the real point: the garden is as artificial as it needs to be to afford the fullest appreciation. The god himself is bewitched by the beauty, and so might well be the human audience. For the garden is an object of contemplation; it is an esthetic object from which one stands aside and admires. As such it again measures the distance between this poem and the *Iliad*, where (as we see it chiefly through the similes) nature is destructive, familiar, awesome, wearying, joyful, but seldom to be admired dispassionately, never felt as over against the observing self. Here, however, as Hermes pauses to enjoy, the garden *is* outside of him, as it would remain equally outside a human observer. It is an object of admiration as it has been, partly, an object of cultivation and "training." It is half-way toward being an artifact.

Wholly finished artifacts abound in the *Odyssey*. The poet's characteristic way of evoking an arch-image is to begin with representative

From *The Descent from Heaven: A Study in Epic Continuity*. Copyright © 1963 by Thomas Greene. Yale University Press.

objects, and when the arch-image is a well-appointed house—like the home of Odysseus and the palaces of Menelaus and Alcinous—its artifacts serve to demonstrate its wealth. The socio-economic arrangement of gift-friendship affords the poet occasion to dwell upon particularly precious things—like the gifts Menelaus and Helen make Telemachus. On Ogygia the poet chooses to enhance most the garden, but he mentions also Calypso's golden shuttle and the "splendid polished throne" whereon Hermes seats himself. The opening scene at Ithaca is richest of all in artifacts, suitable for the entertainment of a goddess:

> Telemachus led the way into the noble house. Pallas followed until he set her spear in *the polished spear rack* beside a *high pillar*, amongst *weapons* once used by the long-suffering Odysseus. Then he spread *smooth draperies* over *a throne of cunning workmanship* and seated her upon it. For her feet there was *a foot-stool*, while for himself he drew up *a painted lounge-chair* . . .
>
> A maid came with *a precious golden ewer* and poured water for them above *its silver basin*, rinsing their hands. She drew to their side *a gleaming table* and on it . . . arranged her store of bread and many prepared dishes . . . A carver filled and passed them *trenchers of meat* in great variety, and set out on their table *two golden beakers* which the steward, as often as he walked up and down the hall, refilled for them with wine.
>
> (1.125–43)

Later, when Telemachus retires, Eurycleia hangs his "long clinging tunic" on a peg by the "fretted, inlaid bedstead" and goes out drawing the door by "the silver beak which served as handle," sliding the bolt by its leather thong, leaving her young master covered by "a choice fleece."

What is the effect of this Balzacian plenitude? It demonstrates wealth, to be sure, but it demonstrates slightly more—something I have adumbrated by the adjective "well-appointed." It suggests that the masters of the home are people of taste and decorum, refined enough to live in the high style, knowledgeable enough to value precious things. It creates a reassuring ambience of amplitude and ritual, courtesy and grace, like the "house where all's accustomed, ceremonious" which Yeats wished for his daughter. The reception of Athene is an aristocratic ritual which is the polar opposite of that other aristocratic ritual—heroic combat. The weapons of Odysseus in their rack do not fit ill into the scene of Athene's reception, but the activity they symbolize is now in abeyance. Hospitality has its own rules, its own form, which Telemachus demonstrably knows.

This feeling for decorum is very highly developed in the *Odyssey*. It informs the otherwise meaningless statement that a fire burns in Calypso's cave *on its appointed hearth*; it informs the epithet "the nymph of the well-braided hair." It informs very strongly the dialogue between the goddess and the god who knows he is bringing her unwelcome news. Her good form as hostess is impeccable and his, in the role requiring diplomacy and tact, is equally fine.

> Calypso, the fair goddess, made Hermes seat himself on a splendid polished throne, and asked him, "Hermes of the gold rod, ever honoured and welcome, from of old you have had no habit of visiting me: why do you come here to-day? Tell me your mind. My spirit is eager to second your desire if its fulfillment be in my gift and such a thing as may lawfully be fulfilled. Yet first enter further into the cave that I may put before you the meed of guests." With such words did the goddess bring forward a table bounteously set with ambrosia. She blended him ruddy nectar. Then did the messenger, Argus' bane, drink and eat: but when he had dined and made happy his spirit with the food, he opened his mouth and said:—
>   "As goddess to god you ask me, you order me, to tell why I have come. Hear the truth of it! Zeus commanded my journey: by no choice of my own did I fare to you across so unspeakable a waste of salt water. Who would willingly come where there is no near city of men to offer sacrifice to the gods and burn us tasty hundreds of oxen? Listen: in no way can another god add or subtract any title from the will of Zeus, the aegis-bearer. He declares that you have with you the unhappiest man of men—less happy than all those who fought for nine years round the citadel of Priam and in the tenth year sacked the city and went homeward . . . The wind blew him and the sea washed him to this spot. Wherefore now the Father commands that you send him hence with speed: for it is decreed that he is not to die far from his friends . . ."
>
> (5.85–113)

Both gods manifest their refinement by their restraint. Calypso is curious but insists that her guest refresh himself before he speaks. Hermes leads up gradually to his painful message, avoiding any breath of accusation in his résumé of the past. ("The sea washed him to this spot. Wherefore now the Father commands . . .") He suppresses the harsh things said of Calypso at the divine council, and he is at pains to dissociate himself from its outcome. At the same time he reminds her that Zeus' will is inalterable. Discreetly he says nothing of what he knows regarding Odysseus' future. His accomplishments as a courier are distinguished. Calypso's anguish is dramatized by the breakdown of *her* manners when she turns upon Hermes to reply: "Cruel are you gods and immoderately jealous of all others . . ."

The value placed on social form by this poet aligns him, *mutatis mutandis*, with other students of aristocratic manners—Castiglione, Lady Murasaki, Saint Simon, James, and Proust. The comparison is not grotesque, but it leads one to consider how many, so to speak, are the *mutandis*.

I think the greatest difference lies in the *insecurity* of form within Homeric society. In the books of these other writers, form is taken for granted and serves simply as a basis for some ulterior comedy or wisdom. But in the *Odyssey* it is much more precious because it coexists with vulgarity, brutality, and monstrosity. It is still something hard-won. So Menelaus' anger is all the more heavy in Book Four when his gatekeeper asks what to do with the unidentified guests.

I have used the word *form* deliberately because it can be applied to the gifts of Menelaus, the bedstead of Telemachus, the garden of Calypso, as well as the diplomacy of Hermes. All these things depend upon knowledge of techniques, upon civilized arts which distinguish cultured men from human or animal brutes. Just as Hephaestus works silver and Demodocus composes lays, just as the natural beauty of the garden has been wrought to a higher loveliness, so the capacity to order and manipulate a social situation is a technique to be learned, a *technē*—and it is the highest of all techniques. Those who are most proficient not only follow the rules but use them to gain prestige, influence, and gifts. Odysseus is the greatest artist or technician of the poem because in addition to his good manners he has the poise, shrewdness, perception, and wit to impose the form of his own will upon a community like the Phaeacian. He is able to be as cruel as, but no more cruel than, he needs to be to Nausicaa. He is a virtuoso and his conduct at Scheria from beginning to end is a little masterpiece of his craft. When he opens his long narrative with a tribute to his auditors:

> Lord Alcinous, most eminent, we are in very deed privileged to have within our hearing a singer whose voice is so divinely pure. I tell you, to my mind the acme of intelligent delight is reached when a company sits feasting in some hall, by tables garnished with bread and meat, the while a musician charms their ears and a cup-bearer draws them wine and carries it round served ready for their drinking. Surely this, as I say, is the best thing in the world.

> (9.2–11)

when Odysseus says this he is at once praising the poetic art of Demodocus and the Phaeacian art of living, and demonstrating his own elegant artistry. The two meanings of *craft* touch; cunning and technique blend into a supreme *savoir faire*. After he leaves Ogygia, the form of the narrative becomes increasingly the product of the hero's contrivance.

Because these ostensibly unheroic qualities count for so much in the poem, the distinction between executive and deliberative episodes tends to blur. Strictly speaking there are only one or two executive episodes in the first eight books: the encounter with Proteus (4.431–586) and the voyage by raft (Book Five). And although Books Nine to Twelve are consistently executive, the second half of the poem is deliberative with the exception of Book Twenty-Two and the closing lines of the last. This predominance explains how Aristotle could have called the *Odyssey* as a whole an ethical epic. But in fact the two types tend to move toward each other. The episode in Polyphemus' cave, which reminds one of folk tale and might have been written as pure narrative, acquires a deliberative tinge through its emphasis on trickery and comedy. And on the other hand, the episodes at Menelaus' and Alcinous' palaces, like the briefer one in Calypso's cave, differ from most deliberative episodes by the strength of their visual image and the dramatic weight they must bear. If social accomplishment can influence one's destiny, then a banqueting hall can test a man's capacity, contain a sort of *agon*. *Ethos* and *mythos*, manners and action, begin to fuse.

In his embassy to Calypso Hermes suppresses his sympathies for Odysseus, just as in the *Iliad* he has concealed his Achaian sympathies from Priam. But his gift of moly on Aeaea indicates that Odysseus is in his favor. I have remarked that epic poems tend to be about politics. The politics of this Olympus are not complex, but the issue of Odysseus' fate does lead to a rudimentary alignment against Poseidon. Athene agitates actively on the hero's behalf, Hermes less consistently; Zeus is hostile after the Thrinacian disaster, but later throws his weight with them at the diplomatic moment. This incipient power struggle works itself out in the human action of the poem, and we might, if we chose, extend the conflict of the Athene-principle and Poseidon-principle even to those episodes where neither god appears. Doubtless such a reading would exceed the cognitive experience of Homer's audience, but it would not violate the poem at its most suggestive and profound.

We might trace then a politics pitting the forces of the land and of civilization against the forces of the sea and brute mindlessness. It is the struggle, in essence, of intelligence against force, order against incoherence, the urban against the rustic, aristocracy against democracy, historical achievement against flux, form against matter. One might sum up the values of the land, the values of Athene and Odysseus, by playing as I have played on the double meanings of the word *form* and the related word *craft*.

The sea is by its nature the element which cannot be controlled; it can at best be put to use through the uncertain art of navigation. When the sea is unruly, Odysseus is most nearly helpless. He has no opposing mind to work upon, nothing to manipulate with his art. He is pitted against pure force. The figure in the poem closest to the sea is Polyphemus, whose brute stupidity is almost as destructive. It is no coincidence that he is Poseidon's son. There are other embodiments of the same unruly force— the Lestrygonians, Scylla and Charybdis, and even those sailors under Odysseus' loose command who open Aeolus' sack of winds, refuse to retire after the victory at Ismarus, and kill the oxen of Helios. Calypso (like Circe) is an ambiguous figure. The remoteness and littleness of her isle in the vast sea, the very water birds roosting at her door, suggest a connection with the sea, which has washed Odysseus to her. But she at least is beautiful and gracious, if subtly dangerous. The one fully realized incarnation of sea-monstrosity is Polyphemus.

The important things about the Cyclops are related before the episode proper begins—in the quasi-sociological remarks Odysseus makes about them at the outset. They are people who cultivate not even the basic arts:

> We came to the land of the arrogant iniquitous Cyclopes who so leave all things to the Gods that they neither plant nor till: yet does plenty spring up unsown and unploughed, of corn and barley and even vines with heavy clusters: which the rains of Zeus fatten for them. They have no government nor councils nor courts of justice: but live in caves on mountain tops, each ruling his wives and children and a law unto himself, regardless . . . The Cyclopes have no ruddle-cheeked ships, nor ship-wrights to make them such seaworthy vessels for pleasuring among the cities of mankind, like those ordinary men who tempt the seas to know others and to be known.
>
> (9.105–15, 125–30)

Odysseus goes on to make clear how rich the soil is, how fine the port, how easy the pursuit of the civilized arts might have been, had the Cyclops chosen to pursue them. Polyphemus' lack of breeding is manifest the moment he opens his mouth: he asks the one question never to be asked a guest before he refreshes himself: "Why strangers, who are you and where have you come from?" This lapse of *savoir faire* is seconded by his boast that he is too big to fear the gods. With this he brands himself a hopeless barbarian and his subsequent violations of the hospitality code come naturally in the course of things.

For religion too is partly a matter of knowledge in the *Odyssey*, of training, culture, rules, and form. The early Greeks never conceived of a human love for the gods (with the possible exception of Athene). But the civilized man was wise enough to know that Zeus must be propitiated. Nestor is the outstanding figure of the devout man in the *Odyssey*, and it is fitting that his sacrifice of a heifer should be the sacrifice most fully detailed in the poem. The details assure you that it is performed according to the rules, punctiliously, *religiously*. And just as Nestor's piety is a form of his wisdom, so the impiety of the suitors is a token of their stupidity.

The suitors have no ostensible link with the sea, as Polyphemus has, but they represent in the Ithacan episodes the same principles of ignorance, disorder, barbarousness, and religious irreverence. These drunken unruly louts never sacrifice a bull and never recognize a divine omen. Antinous reveals his ignorance when he laughs at Telemachus' new assurance after the visit of Athene:

> Why, Telemachus, those very gods must have been giving you lessons in freedom of speech . . .
>
> (1.384–85)

Antinous is precisely the man never to imagine that a visitor might be a god. He is too provincial. The real crime of the suitors, their unpardonable crime, is their lack of breeding. They have no form and no *savoir faire*. They are condemned not only by the poet but by Zeus himself. Hermes descends in part to free Odysseus to kill the suitors.

The suitors are an offense to economy, to morality, and to esthetic decorum, and their liquidation, however unesthetic it looks, justifies itself in all these realms. It is the poem's major imposition of form on disorder, the major victory for the forces of civilization, and it is proper that the definition of this victory require nine or ten books. The form it imposes is a living form, a situation in history, a set of domestic, social, and political relations which are felicitous and proper. It restores that aristocratic elegance, ritual of custom, and appreciation of fine objects, which render living in the high style a form of art.

Odysseus however does not remain long to enjoy these pleasures; he will leave, not altogether reluctantly, to wander until he discovers the symbolic people who know nothing of the sea, who cannot recognize an oar. He must wander to the ends of the world, to encounter more hardships and marvels. Should we regard this fate as a turning away from civilization, from form? It might appear so, but I think the question is not so simple. There has always been in Odysseus, side by side with his nostalgia for civilization, a taste for the exotic and the hostile, a taste for braving the sea to reach the far shore—not touristic curiosity, but an exhilaration in the encounter between Odysseus the man and the marvelous or monstrous, the more or less than human. It affords the pleasure of measuring the self against the non-self, the pleasure of perceiving, apprehending, knowing that other opposing thing, of encountering it without defeat and of possibly overcoming it, through understanding. This virile pleasure, which Odysseus never confesses but readers have always sensed in him, infuses physical strength with intellectual power and renders his craft more robust. It is a craft of body and mind together, and if the form it imposes is intangible, dissipated in a sequence of acts on a picaresque voyage, the form is nonetheless real. All the world becomes the matter of the hero's manipulative skill.

We should not therefore accept too naïvely his polite estimate at Scheria of "the best thing in the world." The forms of Phaeacian culture are graceful, but they are a little pallid seen through his veteran eyes. "I confess" says Alcinous, "that we are not polished fighters with our fists, nor wrestlers: but we can run swiftly on our feet and are experts on shipboard: we love eating and harp-playing and dancing and changes of clothes: and hot baths and beds"(8.246–49). These are arts and customs to be admired, as the Phaeacians as a race are admirable. Zeus, in dispatching Hermes, alludes to them as "godlike in race and habit." But these exemplars of refinement seem almost shallow set against the more robust artist Odysseus. The Phaeacians are indisposed to effort; they avoid contact with other peoples; they shun war; they know of Troy only by hearsay; their ships sail without human work or hazard. Although like the Cyclops they are descended from Poseidon, they are really the opposites of the Cyclops. They have had to flee their original homes for fear of the Cyclops' plundering. In their culture and their treatment of Odysseus they are unlike the Cyclops, unlike Poseidon, and it is not surprising that their divine patron turns against them. Through their culture and destiny, the poem seems to warn against the excessive refinement of arts which in themselves are good. Perhaps a similar mistrust underlies Odysseus' second departure from Ithaca.

Thus you find a certain formalism emergent in the *Odyssey*, a peculiarly dynamic, vital formalism compatible with heroism. There is a conflict between form and its opposite, and there is also a tension between different kinds of form—the Phaeacian and the Ithacan. It is like the tension you find in the language of the poem itself, which is both elegant and powerful; the tension in the landscape by Calypso's cavern, where the artificial garden is roughened by the alders and poplars growing wild, the sea birds perching undisturbed. It is like the tension in the hero, who resembles both the decorous accomplished god and the cormorant which "down the dread troughs of the wild sea chases its fish and drenches its close plumage in the salt spume." Odysseus too drenches his figurative plumage but his will retains something of the predatory bird's firmness. The finest art just skims the element it cannot control, and strengthens itself by the contact. Odysseus will die at an advanced age "far from the sea." The tension is essentially healthy.

The price of formalism, even *this* sort, is emotional hardness; the *Odyssey* is a very hard poem. Odysseus throughout is cold, in spite of his tears; in the recognition scene with Eurycleia and the reunion with Laertes, he is offensively cold. The *Iliad* is a far more tender work in spite of its bloodier action. The *Odyssey* has been sentimentalized by readers who think Odysseus yearns for his wife and son. But Zeus' words to Hermes formulate his goal better:

> The decree is, that so furnished he shall once again behold his friends
> and enter his stately house in the country of his fathers.

(5.41–42)

The poem is not very concerned with personal sentiment, beyond what use can be made of it. It has rather a cool lucid beauty which anticipates the later Attic love of rational form. It announces astonishingly early those themes which were to possess the Greek mind. But its charm lies in its freshness, the luminous objectivity, the narrative verve, the youthful worldliness, the disingenuous faith in life, and the actual flecks of foam on the rapid cormorant's wings.

ERIC HAVELOCK

Epic as Record versus
Epic as Narrative

The reader will remember our appeal
to him to suspend judgment while the *Iliad* was, so to speak, turned upside
down and looked at in the first instance not as a work of poetic invention,
that is as a work of art, but as a kind of metrical text book. The results if
we examine the first book as a sample are now before us. Taking the first
hundred lines alone, we have separated out a total of about fifty and identified their content as didactic in the sense that they recall or memorialise
acts, attitudes, judgments, and procedures which are typical. As they ac-
cumulate, they begin to read like a running report of that society to which
the bard addresses his tale, but a report drafted also as a series of recom-
mendations. This is the way in which the society does normally behave
(or does not) and at the same time the way in which we, its members,
who form the poet's audience, are encouraged to behave. There is no
admonition: the tale remains dispassionate. But the paradigm of what is
accepted practice or proper feeling is continually offered in contrast to what
may be unusual or improper and excessive or rash. So far as the bard's own
invention is concerned, this is more likely to show itself when his characters
depart from the accepted *nomos* and *ethos* than when they conform. In sum,
when Hesiod describes the content of the Muses' song as *nomoi* and *ethe*,
he is describing epic, and Plato's conception of Homer's function as it was
claimed by Homer and for Homer makes sense. He is indeed an encyclopedia

of Greek or at least Homeric *paideia*. This is a poetry of preserved communication and what is preserved has to be typical.

Let us in Homeric fashion attempt three different similes to illustrate
how the substance of this kind of oral poetry is composed. We can speak
of the epic as a mighty river of song. Caught up and borne along in this
flood there is a vast mass of contained materials which as they colour the
waters are also sustained by them. This simile is imperfect so far as it suggests
a qualitative distinction between the river with its power of narrative description and the gross body of information and prescription and catalogue
which depends on the power of the stream for its movement but is not
itself part of that movement. Let us therefore suggest a second simile of an
architectural complex designed, proportioned, and built, which yet depends
for its effect upon the quality of the stones and the wood, the brick and
the marble which have been used in building it. The colours and shapes
of these materials enter into and inform the whole geometric design. This
simile is superior so far as it indicates that Homer's running report is not
something he has worked artificially into his narrative, but is essentially
and inherently part of his style. It is difficult for him to say anything without
infusing it with some colour of the typical.

Yet we need a third simile which shall describe the sharpness of
vision with which these typical elements are framed. They are not as
undifferentiated as bricks and mortar and stone. And yet the vision is not
unique so much as typical. Homer did not personally invent these ways of
recollecting custom and usage. His report of his society must have been
shared by all bards, though no doubt at different levels of virtuosity. He
did not create this code, not can he alter its general colour by imposing
upon it a personal vision, except within narrow limits. Let us think of him
therefore as a man living in a large house crowded with furniture, both
necessary and elaborate. His task is to thread his way through the house,
touching and feeling the furniture as he goes and reporting its shape and
texture. He chooses a winding and leisurely route which shall in the course
of a day's recital allow him to touch and handle most of what is in the
house. The route that he picks will have its own design. This becomes his
story, and represents the nearest that he can approach to sheer invention.
This house, these rooms, and the furniture he did not himself fashion: he
must continually and affectionately recall them to us. But as he touches
or handles he may do a little refurbishing, a little dusting off, and perhaps
make small rearrangements of his own, though never major ones. Only in
the route he chooses does he exercise decisive choice. Such is the art of
the encyclopedic minstrel, who as he reports also maintains the social and
moral apparatus of an oral culture.

In this, we suggest, lies the clue to that peculiar elevation which critics continually recognise in Homeric poetry. For some translators the only possible response has been to attempt versions in the idiom of the King James rendering of the Old Testament. Others with their fingers on the pulse of modernity have felt equally impelled to get away from the grand style as far as possible in order to render Homer in the idiom of modern speech. Both types of version represent some inevitable compromise between failure and success, but the former at least reveals an awareness of the thing in Homer which is unique, namely, an encyclopedic vision, with which goes a total acceptance of the mores of society, and a familiarity with and an affection for its thought-forms. Homer is about as close as poetry can ever come to a report on the normal juxtaposed over against the abnormal. To describe his manner as elevated is to use a poor metaphor. His power derives from his function, and his function does not carry him vertically upward above the spirits of men but extends him horizontally outward to the confines of the society for which he sings. He profoundly accepts this society, not by personal choice but because of his functional role as its recorder and preserver. He is therefore dispassionate, he can have no personal axe to grind, no vision wholly private to himself. The furniture in the house may undergo some rearrangement but there cannot be a manufacture of new furniture. If we ask: Why then is he not dull? we should reply perhaps that he would be dull if he performed these functions as would a literate poet composing for readers. But he is an oral poet composing according to certain psychological laws which were unique, which have literally ceased to exist, at least in Europe and in the West. Plato showed keen awareness of this psychology even as he sought to eliminate it. A little later we must revert to it and consider the psychic mechanisms which this kind of poetry was forced to exploit, and the type of consciousness which it fostered.

Among such poets, superior genius would belong to him who had superior command of the art of relevance. With one part of his attention focused on his tale, itself in part traditional, though amenable to invention, the larger and more unconscious part of his energy would be engaged in bringing the tale into continual contact with the general social apparatus. The more of the apparatus that gets in, the more enriched the narrative mixture becomes. The more aptly and easily the apparatus is controlled by the context of the narrative, the smoother seems the result and the more dramatic the effect. Continually therefore a poet's superior talent can employ the apparatus at two levels, both as a general report and also to gain a specific effect, some heightened parallel or contrast in some specific narrative situation. We have described Achilles' description of the staff of authority as an excursus which interrupts the sweep of his anger. Yet it is also true that the listener hears him describe this piece of a tree which will never burgeon again, for it has become something else, he would catch a note of relevance: the separation of the wood from its tree is irrevocable and so is to be the separation of Achilles from his own parent body the army. A piece of reporting turns into a dramatic device.

It is, however, characteristic of the whole bent of modern criticism that the element of reporting is ignored and the element of artifice is exaggerated. Our conception of poetry does not find room for the oral act of reporting and so does not allow for the complexities of Homer's task. Artistic creation as we understand the term is a much simpler thing than the epic performance and it is one which implies the separation of the artist from political and social action. If this were an essay in Homeric criticism alone one should not perhaps choose to take sides between his encyclopedic functions on the one hand and that artistry on the other with which he weaves his report into his story. These may stand as coeval aspects of his united genius. But the quest we are pursuing here is for a goal which is not Homeric and which grows larger and more oppressive, if that is the word, as Homer is left progressively farther behind. It is the Platonic quest for a non-Homeric mind and language, and in the context of this quest the overwhelmingly important thing about Homer is the thing that Plato said about Homer: in his day and for many days later he was the chief claimant for the role of educator of Greece. Plato did not himself analyse the historical reasons why this was so. We have sought to supply them by considering Homer as the representative of that kind of poetry which has to exist in a culture of oral communication, where if any "useful" statement, historical, technical, or moral, is to survive, in more or less standardised form, this can be done only in the living memories of the members who make up the culture group. The epic therefore is from the standpoint of our present quest to be considered in the first instance not as an act of creation but as an act of reminder and recall. Its patron muse is indeed *Mnemosyne* in whom is symbolised not just the memory considered as a mental phenomenon but rather the total act of reminding, recalling, memorialising, and memorising, which is achieved in epic verse. For a Roman writer the Muse might represent invention applied to content as also to form. But in the antique accounts of her skill in the archaic and high classical period of Greek civilisation this is not stressed. The story of invention belongs properly to the sphere of *logos*, not *mythos*: it was set in motion by the prosaic quest for a non-poetic language and a non-Homeric definition of truth.

Now if the framed word and the important communication could survive only in the living memory, the poet's task was not simply to report and recall, but to repeat. Within the confines of repetition, variety would occur. The typical can be restated within a fairly wide range of verbal formulas. A written encyclopedia on the contrary separates its material into topics and treats each exhaustively with a minimum of repetition. Varying versions of what is "knowledgeable" are pruned down and reduced to mono-types. Oral record demands exactly the reverse procedure and literate interpreters who have not schooled their imaginations to understand the psychology of oral preservation will accordingly divide and prune and excise the repetitions and variants in a text of Homer or Hesiod to make the text conform to literate procedures where the requirements of the living memory are no longer in question. The metaphor which describes Homer as a tribal encyclopedia is in fact loose if we use the term encyclopedia in that bookish sense which is proper to it. For Homer continually restates and rehandles the *nomos* and *ethos* of his society as though from a modern standpoint he were not quite sure of the correct version. What he in fact is quite sure of is the overall code of behaviour, portions of which he keeps bringing up in a hundred contexts and with a hundred verbal variants.

This habit of "variation within the same" is fundamental to Homer's poetry and betrays that root principle of its manufacture as it was analysed by the late Milman Parry. The oral technique of verse composition can be viewed as built up out of the following devices: there is a purely metrical pattern which allows successive lines of poetry of standard time length to be made up of interchangeable metrical parts: second, a vast supply of word-combinations or formulas of varying length and syntax rhythmically shaped so as to fit portions of the metrical line but themselves also made up of interchangeable verbal parts so disposed that either by combining different formulas or combining pieces of different formulas the poet can alter his syntax while maintaining his meter. His overall artistry thus consists of an endless distribution of variables where, however, variation is held within strict limits and the verbal possibilities, while extensive, are in the last resort finite. Or putting it semantically, we can say that the possibilities of variation in meaning, of alteration of statement, are also in the long run finite. This finitude corresponds to the finitude of that pattern of *nomos* and *ethos* which the poet continually recalls.

The virtuosity of this technique in Homer is astonishing and to explore it further can be an esthetic delight. But in our present context, the technique comes into consideration for only one very elementary reason. What was the psychological motive which prompted its development on the part of the Greek minstrels? Homeric criticism has sought to answer this question within the limits of our modern conception of poetry as an act of invention. Ignoring the furniture in the house, we tend to concentrate attention wholly on the narrative path which the poet takes as he threads his way through it. Consequently the epic formulaic technique has been considered almost exclusively as an aid to poetic improvisation, a device to allow the poet to get on easily with his tale. But in fact it came into existence as a device of memorisation and of record; the element of improvisation is wholly secondary, just as the minstrel's personal invention is secondary to the culture and folkways which he reports and preserves.

The notion that Greek epic is to be considered as an act of improvisation, that is of limited but speedy invention, has been assisted not only by modern notions of what we expect of a poet, but by modern analogies drawn from the surviving oral poetry of the Balkans and Eastern Europe. The comparative method used here, which seems so assured and scientific, has in fact been guided by an assumption which is not scientific. It has lumped together two poetic situations which are entirely different, that of the Balkan peasantry and that of the Homeric governing class. It was of the essence of Homeric poetry that it represented in its epoch the sole vehicle of important and significant communication. It therefore was called upon to memorialise and preserve the social apparatus, the governing mechanism, and the education for leadership and social management, to use Plato's word. It is not only that Agamemnon, for example, if he had to muster a fleet at Aulis might be compelled to get his directives organised in rhythmic verse so that they could remain unaltered in transmission. This same verse was essential to the educational system on which the entire society depended for its continuity and coherence. All public business depended on it, all transactions which were guided by general norms. The poet was in the first instance society's scribe and scholar and jurist and only in a secondary sense its artist and showman.

But in countries where the oral technique has survived, it is no longer central to their culture. Modern analogies drawn from these pocket survivals, as exemplified in Yugoslavia or Russia, ignore the vital fact that the central business of government and of social leadership in European countries has for centuries been transacted in letters. Either the governing class has been literate, or it has commanded a literate apparatus centered in the capital cities. The singer therefore becomes primarily an entertainer, and correspondingly his formulas are designed for easy improvisation, not for the preservation of a magisterial tradition. But Homer's were quite otherwise. In them were framed both law and history and religion and technology as these were known in his society. His art therefore was central and functional as never since. It enjoyed a command over education and government, which was lost as soon as alphabetic literacy was placed at the disposal of political power. The role of the Balkan singer shrank and dwindled long ago to the status of a teller of tales. In time of trouble and social dislocation his patriotic themes might briefly revive some of his old prestige as society's leader and teacher. But this is a temporary phenomenon. Leadership normally resides elsewhere.

The Hellenic experience in short cannot be duplicated in modern Europe. That experience had been of a poetry which as it was functional was also magisterial and encyclopedic. The arrival of literacy changed things slowly. The drama even down to Euripides took over for Athens some of the functions of epic and retained some basic elements of what we can call the functional (rather than the merely formulaic) style. The political and moral relations considered proper in society continue to be stated and repeated in aphorisms, proverbs and paragraphs, and in typical situations. The characters themselves are still typical so far as they still have to serve as preserved paradigms of proper and improper behaviour. As criticism of society emerges and the artist begins slowly and imperceptibly to separate himself from his report, even the criticism has still to take the form of juxtaposing what appear to be contradictions within the *nomoi* and *ethe*. These antitheses are themselves still stated as alternative patterns of behaviour and are framed in conventional terms. The artist cannot yet voice some specific and personal creed of his own. The power to do this is post-Platonic.

Thus even the language of Euripides is still woven to a surprising degree out of the conventions of oral utterance. With the advance of literacy, the ceremonial style lost its functional purpose and hence its popular appeal, but to the end of the fifth century the role of the poet as society's encyclopedist, and the function of his formulaic speech as the vehicle of the cultural tradition, remain discernible and important.

NORMAN AUSTIN

The Function of Digressions
in the "Iliad"

$\mathbf{M}$odern Homeric scholarship is characterized by a greater sympathy for Homer's style than was accorded it during the nineteenth century. An important result of the studies begun by Milman Parry on the nature of oral composition is that scholars are more cautious about imposing their own aesthetic bias on Homer and making anachronistic demands of him. There has been an attempt to measure Homer's achievements by his own standards, that is, by the standards of oral poetry, rather than by the standards which may be valid only for later literary productions. The charges of discursiveness, repetition, expansion and even incongruity no longer seem as damning as they were once considered to be.

A danger of this new receptive attitude, however, is that while Homer may be vindicated as an historical personage, as an artist he may be merely excused. Some modern studies, particularly those on the paratactic style of Homer, have not so much settled the question of unity in the Homeric poems as evaded the issue by denying the value of the search for unity, or at least any unity which we could recognize as such, in an oral poet. Far from disposing of the central problems of the Homeric Question this approach has only corroborated the misgivings of earlier Analysts. The suggestion implicit in the oral approach is that we must recognize that there is after all no artistic unity in Homer, just as many Analysts claimed;

From *Greek, Roman and Byzantine Studies*, vol. 7 (1966). Copyright © 1966 by Duke University Press.

moreover, we must learn not to look for any. What was once seen as a pastiche by a collective body of poets, rhapsodes and diaskeuasts is now seen as a loosely tied collection of pastiches, all by the same poet. This denial of organic unity in Homer would appear to prove the Analysts right in their questions even if wrong in their methods of pursuing answers.

The point of view which posits the primacy of the parts over the whole in Homer has been given wide currency by Erich Auerbach's explication of the digression on Odysseus' scar in *Odyssey* 19. Auerbach's contention is that the Homeric style is so compulsively paratactic and explicative that when something such as the scar appears in the narrative, the poet abandons the main narrative entirely in order to bring that object forward and with it all temporal, spatial, and causal relationships. According to Auerbach, this compulsion to "externalize" overrides any other principle in Homer, whether rhetorical, dramatic or aesthetic.

In recent times, the Homeric digression has achieved a certain respectability by virtue of its becoming the focus of much of the work devoted to the paratactic style. Once condemned by the Analysts as irrelevant insertions added by later poets to satisfy personal whims or demands for local tradition, the digressions have become the hallmark of the oral style, the example *par excellence* of the poet's *amor pleni*. But this modern view has not so much acquitted Homer of the charge of irrelevance or incongruity as it has accepted irrelevancy as a characteristic of the oral style and thereby made of it something close to a virtue. It is possible, however, to defend the digression on firmer grounds. I hope to show that the digressions of the *Iliad* are not haphazard accretions, but neither are they merely ornamental decorations subject to the whims of poet or his audience. There is a consistency in their themes, their occurrence and their degree of elaboration which indicates an ordering principle in their use. Both thematically and dramatically they are relevant to the structure of the whole poem.

A justification of the integrity of the digressions must start with an appreciation of the two contrasting styles of narrative in Homer. The one is that which Auerbach has analyzed so well, in which all details, however trivial or incidental, are included and nothing is omitted or left unclarified. The other is a casual, allusive and elliptical way of presenting information. What is particularly curious in the *Iliad* is that for all the importance of the Trojan War as the essential milieu of the quarrel between Agamemnon and Achilleus, it is always referred to in the latter oblique style, while legends and myths which have nothing to do with the War are told in leisurely digressions of ample detail. It is hardly an exaggeration to say that we know from the *Iliad* more about Nestor's youthful exploits in Pylos than we do about the cause and eventual outcome of the Trojan War.

The studies on the paratactic style of Homer have not, I think, taken sufficient cognizance of this fact, that most of the directly relevant background material is presented in the briefest allusions in a quite subordinate manner, often simply included in such indirect ways as part of a taunt by one character to another, while material which we might consider not directly relevant is narrated in the full appositional style. If we believe that Homer is led astray by his own mention of a person or object into a digressional anecdote, his remarkably laconic treatment of interesting stories which are vital to our knowledge of the Trojan War becomes even more inexplicable. Why are the border raids in Pylos so much more entertaining than, say, the judgement of Paris or the rape of Helen? Or conversely, if we are Analysts we must wonder why the later poets who inserted the digressions in the *Iliad* were so partial to Nestor, to women, and to lesser Trojan heroes, and how they could have so successfully suppressed those poets who might have been partial to the important Greek heroes.

It is well to remind ourselves of how scanty the information on the War is. In Book 1, although most of the important heroes are brought on stage, there are only hints rather than facts about the War. We are hardly given the minimum of facts necessary to identify the characters and to establish the moment in the legend when the action of the poem takes place. The only specific reference to the War is Achilleus' angry reminder that he had no quarrel with the Trojans, but that he had come to Troy on behalf of some undisclosed point of Menelaos' and Agamemnon's honor (vv.152–60). Book 2 is equally cryptic, although the Catalogue of Ships offers an excellent opportunity for a full digression on the purpose of the expedition. The Catalogue gives us much extraneous information, but of the War it has little to say. Menelaos is described as longing "to avenge the agonies and sorrows of Helen" (354–56), and figures of Protesilaos and Philoktetes enter to allow brief allusions to the past and future. In Book 3, when Helen, Paris and Menelaos move into center stage, we might expect a detailed account of their rôle in the War, but what facts are stated are presented obliquely. It is Hektor who first mentions the abduction of Helen when he taunts Paris by comparing his present pusillanimity with his past panache (39–57): "Is this the man you were when you sailed across the seas to carry off a foreign woman?" In the *Teichoscopeia* Helen and Antenor give some background information about the Greek leaders, and Antenor reveals quite incidentally that Menelaos and Odysseus had come to Troy to discuss Helen's abduction before the War began. Even this interesting fact is left unelaborated; it is included only because its narration affords a chance to depict Odysseus' abilities as orator.

The first books of the *Iliad* would seem to stand in refutation of Auerbach's thesis when they show so little concern for externalization. Certainly the poem does not show the historical consciousness of the Old Testament, but the obliquity of its style with its gradual revelation of the past and future give a greater depth and perspective than Auerbach would allow.

In marked contrast to the meagre information given about important characters in Book 1, what digressional material the book contains refers to lesser characters or to almost entirely alien legends. Kalchas is given a four-line introduction (69–72); Nestor is introduced in seven lines and then proceeds to a fourteen-line description of how he fought with the heroes of old against the Centaurs (247–53, 260–73); Achilleus reminds Thetis of the occasion when she called upon Briareus to help Zeus against the mutinous Olympians (396–406); Thetis informs Achilleus that Zeus is away on a twelve-day sabbatical among the Ethiopians (423–25); and Hephaistos reminds Hera of the consequences of his having tried to protect her from Zeus's anger in the past, when Zeus threw him from Olympos (590–94).

These digressional anecdotes are short, but yet we may wonder at the disparity between the information given in them and the almost total lack of information about Agamemnon, the other Greek leaders, and the course of the War itself.

The explanation for this disparity is that almost all the digressional material in Book 1 is there not for its historical interest but for its paradigmatic value. Here it is necessary to draw a distinction between digressions into the past and expansions of other kinds of episodes which are subordinate within the poem. The word "digression" is inevitably controversial in poetic criticism and perhaps always a misnomer. Certainly it is an error to apply it indiscriminately to the expanded description of any object, scene or person within a poem. The word, however, may be used with more justification to refer to anecdotes which describe action outside the time of the poem. By this definition, then, the *Teichoscopeia*, though not in itself a digression, has much digressional material in it, while Odysseus' embassy to Chryses in Book 1 is not a digression at all. By this definition four of the five "digressional" anecdotes in Book 1 are true digressions, since they relate to the past. All four, Kalchas' introduction, Nestor's introduction, and the stories of Briareus' rescue of Zeus and Hephaistos' attempt to help Hera are told as paradigms.

The paradigmatic elements of many of the older myths in the *Iliad* have long been noticed, and the obvious instances of the paradigmatic stories which speakers in the *Iliad* use as protreptic arguments have been discussed by others, so that it is necessary only to call attention here to their salient features. The paradigmatic stories are drawn from personal experience, family history, or myths outside the Trojan legend. They are rhetorical devices whose intention is always persuasive; they are either hortatory (or dissuasive) or apologetic. That is, they are a form of argument directed by one person to another to encourage him to, or to deflect him from, some action, or they are offered by someone as self defence for his pursuing a certain course. Some may be both hortatory and apologetic.

The hortatory paradigms are: the story of Briareus against the Olympians (1.397–406); the story of Meleager (9.529ff); Tydeus' exploits against Thebes, told by Agamemnon to Diomedes (4.372–400); the story of Hephaistos' rescue by Thetis (18.395–405); Phoinix's mythic conceit of the Prayers to whom gods and men must submit (9.502–12); Dione's catalogue of human assaults on deities, told as consolation (5.382ff); and all the personal digressions of Nestor (1.260–73; 7.124–60; 11.670–790; 23.629–43).

The important apologetic paradigms which justify a certain action, or defend a right, or offer a rationale for behavior are: the stories of the personal and ancestral kind, such as the story of Tydeus which Sthenelos tells as a sequel to Agamemnon's story of Tydeus (4.405–10), or Diomedes' story of Tydeus (14.113–25); the genealogical stories given by Glaukos (6.150ff) and by Aineias (20.208ff). All these paradigms defend the speaker's honor in war or establish his right to a voice in deliberative council. Other such paradigms are: the story of Lykourgos which Diomedes tells to explain why he will not fight until he knows Glaukos' genealogy (6.128ff); the story of how Atē was thrown down from Olympos, which Agamemnon tells to explain how delusion entered the world (19.86ff); the brief allusion to Herakles' death, which Achilleus tells both as apology and as consolation (18.117–20); the story of Niobe, which is primarily hortatory but also apologetic (24.602–17). Achilleus tells this story to urge Priam to eat, but he is also reassuring himself that he has not betrayed Patroklos by surrendering to his physical needs.

The digressions of Nestor are both hortatory and apologetic. As apology they establish the legitimacy of his position in the Greek hierarchy as the wisest counsellor; as exhortation they offer a challenge to the younger men to live up to the heroic ideal as embodied in his person. His tales, verbose as they may seem to our more impetuous temper, are not senile meandering. We may find his advice inadequate or jejune, but that is not a judgement in which his peers would have concurred. . . .

The digressions, whether drawn from distant myths or family history or from the beginning of the Trojan War, are securely anchored to the present by their pragmatic intent. They reflect a pervasive need to justify an action in the present by an appeal to a past precedent. They go, however, far beyond simple justification of a present course of action. They are cogent examples of that mode of thinking which, as van Groningen has remarked, uses the past occurrence not merely as an edifying example but as the positive proof of a present possibility.

Though the paradigmatic elements of the longer digressions in the *Iliad* have been noted since ancient times, it has not been sufficiently noted that even the brief digressions, and indeed almost every reference to the past, even those made by the poet as narrator, are prompted by the same impulse to find paradigm in the past. As historical clarification of the present they are often too allusive to be satisfactory, so that we must conclude that they are not the product of a mind which is interested in historical completeness. The past intrudes into the present only when it can serve as paradigm.

In Book 1, for example, the poet's introduction of Kalchas is not an overt paradigm, yet its purpose is surely paradigmatic; by citing past precedent (Kalchas' seership which had brought the Greeks to Ilium) it is a guarantee of the reliability of Kalchas' following speech. In the same book the paradigmatic use of the past pervades Agamemnon's retort to Kalchas and the colloquy between Agamemnon and Achilleus. A single action in the past becomes indicative of a permanent *ēthos*. Agamemnon reacts to Kalchas' divination by attacking Kalchas' evil *ēthos* (106–9): "You have habitually given me bad oracles (*sc.* a reference to the sacrifice of Iphigeneia?) and now you are at your oracles again." Similarly, Achilleus reads Agamemnon's single outrageous act as proof of a consistent *ēthos*, with which he contrasts his own *ēthos* (163–9; 225–30): "You have always been a coward who prefers to stay behind and expropriate other men's prizes while I have always fought in the front ranks and have been content with a small prize." This paradigmatic mode of reasoning is fundamental to the quarrel between Agamemnon and Achilleus, and an understanding of its cogent appeal for Homer's heroes will help to explain Achilleus' adamant rejection of Agamemnon's offer in Book 9. How can Agamemnon change now into an honorable man when he is a man *consistently* lacking in honor and honesty?

Paradigmatic logic appears in the hypomnesis of prayers on four occasions in Book 1 alone, three times with positive assertion (39–40, 394–406, 453–4), and once with negative when Hephaistos apologizes to Hera for his helplessness (586–94): "I could not help you in the past, so do not expect me to be able to help you now." In Book 3 the past is constantly introduced as paradigm. We may note Hektor's taunts of Paris, and the obvious examples in the *Teichoscopeia* when Helen and Antenor measure the present against the past as they identify the Greek heroes. In Helen's reminiscences the unhappy present is so at odds with the promise of the past that Helen can scarcely believe that she and the blithe young girl she remembers in Sparta are the same individual, and she is forced to exclaim (180), "If this ever happened."

The other digressions which delve into the background of the War mostly form a complex of stories around Achilleus and are also told as paradigm. The several allusions to Achilleus' raids of Eëtion's city, Thebe, serve first, as J. W. Zarker has shown, as exemplars of the future doom of Troy, and secondly as exemplars to contrast the former chivalry of Achilleus with his present intrasigence. The story of the recruiting mission at Phthia likewise recalls incidents from Achilleus' past to serve as paradigmatic argument.

The reason for the scarcity and allusiveness of the references to the immediate background of the Trojan War becomes more apparent in the light of this Homeric attitude towards the past. Most of the historical digressions are taken from sources outside the Trojan legend because the Trojan War, being still in progress, offers only limited opportunities for paradigm. Notopoulos has suggested that retrospection is one of the devices of the oral poet to fill in essential background and to insure continuity. This is truer of the *Odyssey* than the *Iliad*, but in the *Odyssey* retrospection is the principal technique of narrative and indeed one of the major themes of the poem. In the *Iliad*, however, retrospection plays so little part, except when it can yield a paradigm, that those events which logically belong to the first years of the War are pushed into the present. It would be no structural problem to present the events of Books 2 through 7 in flashbacks, but the *Iliad*, always anticipatory in outlook, eschews the flashback. In the *Iliad* the heroes seem to have almost no past at all, unless the past can provide not just information for its own sake but a persuasive argument for some present action or behavior. In the *Odyssey*, where the heroes have only a past and virtually no present, the Trojan War, now part of the past, becomes the major preoccupation of its characters and a rich source of paradigm.

To explain the paradigmatic intention of the historical digressions is insufficient in itself; we may still question their length and detail. Nestor could say in a simple sentence, once and for all, "I fought with the bravest heroes of the past and they used to follow my advice; so you too should follow my advice." Why a long story to affirm this every time Nestor speaks? We may find the paradigmatic intention relevant but the manner of execution inopportune. It is just the amount of detail, the discursiveness, which has made the digression the subject of such controversy. The length of the anecdote, however, is a relevant as its intent. The expansion of the anecdote is a form of *amplificatio*, or what later Greek rhetoricians called *auxēsis*, a heightening of the subject, and so itself a form of persuasion.

Homer may not have commanded a system of rhetoric as refined and ordered as that of the Sophists, but in this respect his practice is unequivocal. For it is a surprising fact in Homer that where the drama is most intense the digressions are the longest and the details the fullest. In paradigmatic digressions the length of the anecdote is in direct proportion to the necessity for persuasion at the moment. The more urgent the situation, the more expansive the speech and its illustrative paradigm. The two longest digressions, the story of Meleager in Book 9 and Nestor's story of the Pylians and Eleians in Book 11, mark the two most desperate stages in the deteriorating situation. The Greeks are helpless without Achilleus, and only the persuasiveness of Phoinix and Nestor can prevent total catastrophe. In these situations words are the only weapons left; the fighters cannot win without Achilleus, but their warrior skills are powerless to bring Achilleus back into the War. Only the skills of the orator have any chance of success.

It is a modern literary convention that the mode of expression proper to anxiety and desperation is incoherence. The opposite is often true for Homer's heroes. Like the proverbial drowning man, faced with catastrophe they are gifted with total recall and the rhetoric to support that recall. Coherence, lucidity, prolixity, expansive reminiscences couched in a more elaborate, even Pindaric rhetoric of ring-composition, balance, antithesis— these can mark the moment of despair or consternation in the *Iliad* as effectively as those stark silences (as when Achilleus hears the news of Patroklos' death) which strike us with such force.

Paradigmatic digressions, even though they may take us far into the past, function in this respect just as the descriptions of objects or the expansions of such stock oral themes as assembly, arming, sacrifice or battlefield encounters. The mere mention of an object often has a dramatic force, and the expanded description of the object lends an even greater emphasis. Expansions are not ornaments but an essential part of the drama.

That an expanded description of an arming scene or a scepter exalts the character participating in the scene and emphasizes the dramatic situation may be obvious, since the objects described also become participants in the action. Every expanded description, however, whether a genealogy or a myth of by-gone days, follows the same principle. The oral poets of today may call these expansions ornaments, but their practice shows that they observe a careful propriety in the use of such 'ornamentation'. There is a hierarchical procedure in ornamentation; princes receive an amplifi-cation different in degree and kind from that given to squires. There is a similar hierarchy in the use of expansion to depict dramatic situations.

Thus we must recognize that behind the apparent parataxis of Homeric style is a scrupulous dramatic sense which calls attention to a particular situation or person by the multiplicity of peripheral details. There is in Homer a principle which might be called one of *oblique concentration*. To praise Achilleus Homer describes his shield. No expansion of a stock theme is given for its own sake, nor is any story told for its own charm. Elaboration, whether of a scene in the present or of a story from Nestor's past, is a sign of crisis. Homer has too often been considered the exemplar of the clear assertion, the unambiguous statement. There is a certain direct simplicity in the narrative which hides the obliquity of the style, the style which marks the important by evading the explicit statement and glances instead on all the circumferential details.

The effect of this style is to put time into slow motion and to create a ritual out of the moment. A. B. Lord has suggested that the elaboration of certain oral themes may have a significance deriving from ritual. He is referring particularly to those themes of arming and preparation which are greatly amplified when the hero of the poem is about to go to an important encounter. But the arming themes should not be treated as distinct from the other kinds of oral themes. All are subject to expansion and for the same dramatic reason. Though the Homeric poems may derive from mythic sources the drama is what is important in Homer rather than mythic rites of initiation or sacrifice. It is not the survival of an ancient ritual which dictates the degree of elaboration of an oral theme but the dramatic sense which determines the need for ritual. Homer creates ritual by amplification whenever the moment is significant. Thus Helen's conversation with Priam in the *Teichoscopeia* becomes a ritual as much as the arming of Patroklos or Achilleus. Ritual in Homer is ancillary to the drama.

We can see this kind of ritualizing in the description of important scenes of propitiation. The careful description of the mundane details of Odysseus' embassy to Chryses is the dramatic representation of the impor-tance of the mission. The act of propitiation is not merely the return of Chryseis and the sacrifice but the total ceremony, the whole day's cele-bration. In the reconciliation scene between Priam and Achilleus there is the same attention to practical details, the same ritualizing of ordinary activity and for the same reason. This too is a scene of propitiation in which the chances of success remain to the end precarious. This is not an ordinary dinner, but a ceremony in which Priam and Achilleus are officiants. Again the narrative moves slowly to make us experience the ritual, but, more important, the emotional maelstrom which necessitates such elaborate ritual.

Thetis' visit to Hephaistos to obtain arms for Achilleus shows a similar ritualized intensity (18.369ff). All the preliminaries are related at length: Charis' welcome of Thetis, Charis' appeal to Hephaistos to receive Thetis graciously, the description of the workshop with its wheeled tripods and golden automaton handmaidens, Hephaistos' speech of welcome which includes the hypomnetic story of how Thetis had saved him when Hera had thrown him from Olympos, then Thetis' appeal for arms, Hephaistos' promise to provide them, and finally the making of the arms. The social amenities are played out at length, and their elaborate execution is Homer's stylized form of emphasis. When we hear the exchanges between Thetis, Charis and Hephaistos—a total of five speeches repeating the themes of hospitality and past indebtedness and slowly advancing to the present need—we know that the arms must be extraordinary to require such ceremony and the need for them will be proportionately extraordinary.

Bassett has called the Shield an epic hyporcheme inserted as an interlude between two outbursts of passion. In spite of its pastoral tone, however, it is not comparable to the lyric interludes of tragedy, for it is an integral part of the scene in Hephaistos' workshop, a scene which can hardly be called an interlude. As the reason for, and the climax of, that scene it receives the same kind of elaboration as the rest of the scene but in even greater detail. Where the lyric choruses of tragedy telescope our vision to place the specific in its proper relation to the general, the Shield, like the other expansions in Homer, is a microscope to focus more intently on the minutest details of the specific. Though the field of both instruments may be equally varied, the one is cosmoramic while the other is panoramic; the difference in perspective is essential.

The ritualized character of these scenes of a supplicatory nature, is obvious. The scenes are not themselves digressions, but two of the three contain paradigmatic digressions (even Odysseus' embassy scene contains its paradigmatic element in the hypomnesis of Chryses' prayer), and the digressions become elements in the ritual and so subject to the same ritualizing description. It is worth noting that the scenes which include the longest digressions are supplicatory and give great attention to details of hospitality. Hospitality is stressed in the *Nestoris* in Book 11, but it is particularly important in the embassy scene in Book 9. As in other important supplicatory scenes there is not the slightest indication of haste, but an unhurried observance of all the traditional courtesies. There is something of the Oriental habit which marks an important meeting by an extravagant display of the gestures of hospitality while postponing for as long as possible any mention of the topic which is uppermost in the minds of all participants.

A failure to appreciate the fact that the degree of expansion in a digression into the past is dictated by a sense of urgency in the speaker's mind or is an expression of the dramatic tension of the moment has led to a misunderstanding of Homeric style. Homer is not indiscriminate or compulsive about detail. He is quite able to contain himself; both the *Iliad* and the *Odyssey* bear ample testimony to his ability to release background information sparingly, sometimes too sparingly for our curiosity, through the course of an extended narrative. The Homeric poems are not nearly as exhaustive historical source books as they might seem.

HERMANN FRÄNKEL

The New Mood of the "Odyssey" and the End of Epic

If we want to learn the structure of human nature in ancient epic, we must adhere mainly to the *Iliad*, for the picture begins to change markedly in the *Odyssey*. The contrast between the epics can be inferred at once from the programmatic verses with which they begin. As the proems indicate, the hero of the *Iliad* is great because he is wrathful and stubborn; that of the *Odyssey*, not because he is self-willed but because he is "versatile." Achilles shows his worth by sacrificing to his resentment "the souls of many heroes" out of his own camp (and soon he will sacrifice his own soul also: cf. *Il.* 9, 104–16); Odysseus, by contrast, preserves himself because he understands how to save "his own soul and the homecoming of his comrades"—although the comrades perish in the end, through no fault of his. The *Iliad* depicts horrible things which (like everything on earth) came about according to "god's will"; the *Odyssey* does indeed tell (among many other things) of the terrible death of the comrades, but they invited divine punishment "on their part through lack of understanding." Inflexible resentment here, pliable accommodation there; destruction of others and self here, preservation of self and others there; the will of the gods here, and man's own success or failure there.

From *Early Greek Poetry and Philosophy: A History of Greek Epic, Lyric and Prose to the Middle of the Fifth Century*. Translations by Moses Hadas and James Willis. Copyright © 1973 by Basil Blackwell. Harcourt Brace Jovanovich.

• 163 •

The *Odyssey* is no longer romantically lamenting a submerged world which was fatefully ruined by its own stormy nature; instead it celebrates the manful realist of a new present who cleverly and resolutely takes his destiny into his own hands to rise superior to all opposition.

The greater realism and contemporaneity in the *Odyssey* give the entire poem a different character. The distance between the narrator and his subject which is so strictly maintained in the *Iliad* is here perceptibly slackened, and the rigour of the stylization is modified. The Phaeacians are idealized Ionians of the present. Nature is largely restored to its rights. Winter and bad weather afflict Odysseus (*Od.* 14, 457ff.); he is afraid of the cold of night and the wind on the riverbank, and of savage beasts by sea and land (*Od.* 5, 465–73; 421). There are now beggars and humble folk, even a dog, who is the only creature to recognize his homecoming master. The graybeard is no longer above all the bearer of accumulated sagacity, but a fragile man in need of help (*Od.* 17, 195f.). The use of similes is much reduced, for the real world, not a stylized one, enters freely into the narrative itself and does not have to lurk in little digressions.

The people of the *Odyssey* no longer live in an almost empty space; they take pleasure in the abundant variety of things to be seen and heard and experienced. The world is wide and full of wonders, which a man may visit to try his powers against them. The joy of discovery and the love of adventure form the background for a large part of the epic. Odysseus ventures into the cave of the Cyclops out of curiosity and because he hopes to receive gifts of hospitality (*Od.* 9, 224–30), and some of his comrades have to pay for his rashness with a horrible death. Life for these people is full of interest, but also of difficulty. The outside world, which is no longer shadowy but now surrounds and oppresses the individual with its massive presence, constantly thrusts him into situations with which it is hard to cope. So man begins to put a distance between himself and the world. Men are no longer freely receptive and freely outgoing; they are now reserved and calculating. Aloofness and distrust become necessary, indeed a virtue which is glorified in the epic. Even deception and falsehood are now legitimate weapons in the struggle for existence. The modern ideal of the clever and experienced man who makes his way by all means, straight or crooked, displaces the heroic ideal, and antagonism to the outmoded view leads the poets to exaggerate and overvalue the traits which now occupy the foreground. Odysseus the "rogue" (*Od.* 5, 182) is the master of the new art of living, recognized and admired by men and by gods. The proud reserve of unbending rectitude has been given up. For a long while Odysseus plays the role of beggar, and plays it almost too realistically. On occasion his character appears to become quite uncertain.

And yet Odysseus is by no means an actor without a character of his own, or an adventurer ignorant of what he is really seeking; nor is the *Odyssey* a poem of roguery. With all his ingratiating amiability, its hero is a serious, mature, and energetic man, and with all his cunning, he pursues a high goal and, thanks to his toughness with himself, attains it. The iron strength with which he masters feelings, resists seduction, and breaks attachments is a new kind of heroism. This "iron heart" (*Od.* 4, 293) the epic celebrates by regularly attaching the epithet *polytlas* to his name; "much enduring" is only a vague rendering. What *polytlas* really means is shown by a scene at the beginning of Book 20. Odysseus lays himself down to sleep as a beggar in the vestibule of his own house, on the eve of the vengeance through which he will regain his place as master and king. There he hears certain of the maids going, with laughter and jests, to meet their lovers among the suitors. Odysseus' heart begins to rage and to "bark," for as master of the house the maids belong to him, and it is a form of unfaithfulness for them to give themselves to the suitors of their own will. Natural pride would impel him to strike them all down at once, and his heart bays like a hound over what has been tossed to it, irritable and determined to protect is treasure. But he chides his heart and admonishes it to "endure" (*tlēnai*): Even dealings more doglike did you endure when the Cyclops devoured my comrades. You endured until wit brought you out of the cave, which would otherwise have been my death." In Homer the dog is an image of bold audacity and unflinching determination. In the cave the Cyclops had killed and devoured two of Odysseus' comrades. "In my proud temper," so Odysseus tells the story to the Phaeacians (*Od.* 9, 299), "I seized upon the thought of approaching and slaying him. But another purpose restrained me, for then we too would have been irretrievably lost, for we could not have rolled the heavy stone from the high doorway with our arms." So Odysseus controlled himself then, and had to look on while two more of his companions met the same gruesome end before the proper moment came for the appropriate action. Then, as now, something in his heart raged doglike and wished to assert itself in righteous indignation, and now, as then, he constrains his proud temper to "endure." So he spoke, admonishing his dear heart, and it abode in obedience, without yielding." So too Odysseus "endured" (*Od.* 13, 307) when after twenty years he finally entered his own house as a beggar, to suffer many affronts, and revealed his identity to no one until he had obtained exact information and had matured his plan of vengeance. He sits opposite his own wife and plays a subtle game of hide-and-seek with her, because the time has not yet come for an open declaration. In the patience of the "much enduring" Odysseus, in the suppression of his pride and other natural impulses, there is much forceful activity, and this is carried on not for its own sake but to promote an objective. Odysseus is the man who pursues his objectives against all opposition. This quality the epic expresses in other standing epithets which adorn the name of Odysseus: *polymētis*, "rich in ingenious ideas," and *polymēchanos*, 'rich in devices to gain an end.' With such attributes does the new age, which graded its values very differently from the old, bedeck its idol.

In the younger epic Odysseus enters upon the heritage of Achilles, who was the most brilliant figure in the *Iliad*. Odysseus as heir of Achilles: this formulation we do not conceive in retrospect, for it is in this conception that the epic itself at once perpetuated the changed ideal of human excellence as soon as it appeared. This time saga, which reflects so many events of political history after its own fashion, has concentrated a historical evolution in values into a profoundly meaningful legend. One of the epics of Troy, the *Little Iliad*, relates that after the death of Achilles an argument arose as to who was now the best man in the army and so entitled to the armor of Achilles. The candidates were Ajax, the doughty but slow-thinking champion, and Odysseus, the clever but less powerful warrior. The decision was sought from the enemy camp, because the opposition knew best whom they had most to fear. A spy overheard a conversation between Trojan maidens (at the spring); the decisive words were spoken by a Trojan woman who pointed out that Ajax was like a tough and reliable workman, whereas Odysseus was a man of initiative and adroitness. After the armor was awarded to Odysseus, Ajax took his own life in chagrin and shame.

Our *Odyssey* has another confrontation between the two. Odysseus reports to the Phaeacians (11, 543ff.) that he saw the shade of Ajax in the realm of the dead and that Ajax kept his distance in anger at his defeat. And the narrator remarks:

> Would I had never been victor and won so fatal a contest!
> It is for this that the grave now holds so mighty a hero—
> Ajax, in looks and in actions the greatest of all the Achaeans
> Saving only Achilles, the peerless offspring of Peleus.

Nothing could be more significant of the amiable side of the new humanity than these words of Odysseus. They breathe a generous and understanding kindliness—one of the new virtues. There speaks here an insight which recognizes the superiority of a defeated opponent and which would willingly forego the proudest honor if it had to be purchased by the death of such a man. With such feelings Odysseus addresses conciliatory words to the shade of Ajax in the underworld. But this is not the sort of language to prevail over the intransigent pride of the olden days (11, 563):

> So I spoke, but he gave no reply, and turned himself from me,
> Joining the other ghosts of the dead who dwell in the shadows.

On aesthetic grounds we could wish that the scene ended here. But our text contains an after-word which softens the bluntness:

> Yet he might still have spoken for all his angry resentment.
> I might have spoken again; but the heart in my bosom was eager
> Still to see more and to talk with others among the departed.

It is quite possible that these three transitional verses to what follows come from another hand than the scene itself. In any case, they are significant of the optimism with which the new age trusted its new men. Its cleverness and warmth would be able to thaw the rigidity of the old heroism and to reconcile an angry Ajax with an Odysseus. Only the curiosity of Odysseus, wishing to converse with other souls, prevented the continuation of the dialogue.

The hero of the *Odyssey* displays his manifold abilities in having to deal with beings of all kinds, one after the other, and in being involved in difficulties of all kinds. Always he comes to the fore as master, and by his unique greatness leaves all others, friend and foe alike, far behind him; his role is not, like that of Achilles in the *Iliad, primus inter pares*. But if the lesser figures of the *Odyssey* are not the same calibre as Odysseus, they are nevertheless of similar style. They too derive from the new age: the hero's wife holds the suitors off by her ingenuity; Circe is cunning, and Calypso is warm-hearted and kindly—or pretends to be; the suitors, for their part, intrigue against Telemachus, but their attempt on his life mis-carries. The few open and forthright characters fall into special types because of those traits; so, for example, the faithful and amiable swineherd, or the savage and detestable Cyclops, a naïve and conceited blusterer, whose deception is almost tragic (9, 447–60). The lesser like the principal figures move largely among peculiar and precarious circumstances. This makes the action of the *Odyssey* more complicated but also more unified. For every element of the action there are precisely ascribed conditions, and these are all interrelated. The *Iliad,* by contrast, is more loosely jointed, for its theme is simply strife and contention in the war at Troy.

Hence the persons of the *Odyssey* require a different kind of divine assistance for discharging their tasks. Divine providence now takes on the character of a constant surveillance which watches over its protégés with great punctiliousness and intervenes to support them according to a precise plan with either natural or miraculous means. At the same time the people of the *Odyssey*, in their detachment and shrewdness, begin to insulate themselves against the outer world. The individual is no longer an open field of action, but self and not-self are differentiated, so that even divine influence on their conduct is externalized. When Odysseus lands in Ithaca he receives from Athene not inspiration, but detailed information and instructions (*Od.* 13, 372–428), like the information and instructions for his journey given him by the goddess Circe (*Od.* 10, 490–540; 12, 37–141). So in the *Odyssey* a distinction is occasionally drawn which would not have occurred to the older age: ". . . whether it was that a god implanted this thought, or whether he himself devised it" (4, 712). Divine direction and individual action can now be separated from one another, so that man becomes responsible for his acts in a new sense.

Man is not transparent in the *Odyssey*, even when he is not actually lying; he is variable and reserved and sometimes not too certain of himself—like Telemachus and some of the suitors, and probably Penelope also. Not infrequently, then, the representation in poetry must be content without complete clarity and openness. Neither the report of the narrator, who still discreetly restricts himself to externals, nor the speeches of the epic personages, who are far from expressing themselves frankly, can set forth everything the poet has in mind. Instead of the bright footlights before which the heroes of the *Iliad* performed, a softened and shifting half-light plays over the personages of the younger epic, sometimes flaring up only to be dimmed again. For such a presentation traditional epic style was not suited. An astonishing example can show how, in a very late part of the *Odyssey*, the poet drew the utmost refinements from a style not well suited to them.

In the guise of Mentes, a man from a family of friends, Athene comes to the palace at Ithaca, where the suitors have made themselves at home (*Od.* 1, 103ff.). In the midst of the general turmoil Telemachus receives the visitor and does the honors of the house. Between the two a conversation takes place which becomes intimate at once. Telemachus is oppressed by his embarrassing impotence in his own house. He no longer dares hope for the return of his father, which would change everything. The stranger, for his part, is full of friendly reassurances; in his view, he remarks comfortingly, such a man as Odysseus will somehow overcome all hindrances. Homeric etiquette now requires that after a stranger has been received inquiry should be made concerning name, father, home, and other personal details. The visitor had already supplied the information, and now he puts the corresponding questions to his host, in order to satisfy the formal requirements, for in fact he had already treated Telemachus as the man he was (187). He therefore phrases his question to become a compliment on Telemachus' resemblance to his famous father (206): "Tell me this and relate it truly, if you are indeed the son of Odysseus himself. You are marvelously like him in head and handsome eyes. . . ." Whereupon the visitor receives an extraordinary answer (214):

> Friend, I will speak to you as clearly as I am able.
> My mother tells me that I am his son: yet truly for my part
> I cannot say: what man can know for sure his conception?
> Wish that I were a happy man's son—one favored by fortune,
> Sitting among his kin, with a tranquil old age to await him!
> But they tell me that he, instead, the most luckless of all men,
> He was my father: I tell you, for that was the question you asked me.

Telemachus' reply begins with an ordinary epic formula which elsewhere (cf. 179) says nothing more than that one is ready to give the desired information accurately and truly. But this time Telemachus carries accuracy and truth very far, and in a singular direction. Obviously Telemachus had often worried over the misfortune bequeathed to him by an absent man whom he scarcely knew, of whom he was told that his name was Odysseus and that he was his father. His worry now rises to acute doubt: all of this may not be true, and it would be better if it were not. Naturally the doubt is not real, nor was the stranger's question motivated by real doubt; and it is unreasonable, for Penelope is the proverbially faithful wife. But the keen desire of the young man to dissociate himself from his fate and his identity suggest such fancies, for which he eventually apologizes: "[Excuse my outbreak, but you evoked it] because you asked me whether I was my father's son." The response of the stranger tactfully veers back to the normal (222):

> The gods have not given you a nameless ancestry, since Penelope bore
> you to a man such as Odysseus.

Mentes will not deny that no man has personal knowledge of his origin, but in this case the later development of the child banishes every doubt, for Telemachus, as was already noted, has grown up to be a true image of Odysseus. The implications are two-fold: the young man can be proud of his descent, and has no reason to struggle against it.

The section just examined appears so strange and un-Homeric that one is tempted to evade the interpretation here sketched; but the text admits no other explanation. This astonishingly modern piece shows how far Greek epic in its latest stage has travelled from its starting point. It is minded to overstep the boundaries set for this genre. No further advance was possible along this road. Only followers and imitators could be expected.

The new humanity which asserts itself in the *Odyssey* takes away from epic the basis of its existence. The epic form was created in order to give a complete and definitive account of unquestioned actuality either directly or by transparent symbols, not to beat to and fro in a misty environment of hazy possibilities and everyday attitudes. The grandiose language and the powerful verse are not suited to the subtle or the commonplace which they are now used to express. Where previously all that was named or told of was glorified, and only what was praiseworthy had the entrée to epic, now the gates are flung wide to persons and things of every description, and the singer's performance is no longer, as it had been, devotion to and celebration of gods and great men. The poetry is no longer stylized, as it formerly was, but depicts the world more realistically and in a more modern spirit.

The figure of the principal hero embodies the modern spirit at its purest and fullest. From Odysseus contemporary audiences could learn to master life. Why then the roundabout way via an art originally intended for looking backward into a different past? The inherited epic form would have to be alienated from its nature or surrendered entirely, for literature to be able to fulfill the tasks now set before it: to know the world as it is constituted, to confront situations in the way that is most advantageous, and to come to grips with one's life, each with his own.

Into such a situation there now enters the singular figure of Hesiod, and then, with a very different function, lyric poetry: Hesiod to master and encompass the outer world instructively, still in the language and versification of epic; lyric to seize upon the inwardness of personal life in poetry of a new form. The two have now parted. The old unity is broken.

JAMES M. REDFIELD

Achilles

Achilles is difficult to live with partly because he sees situations so clearly. This clarity of vision is the source of his powerful rhetoric and of his greatness as a warrior. Achilles gives himself over to the situation as he perceives it; he acts and speaks without shading or half-measures. A man of this kind is badly placed in a deliberative assembly. He sees the situations so clearly because he sees only a part of it. Achilles, with his instinctive rhetorical resources, dramatizes this partial vision to himself until it fills his view and leaves no place for qualifications. He says to Agamemnon:

> My prize is never equal to yours, whenever Achaeans
> Sack some Trojan castle, well provided—
> And yet the greater part of grievous battle
> Is work of my hands. But when there comes a sharing,
> Your prize is much greater; some small thing of my own
> I take to my ships, whenever I'm worn with battle.
>   (I.163–68)

The formulaic phrase "a small thing of my own"—*oligon te philon te* appears in the *Odyssey* in a context of begging (vi.208 = xiv.58). That is probably the connotation here; Achilles pictures himself as a helpless creature fed on scraps. This is hardly fair. The two girls who are the focus of the quarrel—Chryseis and Briseis—were taken in the raid on Thebe (I.366–69; II.688–93). This raid was itself a theme of epic song; references to it are scattered through the *Iliad,* and Homer seems to assume that his audience knows the story. In Book Six we learn that the most valuable

---

From *Nature and Culture in the Iliad: The Tragedy of Hector.* Copyright © 1975 by The University of Chicago. The University of Chicago Press.

prize of this raid, the king's wife, had been awarded to Achilles, who sold her back to her father, "taking measureless ransoms" (VI.425–27). Achilles was not so unrewarded after all.

In taking Briseis from Achilles, Agamemnon is of course acting outrageously. To Achilles this unfairness is especially bitter because so unexpected. Achilles is trying to rescue Agamemnon's army. If he speaks somewhat harshly to Agamemnon—well, that is the right of the assembly. When Agamemnon insults him, Achilles naturally returns his insults. By the time Nestor gets the floor, it is too late. The best commentary on the whole scene is perhaps Aeneas' remark to Achilles late in the poem:

> We both of us have insulting remarks for the speaking
> In plenty; a hundred-burdened ship wouldn't hold them.
> Flexible is a mortal's tongue; its speeches are many,
> All sorts; the great field of words extends hither and yon.
> Whatever words you speak, such words you will hear.
> But why of strife and quarrels have we two need,
> To quarrel with one another, as if we were women?
> They fall to raging in heart-consuming strife
> And quarrel with one another out in the street
> With much that is true—and is not. For rage compels them
> (XX.246–55)

The word I have translated above as "rage" is *cholos*; Agamemnon and Achilles fall to ranting like fishwives because *cholos* has come upon them both. *Cholos* has a somewhat wider range than "rage"; Achilles feels *cholos* when he looks for the first time upon the arms made by Hephaestus— and delight as well. His eyes "glitter beneath his brows as if flashing" (XIX.16–18). Odysseus fears that Nausicaa might feel *cholos* if a naked salt-covered stranger fell at her feet (vi.147). *Cholos* is a whole-body reaction, the adrenal surge which drives men to violent speech and action. *Cholos*, says Achilles later,

> drives even a sensible man to harshness;
> It is far sweeter than honey pouring within one,
> And in the breasts of men it rises like smoke.
> (XVIII.107–10)

There are two ways of dealing with *cholos*. It can be poured into violent action and in that way "healed" (IV.36). Or it can be "digested" (I.81; cf. IX.565); in the course of time the body will consume the *cholos* and the man will be calm again. Achilles' natural reaction is to take the first course; he decides to kill Agamemnon. But Athena intervenes and promises the "threefold gifts." Achilles replies:

Your word, of course, goddess, must be respected,
However great the *cholos*. For thus it is better.
Who trusts himself to the gods will gain their hearing.
(I.216–18)

Achilles withdraws to his ships, there to "digest his *cholos*" (IV.513) and await events.

We next see Achilles when the embassy comes to him "with glorious gifts and soothing words" (IX.113). The whole rhythm of events up to this point would lead us to expect that Achilles will take the gifts and that his wrath will be over. I believe that Achilles himself thinks he will take the gifts—until he has heard them. Here, I think, is the dramatic force of the long catalogue of gifts repeated almost verbatim by Odysseus from Agamemnon. The first time we hear this catalogue, we respond warmly to Agamemnon's reformation; each additional item is further proof of his new good will. When the same list is recited to Achilles, it falls flat, each item flatter than the last; ideally the audience and Achilles realize at the same moment that the gifts will not work, that the embassy must be a failure.

The phrase of Odysseus'—"if you hate Atreus' son from the heart, himself and his gifts" (IX.300–301)—comes just at the end of the repeated catalogue. Odysseus himself is aware that his presentation is not going well. He inserts this phrase at the moment when he is leaving out the last four lines of Agamemnon's message, which had been:

Let him be ruled; Hades, unsoothed, unruled,
Is therefore hated most of mortals' gods.
And let him accept that I am more of a king
And that I can claim to be elder in my birth.
(IX.158–61)

Odysseus, however, gains no advantage by suppressing a conclusion implicit in the body of the message. By his very act of recompense, Agamemnon asserts his superiority over Achilles. By offering gifts, he shows that he has them, and to spare. By offering Achilles seven towns and his daughter, Agamemnon is not offering to make himself any poorer; he is offering to include Achilles within his own sphere as his son-in-law and subordinate. Achilles twice says that Agamemnon had treated him "like a wanderer without honor" (IX.648 = XVI.59). Such inclusion in the sphere of others is precisely the fate of wanderers, like Phoenix (IX.478–84) and Patroclus (XXIII.83–92), who had been taken in by Peleus. By the offered terms of settlement Agamemnon would convert Achilles into his dependent. That is why Achilles, while still making the somewhat contradictory claim that he has been unrewarded for his efforts, at the same time lays such stress in his reply on his own property and on the fact that he has a father of his own in his own country. Achilles knows that he is being asked to submit.

What does Achilles want from the embassy at this moment? Quite possibly he does not know. Achilles had wanted to kill Agamemnon and would now probably be content with nothing less than Agamemnon's humiliation. Perhaps an embassy that had come, not on Agamemnon's behalf, but, over the king's protests, on behalf of the rest of the Greeks would have been successful. In Book One Achilles says that, were the Greeks not worthless, Agamemnon would have lost the power to commit outrage (I.231–32). Here he says that the other Greeks will no longer trust Agamemnon; Achilles' case should teach them that their king is shameless and deceitful (IX.369–72). Agamemnon, Achilles says, must give back "the whole outrage" (IX.387). Achilles suffers, and his suffering can be soothed only by the suffering of the man who caused it. If Agamemnon lost his authority, he would surely suffer.

Achilles is offered the gifts on condition that he give up his *cholos* (IX.157, 260–61, 299). But he cannot do it; *cholos* is a *pathos*, not subject to rational control. At the end of the embassy Achilles tells Ajax that he is helpless:

> Telamonian Zeus-born Ajax, commander of men,
> In a way your speech is exactly to my mind.
> But still my heart swells with *cholos* at what
> I remember; he made me degraded among the Argives,
> Atreus' son, like a wanderer without honor.
>
> (IX.644–48)

Achilles feels that he has been evicted from his proper place in the world. Until he has recovered from this experience, he cannot return to his friends, however much they need him. In fact he would like to give them all up and go home. His troops have been telling him that, if they're not to fight, they might as well depart (XVI.203–6). The embassy seems to clarify this point in his mind also. There is nothing to wait for; he can leave in the morning.

But he does not go. He longs for home because home means for him his father—but his father sent him out to be a warrior; Achilles' mother may value his life before honor, but Achilles cannot disappoint his father's expectations of him. This idea of going home was always the weak point in his position; on this point, and this point alone, Phoenix and Ajax shift him. He replaces his threat of departure by a vow: he will not fight until Hector comes to the camp of the Myrmidons and the fire reaches his own ships (IX.650–53). He thus commits himself to remain near the battle but not in it. Achilles is caught between a father who has sent him away and a king who wants to take him over and use him. He can think of nothing better to do, for the moment, than to take his stand on the margin of events.

Achilles' great speech, by this reading, is an explosion of rage at the impossible position in which he finds himself. Achilles is an outsize figure. He is stronger, swifter, braver, than the other heroes, and his anger also is larger than any they could feel. And Achilles is a hero with exceptional powers of intellect and speech; he has a unique capacity to generalize his immediate experience and state it in universal terms. If he is deprived on Briseis, well, then, he has been stripped of everything and was given nothing in the first place. If Agamemnon behaves badly to him, well, then, Agamemnon is a fool, a glutton, a cheat, and a coward. Similarly, if he cannot find grounds for a return to battle, then no such grounds exist; nothing can recompense a man for risking his life. The speech is not a step toward a new synthesis but an overpoweringly vivid statement of a partial truth.

I cannot agree with Whitman that Achilles is here "groping for something loftier." He is groping, surely, but nothing comes to his hand. He tries to turn away from war, but war is his life and he cannot leave it. His speech is falsified by his act.

Nor can I agree with Bowra that Achilles here sins and opens himself to proper punishment. As the man he is, in the place he is, I do not see that Achilles could have acted otherwise. In the embassy, as throughout the poem, Achilles is less the creator of situations than their agent and victim; he does in each case what it seems to him must be done.

By Book Sixteen—the following day in the narrative but a long time later in the life of the poem—Achilles' *cholos* is gone; it has been "digested." Patroclus, instructed by Nestor, appeals to him to return to the battle or else send him, Patroclus, in his place; Achilles reviews his grievance once more and then says:

> Let us be done with all that. There was no way
> To keep the *cholos* unceasing at heart. Yet I said
> I would not stop my enmity until
> The war and the battle came to my own ships.
> But you, put my famous armor on your shoulders;
> Lead the warlike Myrmidons to battle. . . .
> (XVI.60–65)

The embassy had come a day too soon; now it might have had better success. But it is too late; Achilles is bound by the vow he made on the previous day. He sends Patroclus instead.

JAMES M. REDFIELD

The Hero

The epic picture of the world was formed and transformed during the Greek dark ages, during the gap or vacant space in Greek history between the fall of citadels—Mycenae, Tiryns, Pylos, Troy—and the revival of towns in the eighth century B.C. Whatever details of Minoan or Mycenaean culture may persist in the poems, the Homeric picture of society in general belongs to the dark age and the early age of recovery. Homer shows us people living in small groups, dependent on one another for their mutual security against a hostile world.

When the background condition of life is a condition of war—when men feel themselves free to steal from anyone with whom they are not acquainted and to plunder and exterminate any town against which they have a grievance—men must place great trust in those close to them. Thus combat generates a tight-knit community. A Homeric community consists, in effect, of those who are ready to die for one another; the perimeter of each community is a potential battlefield. Under these social conditions, war is perceived as the most important human activity because the community's ability to wage defensive war is perceived as the precondition of all other communal values. Within the community there can be families, productive labor, property, religious and social ceremonies, but all these depend for their existence on the valor of the warrior.

The burden of a Homeric battle falls on a few leading men. The anonymous mass may appear on the battlefield, but they are insignificant in the course of the war; battles are won and lost by those who step forward from the mass, the *promachoi*, those who "fight among the foremost." These

From *Nature and Culture in the Iliad: The Tragedy of Hector.* Copyright © 1975 by The University of Chicago. The University of Chicago Press.

are the *aristoi* or princes, men who own armor and chariots, who are trained
to the art and labor of war. To these leading warriors the Homeric language
gives the name of *hērōes*, heroes.

Thus heroism is for Homer a definite social task, and the heroes are
a definite social stratum. The name is given to those who are, have been,
or will be warriors. This is the Homeric governing class, the propertied
class, and also the class on which the burden falls of maintaining the
community. The most lucid statement of the hero's role and task is Sarpedon's speech to Glaucus, spoken in the depths of the battle by the ships:

> Glaucus, why is it we two are most in honor
> In our place at the feast, with meats and many cupfuls,
> In Lycia? Like gods all men behold us.
> Why hold we a great grant-farm by the banks of Xanthus,
> Fair with orchard and corn-rich plow-land?
> For this: that we now with the foremost Lycians
> Must stand and exchange the blows of searing battle
> So that one may say, some Lycian with his armor:
> "They are not so fameless, that rule in Lycia,
> These kings of ours, that eat the fattened flocks
> With the honey-sweet choice wine. It seems their force
> Is good, since they fight with the foremost Lycians."
> Sweet fool, if only escaping this one war
> We two would be able, ageless, immortal,
> To live, then I'd neither fight with the foremost
> Nor would I send you to battle that wins renown.
> As it is, since the winged death-bringers stand beside us,
> Countless, which mortals cannot escape or shun,
> Let us go, to work our boast or submit to another's.
>   (XII.310–28)

Sarpedon sees that the privileges of the warrior serve both to mark the
warrior's special status and role and to hold him to the execution of his
task. The warrior's privileges are a kind of reward granted in advance; the
community accumulates a debt which it collects from the warrior on the
battlefield (IV.338–48). The warrior's advantages and prestige thus serve
to maintain in time of peace a social class which properly functions only
in time of war, on the battlefield.

But as the community's need of warriors generates a social organization, it generates also a paradox. War is initially an unhappy necessity,
the precondition of protected community. But as the warriors become a
class or caste, the advantages—and more important, the prestige—of the
warrior become in themselves desirable. War thus acquires for the warrior

a certain positive value. Heroism is initially a social task; it then becomes a definite set of virtues associated with the performance of this task. The warrior's virtues, further, entitle him to claim a social status. But he can claim that status only if he can show that he has the virtues, and he can demonstrate the warrior's virtues only on the battlefield. If his own community is not at war, the warrior will seek out combat elsewhere. Glaucus and Sarpedon are not fighting in defense of the Lycians; they are far from home, fighting, not on behalf of their community but on behalf of their own status within it. Thus the young Nestor also traveled far to prove himself a hero among heroes (I.260ff.). And so it happens that the community's need for security and for defensive warfare generates a warrior ethic, which then gives rise to aggressive warfare—which is a threat to security. This double meaning of combat—defensive and aggressive, altruistic and egoistic—is fundamental to the *Iliad*.

All this is commentary on the first half of Sarpedon's speech; the tragic power of the speech is in the ending. In the first half Sarpedon praises the warrior's role; in it, he says, a man becomes godlike. In the second half Sarpedon (as it were) steps back from his own picture and says: all this is only a social illusion. The hero may appear godlike, but he is only mortal.

But this shift of perspective enables Sarpedon to justify heroism in another way. Man dies in any case, but he can choose to die well. He becomes a hero because he cannot be a god. In his nature the hero remains like other men, but culture bestows on him a value; he does not survive, but he is remembered. The hero knows this, and his knowledge enables him to go forward. It is a curious kind of knowledge, however; for if the hero knows what he is receiving, he cannot forget that the price he pays is his own existence.

All men are born to die, but the warrior alone must confront this fact in his social life, since he fulfills his obligations only by meeting those who intend his death. The community is secured by combat, which is the negation of community; this generates a contradiction in the warrior's role. His community sustains him and sends him to his destruction. On behalf of community he must leave community and enter a realm of force. The warrior can protect the human world against force only because he himself is willing to use and suffer force, "to work his own boast or submit to another's." The warrior stands on the frontier between culture and nature.

The power of Sarpedon's speech lies in its implicit recognition of the contradiction. To dies for something, he says, is better than to die for nothing—and that is, after all, the alternative. In accepting death he shows himself searingly aware of it. The hero is in a sense rescued from mortality; he becomes godlike in status and immortal in the memory. At the same time he is uniquely conscious of his own mortality.

The greatness of Homer's heroes is a greatness not of act but of consciousness. There is not much nobility in the act of war, which is in itself a negation of human things, barbaric and impure. But there is a nobility in men's capacity to act and at the same time comprehend themselves and their situation. Homer's heroes have the power to step back and conceive themselves, suspended between culture and nature, as godlike and mortal.

Sarpedon and Glaucus, in particular, form a kind of chorus on the Trojan side. To Sarpedon's speech in Book Twelve corresponds Glaucus' speech in Book Six:

> Tydeus' son, great-hearted, why do you ask my breeding?
> Like to the breed of leaves is that of men—
> Leaves that the wind pours earthward, and others the tree
> In its strength puts forth, as the season of spring goes forward—
> Thus the breed of men puts forth and withers.
> If you wish even so to learn, then you may know
> My breeding; there are many men that know it.
>
> (VI.145–51)

For a moment Glaucus moves back and sees men as the gods see them (cf. XXI.464)—creatures as ephemeral and insignificant as all the other creatures of nature. Yet Glaucus goes on to recite his genealogy, and concludes:

> Hippolochus bred me, and I say I am from him.
> He sent me to Troy, and gave me much instruction:
> Always to excel and be held beyond others,
> Nor to shame the race of my fathers, who were much the best
> That grew in Ephyre and in broad-plained Lycia.
> Of this breeding and blood I claim to be.
>
> (VI.206–11)

As the theme of Sarpedon's speech is community, the theme of Glaucus' speech is kinship. Kinship and community generate the institutions of *oikos* and *polis*, household and city, and thus the whole fabric of the human world. Within this fabric, men have identities and roles, relations and obligations, and thus are capable of the virtues.

Glaucus' speech is implicitly a praise of kinship; he displays his pride in his lineage, his breeding. Yet Glaucus also reminds us that kinship, which appears to be founded on nature, is really a fact of culture and another social illusion. Only within the order of culture do men have proper names and individual identities; as creatures of nature they are perfectly ephemeral. Nature cares nothing for the life of the individual and everything for the life of the species. To speak of the generations of men as like the growing of leaves is to see oneself as, after all, insignificant.

Thus the warrior, placed on the edge of culture, is in a position to form a view of culture as a whole. Culture has created a human world within which men can live. The warrior knows that world to be insubstantial. Culture, which appears to us in our social lives so solid and enduring, reveals itself on the battlefield for what it is. The values conferred on life by culture are the only values we have, but they are a secondary product, sustained only by men's common assertion of them. For the warrior, culture appears as a translucent screen against the terror of nature. The heroic vision is of meaning uncertainly rescued from meaninglessness.

JAMES M. REDFIELD

Landscape and Simile

The sharpest demarcation in the Homeric landscape, second only to the distinction between land and sea, is the line between tillable lowland and hill or grazing land. On the alluvial plain there are fields, gardens, cities, and houses; the plain is the properly inhabited world of family life and political community. Around the plain runs the mountain wall, and those who climb this wall find themselves in a separate world: the *agrou ep' eschatiēn*, the land beyond the limit of agriculture. Here the herds live (except in the fallow season) with the herdsmen who care for them. The herdsmen do not live in proper houses but in *stathmoi*, lean-tos or sheds, and there are no families; herding is a task for young men (xvii.20–21), before they reach an age to have a wife, an *oikos*, and a *klēros*—a family, a house, and a tract of agricultural land (xiv.64). The hill land is included in the description of the Shield in a kind of three-line footnote to the third ring (XVIII.587–89). This land beyond the limit of the sown is a no-man's-land between nature and culture; men share it with the wild beasts who also live there: lions, wolves, jackals, wild boar, and deer.

The *agrou ep' eschatiēn*, then, is a marginal environment, and only marginally included on the Shield. Yet this environment dominates the similes. This is because the *agrou ep' eschatiēn* is an image of the battlefield. In order to understand this point, we must consider the application of the similes to their context, and specifically to the situation of combat. We begin with the similes of technical activity.

Combat is not a productive activity, but it is technical, involving planning, skill, and the use of the tools. So combat can be compared to technical activity. But when it is so compared in the *Iliad*, the effect is nearly always shocking, as when the blood runs down Menelaus' flesh like the dye carefully traced over ivory (IV.141–47), or when Achilles' horses trample the corpses like oxen threshing grain (XX.495–502), or

> As when a man gives the hide of a great ox
> To the folk for stretching, once he's soaked it with oil,
> And they pick it up and, leaning apart, they stretch it
> In a circle; the moisture springs out, the oil soaks in,
> When many tug it; it's all stretched out between—
> So this way and that they tugged in a little space
> At the corpse on both sides.
>
> (XVII.389–95)

What is skill in relation to objects becomes ruthlessness once it is applied to persons. The technical similes most often remind us that in combat we treat persons as objects.

The technical simile usually stands in contrast to its context: a peaceful act is unexpectedly compared to the violence of war. The simile of weather and the sea, on the other hand, most often develops and reinforces the tone of its context; weather is even more violent than war. Thus, in Book Eleven, Agamemnon attacks like a forest fire raging through timber (XI.155–59); Hector counterattacks like a whirlwind across the sea (XI.297–98) and like a thunderstorm which drives the foam high up against the shore (XI.305–9). Examples could be multiplied into the scores. Combat is an arena of force, and weather appears in the similes most often as an image of pure force unleashed in the world.

Thus man's war with man is compared to man's struggle with undomesticated nature. Peace, we are reminded, has its violences; man's world is an uncertain achievement, hard won and easily ruined. There is always the threat of the storm which floods the fields (V.87–94) and drowns the children (XXI.281–83). Man's contention with storm can be read as an aspect of man's contention with the gods, particularly with Zeus, who sends the storm (e.g., X.5–8, XII.278–86), perhaps out of his rage with man (XVI.384–93), and who has filled the sky with his portents: thunderbolt, falling star, and rainbow (XIII.242–44, IV.75–77, XII.547–52). There are thus above and below man (as at the center and outer rim of the Shield) horizontal frontiers marking man's relations with forces more powerful than himself: the sky above, from which the weather descends, and the rivers and sea below, which rise in storm and flood to waste his fields and break his ships.

Nature is also menacing in the hunting and herding similes; but these similes, although they also compare man's war with man to man's war with nature, do so in a different way. Their recurrent theme is battle between man and a dangerous wild animal, usually a lion or wild boar. Here the struggle is between equals; sometimes the battle inclines toward man, sometimes toward beast. The wild animals have families of their own; the lioness stands to defend her cubs (XVII.133–36) or searches for them (XVIII.318–22); the birds feed their young (IX.323–24); the wasps swarm out to defend their children (XII.167–70, XVI.259–65). The violence of the wild beast is thus dignified, as the violence of the human warrior is dignified, by reference to the weak who depend upon that violence for their protection. In the similes of hunting and herding, man's war with man is compared to man's struggle with the beasts who live around him, who are alien species yet somehow like himself.

The *agrou ep' eschatiēn* is a vertical frontier; it marks both the limit of the community and a no-man's-land between communities. It makes relatively little difference whether the adjoining community is thought of as animal or human. In either case the herdsman's task stations him on the frontier, subject to attack. Most conflicts between communities take the form of border raids for cattle (cf. I.154); the wild animals also attack the cattle. Deer can be thought of as cattle belonging to the wild predators; huntsmen are then raiders of the wild community and will have to contend with its defenders (cf. XV.271–76). In the weather similes the warrior is presented as sheer force; in the technical similes he is reduced to an object; in the similes of hunting and herding we are reminded that the enemy is like ourselves and that conflict arises from this very likeness, as two groups of similar nature contend for the control of scarce resources.

Thus the warrior who is compared to a wild beast is not demeaned; on the contrary, these transformations (in the form of similes) mark moments of high heroic action:

> Achilles across from him rose up like a lion,
> Ravening, whom men have struggled to kill,
> Collecting all the folk. He first ignores them
> And passes, but then some swift young spearman
> Hits him; he crouches, gaping; the foam from his teeth
> Drips; the spirit of wrath constrains his heart;
> With his tail the flanks and ribs on his two sides
> He lashes, and he drives himself to battle.
> Eyes gleaming, he springs forward, to slaughter
> Some man, or himself to die in the midst of turmoil.
>
> (XX.164–73)

If we turn to the similes involving wild animals among themselves, we find that nearly all of them represent a predator and its prey. Lions attack deer (XI.113–21, etc.); a dolphin attacks little fish (XXI.22–26); a hawk attacks starlings (XVII.755–59) or a pigeon (XXI.493–96). These similes provide a new image of combat. Whereas the struggle between man and lion presents combat as an equal relation, the struggle between lion and deer presents combat as radically unequal. Both images are needed. Combat, when it comes to conclusions, takes parties previously classified as equals and reclassifies them into victor and vanquished. Every warrior seeks in combat to become the predator and risks becoming the prey. The wild beasts among themselves (since they form no part of the human world) do not appear in the Shield, but they are important in the similes. Predator and prey provide an image of the outcome of combat.

Man the huntsman is also a predator of wild prey, but this point is seldom used in the similes. Where we are shown the hunting of deer, goats, or rabbits, the focus is never on the huntsman but on some predatory animal, either a wild predator, who contests his prey with the huntsman (III.23–27, XV.271–78), or else the hunter's own dogs (VIII.338–42, X.360–64, XV.579–81, XXII.189–93). Prey is defined in relation to predator, and man is not himself a predator but is rather one vicariously, through his dogs. This notion of vicarious predation, is the key to understanding the role of dogs in the *Iliad*.

DOUGLAS J. STEWART

The Disguised Guest

Odysseus and Ithaca, each seeking the other, are separated not just by space but by mental confusion, on both sides. Odysseus' confusion is that in all his years outside the real world of human beings he has eventually shed his identification with the code of the epic hero, which is obviously obsolete and flawed—if one can take Achilles' ghost as an expert on the subject. But this change was accomplished by depriving Odysseus of all human contact, so that he now is afflicted by a marked inability to function among men, of every and any class and kind. This was clear in his behavior at the Phaeacian court, and it becomes marked and critical upon his return to Ithaca. Living again even in a quasi-human society like Scheria is an art that Odysseus has forgotten along with his heroic heraldry, and desperately needs to relearn. Unfortunately he does not realize his own needs. All those years of facing danger from nonhuman sources and of overcoming despair in his loneliness have led him to renounce heroic show and self-proclamation for the opposite arts, the inward and inscrutable arts of survival at almost any cost. These arts save his mere existence, of course, but concealment and stealth do not make very healthy constant companions, and in his case they have finally become not simply means of survival, but ends in themselves. Though meant to help him find his way back to his former life, they become instead the substance of his life now! When he returns to Ithaca it is as though to one more foreign island conceivably ruled by one more untrustworthy power who intends evil for him. He sees Ithaca as embodying all the real or imagined threats of all the other islands on his itinerary: that of the Cyclops with its physical terror; the isle of Aeolus with disappointment, frustration, and despair arising from the wind god's curse; Circe's Aeaea with its enchantments; Thrynacia with its temptations to self-destruction; Calypso's Ogygia with its seduction and boredom; and finally, Scheria with its museumlike unreality, its now appalling replay of dead heroic customs, plus the disconcerting apparent prophecy in the Ares-Aphrodite tale sung by Demodocus. But actually the danger on Ithaca stems from another source entirely, the threat of the very lesson he has massively overlearned, that to survive in extraordinary circumstances one must be intensely wary. But not all circumstances are extraordinary, and eventually to live a fully human life one must be able to relax and put one's trust in the company of other men, assuming, for instance, that on most occasions ordinary men speak and act as they really intend. Coming home then will not be the simple act Odysseus had thought. It is he himself who complicates the matter. The real struggle, the most intense adventure, is to come: the struggle with himself to tear away the guise of cunning otherness, of alien strangerhood, of programmatic deceit with others, and to realize in his innards that he really is home, that this is his place. To realize that he can no longer play the empty envelope, the No Man capable of being filled with any arbitrary personal history that might fit the current scheme; that he is no longer in the position of the uncommitted refugee, sharply calculating how to slip away from danger on the next outgoing tide. On Ithaca his problem will be not to find the quickest exit, but to acquiesce in the fact that there are no exits from one's own place, and that there are no good grounds for the use of disguises and false tales with one's own people, even if the suitors remain to be beguiled a bit further. Here the challenge will be to admit his identity courageously, and Odysseus nearly fails the most important challenge of his whole life. (This view of the meaning of the last half of the poem is at variance with the most common understanding of it, and even seems to contradict such things as Athena's willingness to help Odysseus remain in disguise. Such a broad reinterpretation cannot be dealt with in a few footnotes, and I ask the reader to read the whole course of my arguments . . . as my justification for these bold statements.)

The *Odyssey* could be viewed as little more than an endlessly complex study of the possible ramifications of the guest–host relationship, where the guest is nearly always in some form of disguise. This theme is announced, as it were in a minor key, at the opening of the poem, specifically book 1.105ff., where the goddess Athena appears to Telemachus in the guise of Mentes, an old family friend. Nothing so odd, it would at first seem, about this: the gods do that sort of thing all the time, to help, hurt, or spy on men. In fact, at one point a suitor speculates whether the disguised Odysseus might not actually be a god sent to observe their behavior (17.484–86). But the Athena–Mentes scene is only the beginning of a great procession of disguised guests. Even before the Wanderings proper, the guest–host relationship has been turned in every direction, so that every facet is struck by the light, and each reflects some new social and literary insight.

Let us consider only the following cases. Either in direct narrative or flashback one has: Telemachus as a guest of Nestor at Pylos, not literally in disguise but not quickly identified and inhibited by youthful reticence from truly functioning in the fossil society of Pylos. In Sparta Telemachus hears Helen tell the tale of Odysseus' secret mission into Troy—and a spy is a special sort of disguised guest—and how she protected him. (The story is told, no doubt, not for the boy's benefit, but to make the point in Menelaus' hearing that she was always really loyal to the Greek cause, though it seems doubtful he believes her.) Next, Menelaus tells his tale recalling another event involving Odysseus, namely that of the Trojan horse, relating with feeling how Odysseus stopped the mouth of one of the Greeks who was severely tempted to cry out when Helen prowled around the horse cleverly imitating the voices of the men's wives. (This, of course, is meant mainly to rebut Helen's implied claim of loyalty, since her purpose could only serve the Trojan cause.) The Greeks in the horse, surely, were another sort of disguised guest. Moreover they were guests disguised with a beast-guise—this to become a major sub-category of the overall theme of disguises. The subtheme is repeated in Menelaus' tale of how he captured the wily seagod Proteus on his own difficult voyage home. To do so he and his men had to hide in the sea king's cave disguised under sealskins—with insistent emphasis on their sickening smell (book 4.401ff.). This tale, indeed, puts together a complex of motifs that appears with telling effect in the story of the Cyclops, but it also appears with some parts redistributed, in the tale of Circe and in the Odysseus–Eumaeus relationship: that complex is the linkage of animal disguise with guesthood, where the guest needs to overcome the host and win some sort of cooperation from him or them, whether unwilling or only bemused. The Wanderings of course give the theme of the disguised guest still more play and attention. In the Cyclops' cave Odysseus is disguised, first by his use of the trick name, and later by hiding himself and his surviving companions under the sheep, to escape from the cave and the now-blinded Polyphemus—thus he conducts a reprise of the animal-disguise theme, that of Menelaus with Proteus, and of the Greeks in the Wooden Horse. Circe, by turning her guests into beasts will constitute a different twist on this general theme: her guest-victims will be

190 · DOUGLAS J. STEWART

disguised not so much from her, as from other men, and from themselves, in a sense:

> . . . they now had the grunt, bristles, and skin of hogs but their mind remained the same as it had been.
>
> (10.239–40)

Thus they have two natures, one real and internal and the other somehow false but external and visible. They may also be said to represent the dangers that face a disguised guest; he may find his apparent and real identities split so far apart that they can never be reunited, or, like Odysseus, he may come to cling to the difference between the two identities and relish their separation in and for itself.

When Odysseus fails to react as Circe had expected to her drug, Circe is shocked and startled:

> What manner of man, and from where, are you? What is your city, who your parents? I am struck dumb that drinking my drug has not overcome you; for no other man has ever raised this cup but that he was instantly changed, once the draught passed his lips. You must have a heart that cannot be commanded in your breast.
>
> (10.325–29)

The drug, *moly*, given Odysseus by Hermes, is an antidote to Circe's drug, and thus makes him more than, and different from, ordinary men. To Circe his apparent human nature, given his invisible powers of resistance, is as sure a disguise as would be the magical change of his outer appearance by a god or goddess. Once again, and finally, in the Underworld, Odysseus is not precisely disguised (not by his doing, anyway), as much as simply, unreachably, and radically different, because he is alive. His difference from his hosts lies not in physical distance or different appearance but in their state of untouchableness (11.206–8). At each step of the adventures, some new form of isolation becomes his portion and lot, some new experience of the role of the noncomprehended man, the totally foreign nomadic individual having no way of reaching into and relating to any form of community he visits. Much later, on Ogygia with Calypso, though they have been sleeping together for seven years, Odysseus' isolation has gone even further because distrust has now become systematic in him, and has displaced nearly all other visible traits of personality and expressions of feeling. On Scheria, and still more on Ithaca, distrust is almost a metaphysical mood. Moreover distrust, which had a rational basis when Odysseus was dealing with the Cyclops or Circe, lacks that basis when he is dealing later with Calypso, or the sea nymph Ino, or the Phaeacians. They are not unfriendly, but now he is incapable of revealing himself openly to anyone much less of accepting their good will at face value. Odysseus is not simply distrustful of the Phaeacians, he is anesthetized even to their random and innocent diversions, because he cannot really exist yet in any form of company. He is, in an important sense, now inhuman. Distrust has become its own justification, as though it were an art form.

So educated by his experiences, so isolated, so disposed toward other men—this is how Odysseus lands on Ithaca to reclaim his place as king, husband, and father. It is little wonder that the reclamation takes so long, half the poem, and it seems to be no accident that the poet or poets have designed the poem so that the length of time taken—and often objected to by critics—is in proportion to the depth to which the denaturing process has gone, on the general principle that serious illnesses take long conva-lescences. The poem seems to be telling one that a good half of Odysseus' labors and struggles, and perhaps the more important half, take place within a few yards, almost literally, of his and Penelope's wedding chamber, the supposed goal of all his aspirations, which he is so reluctant and wary of approaching once he actually arrives home.

It is obvious to the reader that on Scheria Odysseus was now assured of reaching home, in safety, in health, and even in wealth—and that the only task remaining was to rout the Suitors, a task such a resourceful man as he should not find too difficult. The Phaeacians, who were never really a threat, in fact duly dispatch him with gifts of great value on a stout ship for Ithaca. Yet, on the way, clearly no great distance, Odysseus falls asleep! (13.79) One should have thought that by now, well-rested (he has slept the night before, and such naturalistic information is seldom supplied in the Wanderings unless it has an ulterior purpose), rationally comforted, newly rich, and subject to normal anticipation, he might have stayed awake. But the *Odyssey* is a poem that makes few concessions to naturalism. Sleep in the *Odyssey* is used almost solely as a symbol of transition to new turns of direction in the hero's life and/or a new ordering of events. Although Odysseus like everyone else must sleep to live, sleep, for Odysseus himself, is mentioned only seven times in the poem, and all but one time, it appears to have symbolic status as a pivot—the only exception is the one mentioned above, where he sleeps the night before setting out for Ithaca, which seems to be merely natural sleep, and thus throws the sleep of the second night, on the boat, into contrast as probably unnecessary and unnatural. One may add that during the two nights he and his men spent in the Cyclops' cave, they did not sleep and spent the nights groaning (9.304; 9.436), while the giant does sleep, to his very great sorrow on the second night. Odysseus sleeps, otherwise, only at moments of crisis and transition. (This may be a peasant, or even childish symbolism, with night and sleep representative of leaving one world and entering another.) The first time, Odysseus falls asleep just in sight of Ithaca, whereupon his men untie the bag of winds given him by Aeolus, the event that began the really serious part of his exile, and in a way also foreshadows this occurrence, except that then his troubles were largely elemental while now they will be psychological. Odysseus sleeps again when his men slaughter the cattle of Helios (12.366ff.)—which leads to their destruction and his last contact with human beings. He sleeps when he is washed ashore on Scheria naked and totally defenseless—this time indeed his fortunes will take an upward turn, but upon waking he does not assume that to be the case. In fact, each time, after the first, that Odysseus awakes he begins to fear the worst. And that of course is exactly what he does here. Finally he will sleep again, just before the contest of the bow in book 21, an adventure he has not sought and has tried to avoid, because, there again, he has nothing but misgivings and doubts.

In the first two cases, sleep really did presage disaster. In the third it at least seemed to presage Odysseus' complete disappearance from history, as a household pet of the royal court of the Phaeacians. But now there is a new threat, or so it seems to him. He is safely put ashore sleeping on Ithaca, without treachery, by the Phaeacian sailors. But when he wakes he is totally alone in some kind of grotto that he, the king of the land, does not know. Even the treasures brought with him from Scheria, and scrupulously left by the sailors beside his sleeping form, do not reassure him, about their honesty or about anything else. He appears utterly dejected, fearful to the point of incoherence, and strangely lacking in the determination to do something, which had always been a mark of his character. To believe his own words, one would have to imagine that he suddenly has no idea how to proceed with his own interests. This, I suggest, is the poet's way of signaling that the most strenuous adventure of all is to come, the adventure within himself to open up his mind and identity, and to take the risks that returning to the human community will involve, not with enemies, but with his own people. Coming home, when either home itself or one's own perspectives have changed, can be a terrifying experience. Robert Fitzgerald in his fine translation of the *Odyssey* catches this sense of homecoming with the title he gives book 13: "One More Strange Island."

In a moral sense Ithaca will prove to be the wildest and most dangerous land Odysseus will yet have visited. On Ithaca, he will find not monsters, goddesses, or the dead, but time distorted, emotions wrung dry, society upside down—all the product of his own absence, to be sure—but for a very long time he will feel alien to it all, and thus will be powerless to move in and set things right, because it is not really his simple physical return that is needed for that purpose. No longer—now it is not enough. His mere absence has indeed wrought chaos, but his simple presence cannot right it again, because the figure deposited on the sands of Ithaca by the Phaeacian sailors, at least for the time being, is not a real human being, not a finite, limited, concrete individual with a living history, commitments, and liabilities; he is not a real Odysseus, only a potentiality, a possible husband, father, and king. As he is, he is only a bundle of negative defenses and evasions. For ten years progressive negation and withdrawal from "natural" human behavior has spelled safety. But these things have also "factored out" of his character all that is fixed, unique, particular, and especially important, time-bound, and have left behind only a set of provisional roles, abstractions, and false identities. Having learned all too well how to survive with these tools he has mislaid the personality that was to do the surviving. Having had to deal with nonsocial, nonhuman, and more or less timeless hosts for a decade, he had necessarily become a walking set of contingency plans, a blueprint for the theory of survival, who has ceased to be any particular man with those normal irrationalities, inescapable attachments, cherished idiosyncrasies, and favorite desires, that in fact define a single human being. Desire, especially, that pure irreducible human will to prefer and to choose this rather than that, which compels almost all men at some point to refuse to bend or count costs any further, has been lost. To have a strong desire means to have a particular desire, to want a thing, a person or place, and to refuse to abandon it; it is to be human in the sense that to be vulnerable and threatened in defense of one's place is a sure sign of humanity. Odysseus has managed to avoid vulnerability and outwit threats, but the cost in humanity is high. Odysseus has to learn how to live again a human life that carries with it certain inescapable risks of being caught by unsuspected treachery and unforeseen threats. He is not yet ready for that experience, not prepared to cross that last borderline. Now the man of many turnings must be taught that the time of maneuver is over, that it is now the time for exerting strengths unapologetically, for claiming rights without disguises, and for admitting weaknesses without retreat. The strategy, adapted for all other islands and landfalls in the poem, of keeping open a line of retreat and leaving a margin of noncommitment, will not work on Ithaca, though Odysseus seems to take forever to learn that lesson.

No one denies of course that Odysseus has to overcome the Suitors, whom he finds engaged in a grotesque parody of the siege of Troy, here the comfortable siege of an anguished widow and even more of her pantry and cellar. He will also find the guest–host relationship shunted through a hundred mirrors to produce paradox upon paradox approaching sheer delirium. Odysseus is the unrecognized and unwilling host to the suitors, who in turn play host to him in his last disguise as a shipwrecked vagabond living in beggary. He will find that traditional heroism is dead, since he could hardly come bursting through the doors to confront the suitors like another Achilles, or so he thinks. He will also find the daily routine of the poor and ordinary elevated to a new importance that he will see for the first time, because he will have to share that position.

On waking up, Odysseus begins his plans by assuming, for no reason at all except the general conditions under which his mind now operates, that he has been deceitfully marooned by the sailors, and even after counting over his treasure he is not entirely relieved. While he is thinking generally melancholy thoughts and doing very little, Athena appears to him disguised as a shepherd boy and asks the reason for his evident mood. He relates his suspicions about the Phaeacians and then offers a totally imaginary account of who he is and how he has arrived at this spot. He claims to be a Cretan fleeing a murder warrant. At this point Athena cannot contain herself; she reveals herself and tries to bring him round by mocking gaily at his suspicious nature, urging him instead to press on with his plans:

> It would take a shrewd confidence-man indeed to get past you in tricky dealing—even a god would have trouble. Rascal, nonstop schemer, glutton of guile, won't you ever desist, even in your own homeland, from the lying tales and frauds that are your daily fare?
>
> (13.291–95)

Although, as is undeniable, Athena loves guile herself and cherishes schemers like Odysseus for just that characteristic in them, her main interest here is to stir him up to action, for she seems to realize that here and now still more sterile scheming is not the right strategy and indeed borders on an obsession. These particular suspicions and schemes will get him nowhere. At the same time, she seems either confused, or pessimistic about getting Odysseus to forego scheming entirely when she next counsels him to enter the palace in disguise, to trust no one including Penelope (though in the same breath she says Penelope is faithful), and to lie low waiting for a special chance to kill the suitors. Odysseus generally follows this line of advice in his subsequent actions—as the old Odysseus would no doubt have done—but neither he nor Athena seems to know now what those actions will be, nor *why* this stealth and circumspection will prove useful. It is only after Penelope suddenly proclaims the contest of the bow at the end of book 19, that all these elaborate preparations seem to have had some purpose. And it seems clear, as I will try to show in its proper place, that Odysseus had no idea the contest was coming, and indeed he demonstrates that he is not all that anxious for it to take place, once he knows of it.

Moreover, Athena's advice seems calculated to encourage just those characteristics of diffidence and guile of which she has just complained. In counseling a closed-mouth policy, in advising that he appear as some sort of vagabond, a neutral presence in no real way different from the Cretan fugitive he has just tried to impersonate, Athena seems to be contradicting her own very excellent advice of a few lines earlier. What, precisely, is her point? Why does she stir the plot still thicker by disguising Odysseus as an old and weak man, a disguise that adds little to the subsequent imperson-ation he gives as a sailor down on his luck, and even seems to conflict with it at some points? Again, as was noted [elsewhere] with the case of books 6 and 7, this may be the only way that he can be dealt with at all in his present mood, and she can at least inject a few practical suggestions, like the one that he entrust himself at first to Eumaeus the pig-man. This in particular will have repercussions far different from the considerations im-mediately understood by Odysseus or advanced by Athena as justifying such a tactic.

It was noted [elsewhere], in connection with the adventure of the Cyclops, that the unique narrative gifts employed in the *Odyssey* sometimes work against the larger purpose of the poet or poets who framed it as a whole—at least with traditional audiences. The skill shown in the books of the wanderings, along with their naturally exciting content, has made them the best-known part of the *Odyssey*, such that we tend to know almost too much when we first meet Odysseus in book 5, and thus the sense of wonder it would appear the poet wished to create in us over the hero's diffidence and anxiety is dissipated. In the second half of the poem, perhaps, one poetic skill has outgeneraled another again. The eventual narration of Odysseus' battle with the suitors in book 22 is so vigorous and neatly drawn that we normally know of it ahead of time, and when reading the *Odyssey* in its proper order we look forward to it, and reach it forgetting just how long it took Odysseus to reach that point—eight books! Students and other impatient readers sometimes speak of the intervening books as mere filler, with the poet merely killing time, in order (perhaps?) simply to concoct a poem about as long as the *Iliad*. This criticism should be heard seriously, if not to agree with it, to see what it tells about the subtle differences between the *Odyssey* and a poem in the central heroic tradition like the *Iliad*. The latter poem knows how to organize a tale and make it meandering and majestic, usually by juggling different sorts of material—alternating domestic with military scenes, and the like—which it marshalls in a loose interlocking order that would be quite amenable to different orderings from the one that survives without doing damage to the general demands of the traditional saga or tale. The *Odyssey*, however, steadfastly resists interlarding this long stretch with more interesting material from the world of action, most certainly not because its poet is unfamiliar with writing action scenes, and therefore for some other reasons, which should be tracked down, if possible. (Moreover, this long section of the poem, if dull to some, is not in any sense loose.)

The theory that oral poets sang epics of the *Iliad's* general character and length to crowds at various local or international festivities over and over again down the centuries, eventually to produce the Greek epics now possessed as texts, runs into considerable difficulties if one were to apply the theory seriously to the waiting books of the *Odyssey*, for they would require us to imagine that a poet encountered a unique audience given to hard and serious listening that virtually demanded that he convert to slow-motion tactics like those found in these books, and that this poet or these poets rather quickly acquired a skill both demanding and strangely uneconomical in performing other epics, for whatever memory skills this section would demand would be unnecessarily fine-tuned for the performance of other epics—and would involve something close to sheer memorization of a given and canonical text, which is not how oral poets are said to practice. The point of these books, it seems to me, despite the blood-curdling scenes of book 22, which tend to block one's view, is that Odysseus, though now purged of his ancient loyalties to the heroic life, which is all to the good, as the poet sees it, is now so isolated, so limited in human sympathies as a result of his appalling adventures, so introspective and tentative as an individual (that is, so doubtful and shifting as to his own identity) that he simply could not reenter the palace and claim his former rights by any sort of frontal assault. Nor is it just the problem of the suitors; there are psychological bars to his reentry every bit as strong as the physical ones. In one sense there are no former rights, founded in the customary usages of the dead heroic world: he is in a new era in which a man must earn and deserve what he has or gets, and must make, quite literally, the place he occupies in society. Secondly, a more crucial problem: Odysseus must overcome and reconstitute himself—he must search out and embrace a new personality, new in the sense of being a complex of both the old Odysseus, buried for the moment under a mound of disguises and equivocations, plus a new person who can think, confide, and exchange truths in a new world. Indeed, the killing of the suitors, though posed as

THE DISGUISED GUEST • 197

a narrative necessity, is hardly more than that; they are never a serious threat to him, and the almost comic ease with which they are dispatched—to forget for the moment the elaborate plans discussed anachronistically by Odysseus and Telemachus in book 16—indicates just that. The important victory Odysseus must win is a paradoxical conquest of the self: he must yield his by-now habitual slyness and mistrust, and make an acceptance full of risk, or so he feels, of the need to entrust himself to others in general, and to Penelope in particular.

I would argue that the last twelve books of the poem are anything but a hodgepodge of trivia and padding, a bad case of longueurs from a poet who has lost the touch for the definite. Rather, the second half of the poem is a steady and profoundly sensitive study of the hero, shorn of his heroic—that is, automatic—signs of virtue and consequence, who is forced to reenter human society and climb, rung by rung, back up the ladder of both social and emotional dependence, before he can repossess home, wife, and property. He is being conducted here by the poet and by circumstance on a different series of adventures, a set of fundamentally more serious escapades than those of the Wanderings. He is being forced to learn, from the inside as it were, the whole of the human condition, its weaknesses and vices, its pleasures and strengths, as they are contained in his own little world of Ithaca, which were once unseen by him though they lay within a few yards or miles from the palace where he reigned long ago. Having passed through experiences unimaginable by any man, he must now pass through feigned conditions, as a beggar and vagabond, roles very real for certain men, but unimaginable to epic heroes, so distant are these conditions from their social rank and ordinary field of vision. The unsettling irony of the last half of the Odyssey is the fact that in a very real sense, any worthy man, no matter what his name or origins, on the day Penelope sets the contest of the bow just might have won her. Odysseus' last adventure is conducted by a poet concerned with teaching him not how to be Odysseus, son of Laertes, the old heroic formula, but how to be a trusting, humane, and sympathetic man, however anonymous, one capable of understanding all the possible conditions of human life because he has either experienced them himself or has been forced to encounter them and show sympathy with them. Odysseus' ten years of wandering commence with his claiming, in deceit, to be nobody; they end with his being forced to accept the risk of appearing to be anybody.

Upon his return to Ithaca and upon Athena's orders, Odysseus finds it necessary to entrust either his life or his secret, or both, in succession, to a slave, to his son, to the suitors when disguised as a beggar and freebooter, to the old maid Eurycleia, and finally to his own wife, who at more than one point must protect him with her authority. This is doubly wrenching. He who has come to trust no one, not even the gods, must now rely on just about everyone, including some very slender reeds indeed, at least as an epic hero would have thought. And he must do so just like every other dependent and unfortunate person, with at least the appearance of gratitude and subservience. The shipwrecks and beggars he impersonates are, by heroic standards, unimportant persons. How bitter it will be to learn by reenactment the fact that this world often errs in allotting station and merit to the opposite persons. Indeed in the heroic world of the *Iliad* it would have been something next to impossible to disguise greatness and hero status: the operative social ideologies in the *Iliad* imply that a hero would naturally refuse to mask his status and set aside the social dues that his status is owed at all times from all other men, for to mask status even as a strategem for a time would in fact make life meaningless and thus contradict the basic realities of heroic life; but still more, such strategems would not work, for heroic grandeur, it was felt, must shine through no matter what else may happen, and no one could really fail to recognize a hero when he saw one. All this is controverted by these books of the *Odyssey*, which force the hero to contemplate society, ironically a society he formerly ruled, from the bottom up. He is forced to experience almost every known form of social inferiority and powerlessness in the kingdom over which he is still at least the titular ruler. Imagine Achilles or Diomedes or Ajax consenting to appear as the dependent of slaves, of a boy, of a servant woman, or even—or much less—of a wife! And that, simply to survive, possibly to do no more than endure more and more of the same kind of treatment, frustration, and humiliation (since, of his own actions, Odysseus does nothing to bring about a confrontation with either the Suitors or Penelope it appears at least possible that he could swallow his pride forever; it is Penelope's decree of the contest of the bow that forces his hand). No Iliadic hero could have endured this situation ten seconds. Any of them, in a similar situation, would simply have burst through the front gate of the palace, shouting his glorious name and title, no matter the consequences. But not Odysseus now. We, and no doubt he, recall the angry regretful words of Achilles' ghost, that life, even as the servant of a tenant farmer, is better than death, no matter how glorious the gaining of it. In his first step toward his return to real life, what does Odysseus do but become the servant and guest, so far as any observer could tell, of the slave Eumaeus, upon whom he must depend for literally everything from food and shelter, information and advice, protection from other slaves, to protection from dogs, and finally for a chance to see his own son!

Eumaeus is a kind of benign Cyclops, a pastoral figure, close to nature and animals and possessed of a natural patience inculcated by the rhythms of the seasons; a counterfoil to the Cyclops, which represented nature's violent disregard of civilized conventions, he represents nature's preference for real merit versus socially acquired status. Odysseus on the other hand only tells Eumaeus lies about his person and origins, and none of them are in the heroic mode, interestingly enough: his stories all make him out a wretched adventurer, a cursed loser in life, and so he cannot expect the pig-man to worship him like a lord. But for this sacrifice, he is rewarded: a new intimacy and friendship arises—with his own slave, a man he has barely known!—and a new revelation of humanity is granted. Eumaeus, he now learns for the first time, is himself the long-lost son of nobility, kidnapped by pirates as a boy and sold into lifelong slavery. Here is a tale even sadder than that of Odysseus himself—sadder than his made-up tales, too! Eumaeus' tale repeats and emphasizes the theme of the reversal of fortune, that Odysseus is by now so well acquainted with, and as well it enlightens the hero as to the virtue and history of one of his own slaves, with whom he forms the first real friendship, I believe, of the poem, and probably only the second or third in Greek epic. Finally, the story of Eumaeus tells Odysseus that he is not the first or necessarily the best man whose real and rightful identity has been cloaked in disguise and hidden from the world of men by fell circumstance. The reeducation of Odysseus' emotions has begun. His capacity for sympathy has been enlarged, if only slightly—he is still suspicious enough to tell Eumaeus only lies—but he has at least taken the first few steps in learning an important general lesson, one that is true not just in his peculiar case, that virtue and merit are where you find them, but that men, while professing to identify and preserve virtue and merit, more or less routinely and predictably fail to recognize either of them when they actually and infrequently occur.

At this point, the opening of book 16, by a seeming accident, Telemachus appears at the door of the pig-man's hut. The reader knows, though Odysseus could not, that Telemachus, warned by Athena not to land in the main harbor on his return from his fruitless errands to Pylos and Sparta but on the other side of the island, and sneak back to town in secret, is simply stopping by to greet his friend and confidant, Eumaeus. (Why the Suitors are pictured as a threat to Telemachus by sea, but not by land, is a minor puzzle of construction. The Suitors' overelaborate preparations for the ambush seem excessive, by a wide mark, just to motivate this chance meeting in the mountains between father and son. The case could be made, persuasively, that the easy frustration of their ambush is meant to show the Suitors as ineffectual, and their inability to change their plan and deal with Telemachus on dry land may point to their essentially comic function in the poem.)

The meeting between father and son is tense and excruciating. Odysseus, who at this point has no mind to reveal himself to anyone, only agrees to greet his son when directly ordered to do so by Athena appearing in a special vision he alone can see. This portrait of his caution allows us, by contrast, to estimate his candid son's exquisite virtues. Telemachus is not a paragon of all possible virtues, but those he possesses are remarkable, not the least of which is patience and steadiness, needed at first for with-standing the suitors as best he could, and now for dealing with his father's eccentricities—for so they must appear to him—as Odysseus is now given to almost sadistic deviousness of speech and action. The scene is tense for another reason, because it shows Odysseus how, in contrast with his emo-tional distance from his son, Telemachus and Eumaeus express open and intense affection for one another. Indeed, the scene makes it clear that Eumaeus is the nearest thing Telemachus has to a father, as confidant, model, and guide. Odysseus is only a name to him—another sort of disguise, reputation, the well-known curse of the sons of famous fathers—plus a memory suggesting mainly backbreaking financial obligations and neurotic distress in his relations with his mother. Eumaeus, on the other hand, has been a real and reassuring presence and has in turn shown an unbought affection and concern for the young man, completely obliterating the vast difference in their present social standing—another reminder of the collapse of the heroic consciousness.

Finally, Athena forcing the issue, Odysseus reveals himself to his son, Eumaeus having been sent outside the hut on some errand or other, and after a moment's amazement on Telemachus' part, father and son put their heads together to plan a surprise revenge on the Suitors. In this exchange, Telemachus, not surprisingly, shows respect, intelligence, and attention toward this strange man, who impresses him primarily as a novel creature, but at first he seems unable to show any real affection for the man as his father. He is respectful mainly because he is an older man, and he is always respectful to such persons unless seriously provoked to behave otherwise. Indeed, it is interesting that unlike his father, even in a new and conceivably dangerous and doubtful situation, he feigns no emotions, for possible tactical reasons, that he does not genuinely feel. He neither imagines that Odysseus might be a trickster, though well he might, since he too has been hardened by having to endure some serious pressures and threats himself; nor does he pretend to feel a great wave of warmth and affection for his father, either, only reflecting the fact that hardly anyone could feel such emotions for a father missing from the scene all of one's remembered life. And it would be especially difficult with a father so inward and furtive as Odysseus has now become. Nor should we find this odd, that Telemachus, while son of the heroic world's most accomplished liar-for-policy, is probably the most candid and truthful character in all of Greek epic, a man of no personal policy whatever. Odysseus' problem, skillfully etched in this book as a kind of object-lesson, is now no longer really that of conquering physical threats or mental traps almost too formidable for even his ready wits, but that of dealing with real, limited, finite, and candid people, like Telemachus or Penelope, who have suffered their own special terrors and yet have remained attractively and vulnerably human through it all. Though Telemachus naturally and dutifully falls in with his father's plans and orders, that is only the result of his general piety toward his elders; affection, if it is to come, will only come much later. The behavior of Telemachus, proper and attentive but also reserved and diffident, is an early warning to Odysseus that the dangers of this last island, Ithaca, are clearly the opposite of those he has faced on all those other islands, from the land of the Cicones to the isle of Phaeacians.

The plans Odysseus and Telemachus make are complicated, and surely unreal, because their scheme to round up the armor hung in the great hall of the palace and lock it away has no tactical meaning here unless Odysseus could have known ahead of time that he would at some point find every last Suitor present in the hall and otherwise defenseless, while he himself would be present splendidly armed with a weapon, that is, unless he foreknew of the contest of the bow, but no one could know such a thing because Penelope will think it up only at the last moment. This passage of book 16 was written with book 21 in mind, and we can be sure as well that Odysseus had no such visions of the future at this time. This is probably one of the latest passages in the *Odyssey*, composed by a rather literal-minded man who found a technical difficulty in book 21: why could the Suitors not have defended themselves with the ceremonial armor that is always hung on the walls of the dining hall? And this scheme was his lumbering, straightforward answer. (This suspect passage, while straightening out one difficulty, creates a worse one: presumably Odysseus' bow will have to be locked away with all the other arms—as indeed it is; Penelope has to send specially for it—so how could Odysseus assume he would be present, and be handed the bow by Penelope or anyone else, unless he knew about the contest and the fact that he, still disguised as a beggar, would be allowed to participate, despite the loud objections of the Suitors because they had not penetrated the disguise? This peculiar passage, if there is any merit in seeing it as part of the essential *Odyssey*, should best be seen simply as a vehicle demonstrating how Odysseus now makes slow-motion and overelaborate preparations—analogous to those of the Suitors scheming against Telemachus—against contingencies that even he cannot imagine. It is a passage cut from the same cloth as his use of the name "No man" with the Cyclops, long before he had any idea how useful it would be to him.) Odysseus then adds a further touch, demanding that Telemachus not tell another soul that he is present on Ithaca, not his father, Laertes, not the swineherd, not even Penelope, because, he says, they must test the loyalty of the maidservants and the men who work the estates (book 15.300–307).

To deny Laertes the news seems sadistic, given the universal Greek obsession with having surviving children to perform one's funeral obsequies. And Eumaeus has surely already proved his loyalty. And Penelope? On his adventures Odysseus had been subjected to countless reminders of the infidelities of famous women, and other analogies, like that suggested by the song of Ares and Aphrodite in book 8; such exposure had made him even more nervous about his own reception at home by his own wife, but all that was on the high seas, when he had no fresh information. Here, he has Telemachus to tell him whether or not Penelope is faithful. But no, he trusts almost nobody, and was not ready to trust Telemachus except for a divine command. Moreover, the reasoning he offers is a bit thin; testing the loyalties of servants and distant sharecroppers hardly seems connected with a decision to withhold his identity from his nearest kin—nor indeed is that loyalty really tested: Melanthius and some of the servant girls all too readily reveal their disloyalty, but not as the result of anything the Great Tactician has devised as a proper test, and no other real tests are applied in the text. Telemachus, who would hardly dream of contradicting his father directly, still manages to insinuate a note of impatience with all this deliberateness: he disagrees that there is time to test the opinion of every sharecropper, though he consents to some testing of the servant girls (this is not carried out, since Eurycleia knows the facts anyway and saves everybody the trouble). Telemachus is humoring his father, but is adding, as best he can, a mildly sarcastic note of urgency—as Penelope will do later on—saying that it is hardly time to go counting noses in a kind of political poll on the outlying farms, while,

. . . that luxurious bunch there in the house eats up our substance without
thought of restraint. . . .

(16.314–15)

Telemachus urges his father to forego these roundabout schemes, his most
characteristic mode of thought at this point, and to do something positive,
and quickly! All this is set in ironic contrast with the events that actually
occur in the balance of book 16—the attempt of the Suitors to waylay and
butcher Telemachus, not his father. It is Telemachus who is in danger at
the moment, not his father, since virtually none of the Suitors can imagine
that Odysseus is still alive. With something more than restraint, Telemachus fails to tell Odysseus of his own personal danger, and consents to
palaver about the hypothetical dangers against which his father is laying
almost preposterous plans. Yet the son is prepared to enter the palace himself
in no disguise at all, with no protection other than his bold honesty, in
order to carry out his father's plans, while his father has no intention of
giving up his own disguises, and indeed he is already planning to burrow
still deeper into them.

At the end of their strategy session, Eumaeus returns, and the three
share a rustic meal and settle down to sleep. The next morning, the beginning of book 17, Telemachus arises with a firm decision already in his
mind and upon his lips. He plans to force his father to approach at least
a bit closer to his own home. With a gruff air he addresses Eumaeus:

. . . I have a task for you. Conduct this unfortunate fellow, this vagabond,
down into town, so he can beg his victuals from whomever of the townsfolk
wishes to share a bit with him. It is not my place to feed all men, with
all the troubles I have.

(17.9–13)

This superb little speech shows that Telemachus has understood the situation perfectly, and forces the action in just the right direction, by pre-
tending to forget all about Odysseus' plans. If Eumaeus is not to know the
identity of Odysseus, the only way to break his father free from the pig-
man's rather comfortable hospitality, which could go on forever in perfect
security with plots for an eventual return growing thicker and thicker, is
a direct order from the lord pro tempore, which the stranger cannot coun-
termand without giving away his identity, and so Odysseus is forced to go
along with the quite different plan Telemachus implies in what is on the
surface simply a housekeeping directive to one of his servants, and even
has to do so with a good grace. He puts the best face he can upon the
situation, and orates for a few moments praising the wisdom of the boy's

idea and voicing general agreement that it is best to seek his sustenance in the town for the indefinite time he says he plans to spend on the island, though probably it all came as a complete surprise to him. Does Odysseus really want events to take this particular turn? No such specific plan was discussed in the previous book, and indeed at one point Telemachus had offered to send the still unidentified stranger a regular ration, plus clothing and a weapon as though he were to remain with Eumaeus for an indefinite time (17.78–84). None of this was even in the plans of Odysseus at all. This move on Telemachus' part is noteworthy because it triggers another stage in the reinduction of Odysseus into society, who will be forced by it to climb the social ladder rung by rung. With Eumaeus he is the dependent of a slave—virtually the same social position Achilles' ghost had named in book 11 as preferable to being gloriously dead; now he is subject to the authority of his son, a son who at the moment proves a good deal more decisive and direct than he is. He is being forced not just to see but to feel inferior conditions of life that no Iliadic hero, in life, could imagine tolerating for any reason whatsoever, certainly not for a cause so dubious as mere survival. Moreover, Odysseus is being subtly told by his son's words that until such time as he chooses to reveal himself and take the risks such an action would entail, he not only will lack the ability to exercise his rightful authority, so-called, but still worse, with respect to the corporate reality of the house of Odysseus, as an unprofitable dependent, he will be no more than one more Suitor. Quite apart from his personal problems, Odysseus, father though he may be, while remaining anonymous, is no real father but simply one more consumer of a dwindling supply of goods and certainly no help to his son in stanching the continuous material outflow from his own estate. Telemachus has begun the slow process of provoking Odysseus to come forth from his shell and be himself again, a process that he and Penelope will have to continue for some good long time before it is successful. Telemachus obviously does not begrudge his father the food that is rightfully his (for Odysseus actually does all his begging in the palace, which means that he still consumes his own food), but this short speech also lets him know what his technical social position is and what it will remain until the time that he decides to reveal his identity, and the sense of urgency is not without its tone of reproach.

GREGORY NAGY

Poetic Visions of Immortality for the Hero

Upon having their lifespan cut short by death, heroes receive as consolation the promise of immortality, but this state of immortality after death is located at the extremes of our universe, far removed from the realities of the here-and-now. We in this life have to keep reminding ourselves that the hero who died is still capable of pleasure, that he can still enjoy such real things as convivial feasts in the pleasant company of other youths like him. It is in this sort of spirit that the *Banquet Song for Harmodios* is composed, honoring the young man who had achieved the status of being worshiped as a hero by the Athenians for having died a tyrant killer:

> Harmodios, most *philos* [dear]! Surely you are not at all dead,
> but they say that you are on the Isles of the Blessed,
> the same place where swift-footed Achilles is,
> and they say that the worthy Diomedes, son of Tydeus, is there too.
>
> (*Skolion* 894P)

The perfect tense of the verb [meaning] 'you are not dead' leaves room for the reality of the hero's death: it is not that he did not die, but that he is not dead now. The fact of death, even for the hero, is painfully real and preoccupying. Consider this excerpt from a *threnos* 'dirge' by Simonides:

> Not even those who were before, once upon a time,
> and who were born *hēmítheoi* [demigods] as sons of the lord-gods,
> not even they reached old age by bringing to a close a lifespan that is without
> toil, that is *aphthitos* [unfailing], that is without danger.
>
> (Simonides *fr.* 523P)

Not even heroes, then, have a *bios* 'lifespan' that is *aphthitos* 'unfailing'; they too have to die before the immortality that is promised by the *threnoi* comes true.

Even in the *Aithiopis*, the immortality reached by Achilles is not an immediate but a remote state: after death, the hero is permanently removed from the here-and-now of the Achaeans who mourn him. For them, the immediacy of Achilles after death has to take the form of a funeral, which includes not only such things as the singing of *threnoi* over his body but also—even after Achilles has already been transported to his immortal state—the actual building of a funeral mound and the holding of funeral games in his honor. I conclude, then, that even in the *Aithiopis* the immortality of Achilles is predicated on his death, which is the occasion for the *threnoi* sung by the Muses as a consolation for his death. In the *Iliad*, the theme of immortality is similarly predicated on the death of Achilles, but here the focus of consolation is not on the hero's afterlife, but rather, on the eternal survival of the epic that glorifies him.

As we now proceed to examine the diction in which this theme is expressed, we must keep in mind the words in the *threnos* of Simonides (523P): even the heroes themselves fail to have a *bios* 'lifespan' that is *aphthitos* 'unfailing'. In the *Iliad*, Achilles himself says that he will have no *kleos* 'glory' if he leaves Troy and goes home to live on into old age (IX 414–416)—but that he will indeed have a *kleos* that is *aphthiton* 'unfailing' (IX 413) if he stays to fight at Troy and dies young. The same theme of the eternity achieved by the hero *within epic* recurs in Pindar's *Isthmian* 8, and again it is expressed with the same root *phthi-* as in *aphthito-*; he will have a *kleos* that is everlasting (cf. xxiv 93–94):

> But when he [Achilles] died, the songs did not leave him,
> but the Heliconian Maidens [Muses] stood by his funeral pyre and his
>   funeral mound,
> and they poured forth a *threnos* that is very renowned.
> And so the gods decided
> to hand over the worthy man, dead as he was [*phthimenos*], to the songs
>   of the goddesses [Muses].
>
> (Pindar I.8.62–66)

The key word of the moment, *phthi-menos*, which I translate here in the conventional mode as "dead," is formed from a root that also carries with it the inherited metaphorical force of vegetal imagery: *phthi-* inherits the meaning "wilt," as in *karpou phthisin* 'wilting of the crops' (Pindar *Paean* 9.14). Through the comparative method, we can recover kindred vegetal imagery in another derivative of the root, the epithet *a-phthi-ton* as it applies to the *kleos* of Achilles at IX 413.

As in the *Iliad*, the contrast in this Pindaric passage concerns the mortality of Achilles and the immortality conferred by the songs of the Muses. More specifically, Pindar's words are also implying that the epic of Achilles amounts to an eternal outflow of the *threnos* performed for Achilles by the Muses themselves. In this light, let us now consider again the Homeric evidence. In the *Odyssey*, the description of the funeral that the Achaeans hold for Achilles includes such details as the *threnos* of the Muses (xxiv 60–61) and ends with the retrospective thought that "in this way" (xxiv 93) the hero kept his fame even after death and that he will have a *kleos* that is everlasting (xxiv 93–94). We get more evidence from the *Iliad* in the form of a correlation between theme and form. The forms are the actual names of *Akhi-l(l)eus* (from Akhi-laos 'having a grieving *laos*') and *Patrokleēs* ('having the *kleos* of the ancestors'). As I have argued, the figure of *Patro-kleēs* is in the *Iliad* the thematic key to the *kleos aphthiton* of Achilles, while *Akhil(l)eus* is commensurately the key to the collective *akhos* 'grief' that the Achaeans have for Patroklos on the occasion of his funeral. Since this *akhos* takes the social form of lamentations even within the epic of the *Iliad*, we can say that the theme we found in Pindar's *Isthmian* 8 is already active in the Homeric tradition; here too, lamentation extends into epic.

Up to now, I have been stressing the remoteness inherent in the concept of immortality after death, as we find it pictured in the formal discourse of the *threnos* and then transposed into the narrative traditions of epic. In contrast to the remoteness of this immortality stands the stark immediacy of death, conveyed forcefully within the same medium of the *threnos* and beyond. We are again reminded of the excerpt from the *threnos* of Simonides, which says that even the *bios* 'lifespan' of the heroes themselves fails to be *aphthitos* (523P). The latent vegetal imagery in this theme—that the life of man "wilts" like a plant—brings us now to yet another important contrast in the poetic representations of immortality and death. Traditional Hellenic poetry makes the opposition immortality/death not only remote/immediate but also artificial/natural. To put it another way: death and immortality are presented in terms of nature and culture respectively.

In *Iliad* VI, Diomedes is about to attack Glaukos, but first he asks his opponent whether he is a god, not wishing at this time to fight an immortal (VI 119–143; see the words for "mortal"/"immortal" at 123, 142/ 128, 140 respectively). In response, Glaukos begins by saying:

Son of Tydeus, you with the great *thumós*! Why do you ask about my
    geneē [lineage, line of birth]?
The *geneē* of men is like the *geneē* of leaves.
Some leaves are shed on the earth by the wind,
while others are grown by the greening forest
—and the season of spring is at hand.
So also the *geneē* of men: one grows, another wilts.

(VI 145–149)

Here the life and death of mortals are being overtly compared to a natural
process, the growing and wilting of leaves on trees. In another such Homeric
display of vegetal imagery, in this case spoken by the god Apollo himself
as he talks about the human condition, this *natural* aspect of death is
expressed specifically with the root *phthi-*:

. . . if I should fight you on account of mortals,
the wretches, who are like leaves. At given times,
they come to their fullness, bursting forth in radiance, eating the crops
    of the Earth,
while at other times they wilt [*phthi-nuthousin*], victims of fate.

(XXI 463–466)

      Let us straightway contrast the immortalized heroes on the Isles of
the Blessed, whose abode flourishes with *golden* plant life (Pindar O.2.72–
74; *Thrênos fr.* 129.5SM). Also, let us contrast the First Generation of
Mankind, whose very essence is gold (Hesiod, *Works and Days,* 109). The
immortality of the Golden Age is specifically correlated with the *suspension
of a vegetal cycle:* in the Golden Age (*W&D* 117–118) as on the Isles of
the Blessed (*W&D* 172–173), the earth bears crops *without interruption.*
The description of Elysium supplements this picture: in the state of immortality, there is simply *no winter,* nor any bad weather at all (iv 566–
568).

      In these images, we see gold as a general symbol for the artificial
continuum of immortality, in opposition to the natural cycle of life and
death as symbolized by the flourishing and wilting of leaves on trees, where
the theme of wilting is conventionally denoted with derivatives of the root
phthi-. As we now set about to look for specific words that express this
cultural negation of the vegetal cycle, we come back again to the negative
epithet *aphthito-.* Let us begin with the *skeptron* 'scepter' of Agamemnon
(I 245–246), by which Achilles takes his mighty oath (I 234–244), and
which is specifically described as "gold-studded" (I 246) and "golden" (II
268). This *skeptron,* by which Agamemnon holds sway in Argos (II 108)
and which an Achaean chieftain is bound by custom to hold in moments
of solemn interchange (I 237–239, II 185–187), also qualifies specifically

as *aphthiton aiei* 'imperishable forever' (II 46, 186). It was made by the ultimate craftsman, Hephaistos (II 101), whose divine handicraft may be conventionally designated as both golden and *aphthito-* (e.g., XIV 238–239). Significantly, this everlasting artifact of a *skeptron* provides the basis for the Oath of Achilles in form as well as in function:

> But I will say to you and swear a great oath:
> I swear by this *skeptron*, which will no longer ever grow leaves and shoots,
> ever since it has left its place where it was cut down on the mountaintops—
> and it will never bloom again, for Bronze has trimmed its leaves and bark.
> But now the sons of the Achaeans hold it in their hands as they carry
> out *dikai* [judgment].

(I 233–237)

Achilles is here swearing not only by the *skeptron* but also in terms of what the *skeptron* is—a thing of nature that has been transformed into a thing of culture. The Oath of Achilles is meant to be just as permanent and irreversible as the process of turning a shaft of living wood into a social artifact. And just as the *skeptron* is imperishable *'aphthiton'*, so also the Oath of Achilles is eternally valid, in that Agamemnon and the Achaeans will permanently regret not having given the hero of the *Iliad* his due *timē* 'honor' (I 240–244).

For another Homeric instance featuring *aphthito-* as an epithet suitable for situations where the natural cycle of flourishing and wilting is negated, let us consider the Island of the Cyclopes. In *Odyssey* ix 116–141, this island and the mainland facing it are described in a manner that would suit the ideal Hellenic colony and its ideal *peraia* mainland respectively, if it were not for two special circumstances: the mainland is inhabited by Cyclopes, who are devoid of civilization (ix 106–115), while the island itself is populated by no one at all—neither by humans nor even by Cyclopes, since they cannot navigate (ix 123–125). At the very mention of navigation, there now follows a "what-if" narrative about the idealized place that the Island would become *if it were colonized* (ix 126–129). If only there were ships (ix 126–127), and these ships reached the Island, there would be commerce (ix 127–129), and then there would also be agriculture, yielding limitless crops (ix 130–135). What is more, the grapevines produced by this ideal never-never land would be *aphthitoi* 'unfailing' (ix 133). Thus if culture rather than nature prevailed on the Island of the Cyclopes, then its local wine would bear the mark of immortality. Again we see the epithet *aphthito-* denoting permanence in terms of *culture* imposed on *nature*.

In fact, the epithet *aphthito-* functions as a mark of not only culture but even cult itself. In the Homeric *Hymn to Demeter*, the infant Demophon is destined by the goddess to have a *timē* 'cult' that is *aphthitos* (*H. Dem.*

261, 263), and this boon is contrasted directly with the certainty that he is *not* to avoid death (*H. Dem.* 262). As Demophon's substitute mother, Demeter had actually been preparing him for a life that is never to be interrupted by death (*H. Dem.* 242, 261–262), but the inadvertence of the infant's real mother had brought that plan to naught (*H. Dem.* 243–258). Still, Demophon is destined by the goddess to achieve immortality on the level of cult, so that her preparation of the infant was not in vain. We in fact catch a glimpse of the child's destiny as a hero of cult in the following description of how the goddess had been preparing him to be immortal:

> She nurtured him in the palace, and he grew up like a *daimōn* [god],
> not eating food, not sucking from the breast. . . .
> She used to anoint him with ambrosia, as if he had been born of the goddess,
> and she would breathe down her sweet breath on him as she held him at her bosom.
> At nights she would conceal him within the *menos* [spirit] of fire, as if he were a smoldering log,
> and his parents were kept unaware. But they marveled
> at how full in bloom he came to be, and to look at him was like looking at the gods.
>
> (*H. Dem.* 235–236, 237–241)

The underscored phrase at verse 235, meaning "and he grew up like a *daimōn*," contains a word that we have in fact already seen in the specific function of designating heroes on the level of cult (Hesiod *W&D* 122, *Th.* 991).

   This same underscored phrase, as Sinos points out, has an important formal parallel in the *Iliad*:

> Ah me, the wretch! Ah me, the mother—so sad it is—of the very best.
> I gave birth to a faultless and strong son,
> the very best of heroes. And he shot up like a seedling.
> I nurtured him like a shoot in the choicest spot of the orchard,
> only to send him off on curved ships to fight at Troy. And I will never be
> welcoming him back home as returning warrior, back to the House of Peleus.
>
> (XVIII 54–60)

The context of these words is an actual lamentation (*goos:* XVIII 51), sung by the mother of Achilles himself over the death of her son—a death that is presupposed by the narrative from the very moment that the death of the hero's surrogate Patroklos is announced to him.

   It appears, then that the mortality of a cult figure like Demophon is a theme that calls for the same sort of vegetal imagery as is appropriate to the mortality of Achilles. The examples can be multiplied: like the hero of the *Iliad*, who is likened to a young shoot with words like *phuton* (XVIII 57, 438) and *ernos* (XVIII 56, 437), the hero of the *Hymn to Demeter* is directly called a *neon thalos* 'young sprout' (*H.Dem.* 66, 187). Moreover, we have seen that this theme of mortality common to Demophon and Achilles is replete with the same sort of imagery that we find specifically in the genre of lamentation (consider again the *goos* of Thetis, XVIII 54–60).

In this light, let us reconsider the epithet *aphthito-*. We have already seen that it conveys the *cultural* negation of a *natural* process, the growing and the wilting of plants, and also, by extension, the life and the death of mortals. Now we must examine how this epithet conveys the theme of immortality in its application to Demophon and Achilles as heroes of cult and epic respectively. As compensation for the death that he cannot escape, Demophon gets a *timē* that is *aphthitos* (*H.Dem.* 261, 263); likewise, Achilles gets a *kleos* that is *aphthiton* (IX 413). Thus both heroes are destined for immortality in the form of a *cultural* institution that is predicated on the *natural* process of death. For Demophon, this predication is direct but implicit: by getting *timē* he is incorporated into hero cult, a general institution that is implicitly built around the basic principle that the hero must die. For the Achilles of our *Iliad*, this same predication is explicit but indirect: by getting *kleos* he is incorporated into epic, which is presented *by epic itself* as an eternal extension of the lamentation sung by the Muses over the hero's death (xxiv 60–61, 93–94). Thus the specific institution of lamentation, which is an aspect of hero-cult and which is implicit in the very name of Achilles, leads to the *kleos* of epic. For both heroes, the key to immortality is the permanence of the cultural institutions into which they are incorporated—cult for Demophon, epic for the Achilles of our *Iliad*. Both manifestations of both institutions qualify as *aphthito-*.

For the Achilles of our *Iliad*, the *kleos aphthiton* of epic (IX 413) offers not only an apparatus of heroic immortality but also a paradox about the human condition of the hero. Achilles himself says that the way for him to achieve this *kleos aphthiton* is to die at Troy (IX 412–413), and that the way to lose *kleos* is to live life as a mortal, at home in *Phthiē* (IX 413–416). The overt Iliadic contrast of *kleos aphthiton* with the negation of *kleos* in the context of *Phthiē* is remarkable in view of the element *phthi-* contained by the place name. From the wording of *Iliad* IX 412–416, we are led to suspect that this element *phthi-* is either a genuine formant of *Phthiē* or is at least perceived as such in the process of Homeric composition. We see the actual correlation of the intransitive verb *phthi-* (middle endings) 'perish' with *Phthiē* at XIX 328–330, where Achilles is wishing that he alone had died at Troy and that his surrogate Patroklos had lived to come home. Again, coming home to *Phthiē* (XIX 330) is overtly contrasted with dying *'phthisesthai'* at Troy (XIX 329). If indeed the name for the homeland of Achilles is motivated by the theme of vegetal death as conveyed by the root *phthi-*, then the traditional epithet reserved for the place is all the more remarkable: *Phthiē* is *bōtianeira* 'nourisher of men' (I 155). The combination seems to produce a *coincidentia oppositorum*, in that the place name conveys the death of plants while its epithet conveys the life of plants— as it sustains the life of mortals. The element *bōti-* in this compound *bōtianeira* stems from the verb system of *boskō* 'nourish', a word that specifically denotes the sustenance, *by vegetation*, of grazing animals, as at xiv 102, and of men, as at xi 365. In the latter instance, the object of the verb *boskei* 'nourishes' is *anthrōpous* 'men', and the subject is actually *gaia* 'Earth'. Thus the life and death of mortal men is based on the life and death of the plants that are grown for their nourishment: this is the message of the epithet *bōtianeira* in its application to the homeland of Achilles. *Phthiē* is the hero's local Earth, offering him the natural cycle of life and death as an alternative to his permanent existence within the cultural medium of epic.

GREGORY NAGY

The Worst of the Achaeans

Although Homeric Epos is not in-
trinsically suited for the comic element, Aristotle does find an attested
poetic form, *within the Homeric tradition*, that has a function parallel to that
of comedy. The form in question is represented by the Homeric *Margites*,
which shares with comedy the prime function of *to geloion* (*Poetics* 1448b28–
38). From both Aristotle's brief account (ibid.) and the few fragments that
have survived (most notably *fr.* 1W), we know that the *Margites* even
combines the meters of both Epos and Iambos. It consists of dactylic hex-
ameters interspersed with iambic trimeters. From the fragments and the
overall testimonia, we also know that the contents of the *Margites* resemble
those of the Iambos: both the story and its characters are base and ridiculous.
Finally, we may note that the very name *Margitēs* is built from the adjective
margos 'gluttonous, wanton'—a word that serves to designate a base ex-
ponent of blame poetry.

In fact, the name *Margitēs* has a strikingly close formal parallel in
Thersitēs, the name of a figure described in the *Iliad* itself as the most base
of all the Achaeans who came to Troy. The actual word here for 'most
base' is *aiskhistos* (II 216), belonging to the family of the same noun *aiskhos*
that conventionally designates the baseness of blame poetry. This man who
is *the worst of the Achaeans* (cf. also II 248–249) is also described as *ekhthistos*
'most hateful' to Achilles and Odysseus specifically (II 220), who happen
to be *the best of the Achaeans* in the *Iliad* and *Odyssey* respectively—and
thereby the two preeminent figures of Panhellenic Epos. In this respect
also, the word *ekhthistos* is significant. It belongs to the family of the same
noun *ekhthos* 'hatred' that conventionally designates the nature of blame

poetry compared to that of praise poetry: "being *ekhthros*" as against "being *philos.*" Moreover, Thersites is said to be *ekhthistos* 'most hateful' in particular to Achilles and Odysseus (II 220) for the following reason:

> . . . because he made *neikos* [strife] against these two
>
> (II 221)

Thersites is the most inimical figure to the two prime characters of Homeric Epos *precisely because it is his function to blame them.* Epos is here actually presenting itself as parallel to praise poetry by being an institutional opposite of blame poetry. This passage, then, even supports Aristotle's formulation of Epos as a descendant of *enkōmia* 'praise poetry' (*Poetics* 1448b24–38). We should add the qualification, however, that Epos is more likely a partial and maybe even an indirect descendant. Nevertheless, it implicitly recognizes its own affinity to praise poetry.

The name of *Thersitēs* connotes blame poetry not only by way of its parallelism with the formation *Margitēs*. The boldness conveyed by the element *thersi-* is not the same as a warrior's *thersos/tharsos* 'boldness'. Rather, it is akin to the *thersos/tharsos* 'boldness' of the blame poet. Consider the expression *thersi-epēs phthonos* 'bold-worded envy' at Bacchylides 13.199, which serves as a foil for *aineitō* 'let him praise' at line 201. Or again, we may note that Antinoos calls Odysseus *tharsaleos* 'bold' (xvii 449) after hearing a speech directed at him by the would-be beggar, who is asking him for food (xvii 415–444). When the base suitor refuses, he is reproached by Odysseus (xvii 454–457), whose words are actually acknowledged as *oneidos* [plural] 'blame' by Antinoos. Finally, consider the collocation *Polutherseidē philokertome* at xxii 287, applied in derision to Ktesippos, another of the base suitors, at the moment of his death by the man who killed him, the loyal Philoitios. The *lōbē* 'outrage' of Ktesippos against the disguised Odysseus (xx 285) had been verbal as well as physical: while sarcastically advocating that the apparent beggar be treated as a *xenos* 'guest' (xx 292–298), Ktesippos had thrown a foot of beef at him (xx 299–300). Having now avenged this insult, Philoitios ridicules the slain Ktesippos by calling him *Polu-therseidēs* and *philo-kertomos* (xxii 287) in the context of reproaching him specifically for improper speech at the time of his physical attack on Odysseus (xxii 287–289). The mock patronymic *Polu-therseidēs* 'son of Bold-in-many-ways' reinforces the epithet *philo-kertomos* 'lover of reproaches'. In sum, a man who had reproached Odysseus is now getting a taste of his own medicine.

Similarly, Thersites in the *Iliad* gets blame for having given blame. He dares to reproach Agamemnon (II 225–242), and the narrative introduces his words with *neikee* 'made *neikos*' (II 224), then concludes them with *phato neikeiōn* 'spoke making *neikos*' (II 243). Thersites is in turn reproached by Odysseus himself (II 246–264), whose own words of blame are introduced with *ēnipape* 'reproached' (II 245) and concluded with his actually beating Thersites (II 265–268). Significantly, this combined physical and verbal abuse of Thersites results in pain and tears for the victim (II 269) but laughter for the rest of the Achaeans (II 270). Here again, we see a theme of reversal, since the function of Thersites himself was "to make *eris* 'strife' against kings" (II 214)—in accordance not with the established order of things but rather with *whatever he thought would make the Achaeans laugh* (II 214–215).

We may note that the word here for 'laughable' is actually *geloiion* (II 215), corresponding to Aristotle's term for the function of comedy, *to geloion* (*Poetics* 1448b37, 1449a32–37). We may note also that Aristotle's concept of *aiskhos* 'baseness', to which the concept of *to geloion* 'laughter' is intrinsic (*Poetics* 1449a32–37), corresponds to the characterization of Thersites as the *aiskhistos* 'most base' of all the Achaeans who came to Troy (II 216). I infer, then, that Homeric Epos can indeed reflect the comic aspect of blame poetry, but that it does so at the expense of the blame poet. In the Thersites episode of the *Iliad*, it is Epos that gets the last laugh on the blame poet, rather than the other way around. Not only the maltreatment of Thersites by Odysseus but even his physical description by the narrative makes him an object of ridicule. Epos dwells on his deformities in repulsive detail (II 217–219), thus compounding the laughter elicited by his baseness. He is *aiskhistos* 'most base' not only for what he says and does (or for what is said and done and to him by Odysseus!) but also for his very ugliness. And surely the base appearance of Thersites serves to mirror in form the content of his blame poetry. The content, in fact, is a striking illustration of what is called in Pindaric praise poetry *ekhthra . . . parphasis* 'hateful misrepresentation' (*N*.8.32)—the negative essence of blame poetry. In the words that Thersites is quoted as saying, we actually find such a misrepresentation: the anger of Achilles, he says, is nonexistent, since such a superior hero would surely have killed Agamemnon if he had really been angry (II 241–242). Since the *menis* 'anger' of Achilles is the self-proclaimed subject of the *Iliad* (I 1), these words of Thersites amount to an actual misrepresentation of epic traditions about Achilles. As a blamer of the *Iliad*, Thersites is deservedly described at II 220 as *ekhthistos* 'most hateful' to the prime hero of our epic.

From what we have seen up to now, the story of Thersites in the *Iliad* surely stands out as the one epic passage with by far the most overt representation of blame poetry.

MARTIN MUELLER

The Simile

At the simplest level the simile marks its context as worthy of special attention. Whenever Homer wants to say something important he slows down the pace of the narrative—a procedure that has been much misunderstood. We are all familiar with the term 'epic length', a term which implies that the epic world, unlike the world of drama, is always leisurely and that the urgency of action is subordinated to a stately and imperturbable flow of narrative. The opposite is the case. Homeric narrative has a keen sense of narrative tension and hierarchy, but slowing down is its major tool of emphasis (Austin, 1966). Its seeming digressions and endless descriptions are, like still shots or slow-motion sequences, moments of heightened suspense. When Pandaros prepares to shoot Menelaos, half a dozen lines are given over to an account of how he made his bow (4.106–11). The description underscores the gravity of the broken truce. The elaborate account of Agamemnon's arming (11.16–45) signals the opening of the Great Battle. The description of Achilles' arms, including 130 lines about his shield, pushes the principle to its extreme.

Like these descriptions, the similes arrest the reader's attention and by their mere presence make him recognise a momentous point in the narrative. Similes occur predominantly in battle scenes. Here they articulate change and are found when a warrior joins or withdraws from battle, defeats his opponent or is defeated by him. When Sarpedon joins the attack on the wall, his entrance is marked by the unusually long simile of a hungry lion attacking the stable (12.299–306). The longest lion simile in the *Iliad* marks the re-entry of Achilles into battle (20.164–73). The retreats of Aias and Menelaos are marked by the identical simile of a lion beaten back by herdsmen (11.548 = 17.657). The fall of a major warrior is an important moment. Simoeisios, important only because he is among the very first to fall, receives a tree simile (4.482). Asios, Sarpedon and Euphorbos have their narrative role confirmed when a tree simile accompanies their fall (13.389 = 16.482, 17.53). The temporary fall of Hektor at the hands of Aias merits no less than the image of an oak struck down by lightning (14.414).

The point of decision can be seen from the perspective of victory or of defeat. The latter, illustrated by the previous examples, is the standard procedure when the fallen warrior is of any note. To honour him with a simile or necrologue is the least the poet can do for him. Similes of victory occur at lesser moments and mark the warrior's progress towards a final encounter. Thus Agamemnon and Hektor are lions singling out a cow from a stampeding herd (11.172, 15.630). The victim in both cases is of no consequence.

While the simile generally marks change, it will sometimes focus on a state of equilibrium that is the result of an extraordinary expenditure of energy on both sides. Thus the first clash of armies is compared to a confluence of torrents (4.452). In the fight over the wall the Achaeans and Trojans have at each other noisily but indecisively. The event is compared to a snowstorm that blankets both land and sea. Indeed, the image appears twice, and its elaboration on the second occasion marks the growing intensity of the battle (12.156–8, 278–86).

Two similes of precise measuring mark the balance of battle before Hektor smashes the gate of the wall. In the first, two men dispute the proper location of a boundary stone (12.421); in the second a poor woman measures wool on a pair of balances (12.433). Some of the most vivid similes in the *Iliad* illustrate intense but indecisive fighting over the body of a fallen warrior. The dead Sarpedon is hidden from view in the heat of the fighting while the noise of battle about him is compared to the work of woodcutters and the warriors swarm around him like flies around a milk-pail (16.633, 641). The most remarkable instance of a fiercely contested draw occurs in the fight over the body of Patroklos:

> As when a man gives the hide of a great ox, a bullock,
> drenched first deep in fat, to all his people to stretch out;
> the people take it from him and stand in a circle about it
> and pull, and presently the moisture goes and the fat sinks
> in, with so many pulling, and the bull's hide is stretched out level;

so the men of both sides in a cramped space tugged at the body
in both directions; and the hearts of the Trojans were hopeful
to drag him away to Ilion, those of the Achaians
to get him back to the hollow ships.

(17.389–97)

If one simile is not enough to underscore the significance of the moment, the poet can use two or more. The most stunning example of this technique occurs in the *Odyssey*. At the climactic moment of Odysseus' revenge on Polyphemos, at the point when the smouldering tip of the olive staff is plunged into Polyphemos' eye, the poet transforms this instant of agonising pain into a detached technological description: the rotation of the staff is compared to a shipbuilder's drill; the sizzling of the eye to a red-hot axe tempered in cold water (*Odyssey* 9.384).

In the *Iliad*, the most effective double simile is used on the occasion of Aias' reluctant retreat on the morning of the Great Battle. First he appears as a lion who after a night of being beaten back by men and dogs abandons his attack on a herd of cattle (11.548). Immediately afterwards, he is a donkey who goes into a cornfield

in despite of boys, and many sticks have been broken upon him,
but he gets in and goes on eating the deep grain, and the children
beat him with sticks, but their strength is infantile; yet at last
by hard work they drive him out when he is glutted with eating.

(11.558–62)

Here the wonderful contrast of heroic frustration and comic satisfaction serves to underscore both the reluctance of Aias' retreat and the ambiguity of heroic existence: if you can limit your desire to corn rather than meat, you will get what you want.

The most elaborate simile cluster in the *Iliad* occurs in Book 2 when the marshalling of the army on the plain of Skamander is expressed through a sequence of five similes. This unique cluster expresses not only the sheer mass of the army but also the process by which the confused multitude is turned into an orderly force (2.455).

Similes are often found in complementary distribution balancing one another and their context not unlike the *men . . . de* [on the one hand . . . on the other hand] of the typical Greek sentence. Thus at the opening of Book 3 the progress of the armies towards each other is marked by a simile for each side (3.3, 10). As the armies approach, Paris and Menelaos jump ahead of their men, and each of them receives a simile (3.23, 33). The procedure is repeated in the encounter of the armies in Book 4, where a simile describing each side is followed by a simile describing their clash

(4.422, 433, 452). In the final duel of Hektor and Achilles, the initial position of each man is marked by a simile. Hektor is a hissing snake waiting for its attacker (22.93), Achilles is seen at the moment of Hektor's flight as a hawk pursuing a trembling dove (22.139). The race that delays their encounter receives three similes, and in the encounter itself each man is once more defined by a simile. Hektor, no longer the trembling dove, has turned into a high-flown eagle (22.308–10), but Achilles has been removed from the world of nature altogether and has become a cosmic force:

> And as a star moves among stars in the night's darkening,
> Hesper, who is the fairest star who stands in the sky, such
> was the shining from the pointed spear Achilleus was shaking
> in his right hand with evil intention toward brilliant Hektor.
>   (22.317–20)

To these instances in which the placement of similes articulates the structure of a particular scene, we must now add instances in which a chain of similes underscores narrative continuity through successive scenes. The most striking example is the chain of similes that associate Achilles' re-entry into battle with fire and range from a burning city to the light of the stars. The simile quoted above is the final link in this chain and prefigures night in its choice of constellation. The chain begins with the apparition of Achilles that puts a sudden end to the fighting over the body of Patroklos. There the divinely caused radiance (*selas*) from his head is compared to fire signals sent by a beleaguered city (18.207). When he receives his new armour from Thetis, the Myrmidons dare not look at it, but Achilles' eyes light up with fire (*selas*) as he gazes at it (19.16). The same word is mentioned in the arming scene, where the brilliance of his shield is compared to a mountain fire seen by sailors in distress, and his helmet shines like a star (19.375). In the aristeia [heroic action] of Achilles the fire metaphors are 'reliteralised' when Hephaistos in his elemental form helps Achilles in the fight with the river. After this literal interlude the metaphors resume. The slaughter Achilles causes among the Trojans becomes a burning city doomed by divine wrath (21.522). As Priam watches Achilles' approach to the city he sees him as the Dog Star (22.26). Hektor is turned to flight by the brightness from Achilles' spear 'shining like a fire or the rising sun' (22.135). (Note how rising sun and evening star frame the duel itself!)

This chain of images associating the aristeia of Achilles with various forms of fire is framed by two images of a burning city, which provide a prologue and epilogue to the chain. As Menelaos and Meriones carry the body of Patroklos towards the ships the fighting around them is compared to fire that rages through a city (17.737). The simile is clearly proleptic and looks ahead to the conflagration of Troy that begins when Achilles learns about the death of Patroklos. The epilogue shows us the smouldering ruins of Troy in a simile that illustrates the desolate laments of the Trojans when Hektor dies (22.410).

THE CONTENT OF SIMILES

Similes are drawn from a wide range of phenomena but with a very uneven distribution. A handful of simile families account for well over two-thirds of all occurrences. By far the largest group is made up of hunter–hunted similes. Here we may further distinguish between a smaller group in which the hunter is human and a much larger group in which he is an animal. The latter category is dominated by lion images but also includes birds of prey, dogs, wolves and, on one occasion, dolphins (21.22). The most interesting of the hunted animals is the boar because it allows the poet to represent a strong and aggressive animal in a posture of defence or counter-attack (11.324, 414, 12.146, 13.471). Odysseus surrounded by Trojans turns on them like a savage boar (11.414); a little later, when he is injured, exhausted, and lost but for the timely help of Aias, the poet sees him as an injured stag (11.474).

Not all animal images involve hunting. We also find bleating sheep (4.433), flies around a milk-pail (2.469, 16.641), swarming bees (2.87), goats (2.474), wasps attacking boys who disturbed them (16.259), prancing horses (6.506 = 15.263), a cow giving birth (17.4), snakes attacking or waiting for a by-passer (3.33, 22.93), a donkey shrugging off the sticks of little boys (11.558).

Vegetation imagery is dominated by the family of tree images. The warrior falls like a tree (4.482, 13.178, 13.389 = 16.482). The first occurrence of this simile is particularly moving. Simoeisios falls at the hands of Aias and 'did not repay his parents' care for him' (4.477). He crashes to the ground like a poplar that a carpenter cut down for use in making a chariot. The implicit contrast with the uselessness of the corpse continues the theme of wasted care. The falling tree can be elaborated in the direction of pathos or terror. When Hektor is felled by Aias he is like an oak uprooted by a thunderbolt (14.414), but the half-grown Eurphorbos is compared to a sapling tended carefully by a man in a lonely place and torn up by a sudden gust (17.53). The simile casts a shadow over Thetis' comparison of her son to a young tree (18.57). Trees do not always fall: Leontes and Polypoites, defenders of the wall, are like sturdy oaks that no storm can uproot (12.131). If the falling tree is the chief image of violent death, the cycle of leaves is a haunting reminder of the ephemerality of human life (6.146).

The weather, especially in its violent forms, provides the subject of a loose and extended simile family. Wind and water combine in images in which warriors are seen in various phases of a wave (2.144, 209, 394, 13.795, 15.381, 618, 624). There are dust storms (13.334), snow storms (12.156, 278), rivers in spate (4.452, 11.492), lightning (13.242), and forest fires (2.455, 14.396). From violent weather it is only a step to catastrophes such as earthquakes, mentioned once in a simile (2.781) and once directly in the preparation for the battle of the gods (20.57). Sometimes the weather spells relief in the form of a clear night (8.555) or a helpful breeze (7.4). When Patroklos beats back the attack on the ships, Zeus in his frequent role as weather god suddenly lifts clouds from a mountaintop (16.297). But for the Trojans the intervention of Patroklos is an almost apocalyptic flood sent by Zeus to punish wicked mortals (16.384). On two occasions, uncertainty of mind is expressed in the striking image of the sea torn by winds from different directions (9.4, 14.16).

It is often said, and with some justice, that the similes are drawn from a wider experience of the world than the narrative itself reveals. It is more questionable to argue that the major collective function of the similes is to add variety and provide some relief from the grim and monochromatic business of battle. The dominant simile families of hunter–hunted and violent weather are themselves drawn from a very narrow segment of the world and one that is very close to the phenomena of war the similes are meant to illustrate. Rather than provide variety and relief, the dominant simile families underscore the austerity of the poem and intensify its obsession with force and violence. Redfield has interpreted the *Iliad* as an inquiry into the paradoxical place of war in human society: dedicated to the preservation of a particular culture, it is an activity opposed to the work of culture as such. He points out that many of the similes are located *agrou ep'eschatiēn,* in the marginal zone between human habitation and the wilderness. The collective effect of the dominant simile families is to establish the battlefield as a similar marginal zone.

One way of developing this theme further is to look at the role of eating in the similes and in the narrative. The frequent descriptions of food are a justly famous element of Homeric style, but it is well to remember how little the poet says about eating itself. Take the following example. When the Achaean delegates come to Achilles they are first treated to a dinner. Chines of mutton, goat and pork are carved, put on spits, salted, and roasted when the fire has died down. The meat is put on platters and served together with bread in 'beautiful baskets'. After sacrificing to the gods,

> They put their hands to the good things that lay ready before them.
> But when they had put aside their desire for eating and drinking . . .
>
> 9.221–2)

No less than fifteen lines are devoted to food (9.206–20), but eating occurs in the space between one line and the next. In the narrative of the *Iliad* eating is a purely cultural phenomenon the natural basis of which is taken for granted and ignored. By contrast, the hunting similes often stress the hunger of the predator and sometimes conclude with the image of a feeding animal:

> like a lion who comes on a mighty carcass,
> in his hunger chancing upon the body of a horned stag
> or wild goat; who eats it eagerly, although against him
> are hastening the hounds in their speed and the stalwart young men.
>
> (3.23–6)

> First the lion breaks her neck caught fast in the strong teeth, then
> gulps down the blood and all the guts that are inward.
>
> (11.175–6)

> And as herdsmen who dwell in the fields are not able to frighten
> a tawny lion in his great hunger away from a carcass . . .
>
> (18.161–2)

The *Iliad* thus shows a contrast between immediate and mediated satisfaction of physical needs. Mediation is specifically human: in the ritual eating scenes of the *Iliad* it has reached such a degree that the "original" purpose of the mediated activity is almost forgotten. Despite the frequency of meals in the *Iliad*, one cannot really say that the warriors like to eat. The opposition between mediated and unmediated food clarifies the role of the animal images of the *Iliad*, which do not simply show that the warrior is as strong as a lion, swift as a hawk or dangerous as a boar. Rather, they say that he has returned to a state of nature and has abandoned the mediations of law, custom and ritual that make up human society. It is fully in keeping with this theme that Achilles in his fury expresses a desire to eat Hektor raw, but that action of the poem comes to a close with the ceremonious meal of Achilles and Priam (24.621).

An odd simile in Book 11 appears in a new light from this perspective and permits some further modification of the food theme. Odysseus has been injured but is saved by Aias. This situation generates the following simile:

They found Odysseus, beloved of Zeus, and around him
the Trojans crowded, as bloody scavengers in the mountains
crowd on a horned stag who is stricken, one whom a hunter
shot with an arrow from the string, and the stag has escaped him, running
with his feet, while the blood stayed warm, and his knees were springing
    beneath him.
But when the pain of the flying arrow has beaten him, then
the rending scavengers begin to feast on him in the mountains
and the shaded glen. But some spirit leads that way a dangerous
lion, and the scavengers run in terror, and the lion eats it.

                                     (11.473–81)

Odysseus is the wounded stag. But to persist in this identification raises difficulties. First he is eaten by his enemies, which is not true because he does not die, and then he is eaten by his friend, which is absurd. Clearly this is not the way to read the simile, but neither can we read the detail as gratuitous elaboration. While not homologous with the immediate context, the simile fits into the wider theme of the brutalising power of war, sounded by the poet when in his proemium he envisages the warriors' corpses as food for dogs and carrion birds. If we are in a speculative mood we may go farther and ask why the fate of being eaten twice should happen to Odysseus of all warriors. The question leads to the exceptional relation of Odysseus to food, both in the *Iliad* and in the *Odyssey*. Odysseus is the only Homeric warrior whom we ever see eating and drinking (*Odyssey*, 7.177, 14.109). He speaks of his belly as an independent and shameless agent who cannot be gainsaid (7.216). He is on one occasion compared to a haggis, a stomach filled with blood and meat, turning over the fire (20.25–7). These are of course Odyssean passages that fit into the wider theme of Odysseus as the survivor. The brainiest of the warriors, he has also the most accepting attitude towards the body. But even in the *Iliad* Odysseus is the one warrior who stresses the physical necessity of food. After the reconciliation of Achilles and Agamemnon he insists, against the impetuosity of Achilles, that the army must eat before going into battle. This unique connection between Odysseus and food remains striking, whether or not we see it as related to the simile in which he is a stag eaten first by dogs and then by a lion.

THE FUNCTION OF DETAIL: THE LION SIMILES

There is an old question about the degree to which detail in similes is relevant to narrative context. It was raised with polemical intent by Charles Perrault, who in his *Parallèle des anciens et des modernes* (3.65–7) ridiculed the 'simile with a tail'. The tail for him is the elaboration that does not contribute to the point of the simile. Thus, in the simile that illustrates the thigh-wound of Menelaos (4.141) he does not object to the basic conceit of comparing the blood on the white thigh to a piece of ivory stained with purple. But why does the poet tell us that the piece was stained by a Maeonian or Karian woman, that it is a cheek-piece for a horse, that many horsemen desire it, that it lies in the king's treasure chamber, and that it brings beauty and prestige both to the horse and to the horseman? What has any of this to do with the simple notion of 'red on white'? The question depends on two premisses of dubious merit. The first is that every simile is dominated by a specific point of departure. The second premiss is that the point of departure governs a homological relationship between simile and narrative hammered out in close detail just as Shakespeare's Richard II in his prison cell hammers out the conceit of the prison-as-world. Because Perrault cannot reconcile the subsequent detail of the simile with its alleged point of departure he shrugs it off as useless. But the search for a dominant point of departure and for a hierarchy of corresponding detail often leads nowhere with Homeric, as indeed with later, similes. It is more useful to think of the simile as an entity with its own structure capable of illuminating the immediate or wider content of narrative without being isomorphic at every point. It is also important to distinguish between the point of departure of a simile and its main idea. Often the two are the same, but sometimes they are not. Thus 'red on white' is not the central element in the purple ivory simile, which develops a precious mood that stresses the triviality of the injury and ironically undercuts the hysterical despair of Agamemnon's reaction to his brother's wound.

A good way of sharpening our eyes for the manner in which detail is relevant is to look at the individual simile in relation to its siblings and ask whether it could be interchanged with them or whether its individual features are strongly motivated by the particular narrative context. My discussion of tree and fire images has already given some answer to that question, but the demonstration can be made more systematically by a survey of the two dozen lion similes, by far the largest and most complex family of similes in the *Iliad*.

The lion either wins or loses. The class of winning similes is differentiated by the nature of the victim: fawn, cow, bull or boar. The differentiation fits the hierarchy of victims in the narrative. The hapless warrior on whom Agamemnon and Hektor fasten in their rout of the enemy is a cow (11.172, 15.630). Euphorbos, greatest of the minor warriors, is also a cow when he falls to Menelaos. But, unlike the random victims in the other two examples, he is the 'best cow' (17.62). Sarpedon is a bull (16.487), Patroklos a boar (16.823). The ascending hierarchy is completed in the only simile that pits a lion against another lion and ends in a draw: it applies to Patroklos and Hektor as they fight over the body of Kebriones (16.756).

The simile in which the victims of the lion are fawns deserves special attention. Agamemnon kills Isos and Antiphos, whom Achilles on a previous occasion had captured and ransomed. They are like the helpless young of a hind who helplessly looks on while they are killed in their lair (11.113). The pathos and cruelty of this simile are relevant to the characterisation of Agamemnon in his aristeia and throughout the poem. In the scene following the killing of Isos and Antiphos, Agamemnon denies ransom to the sons of Antimachos. The scene recalls the earlier supplication of Adrestos that Menelaos was willing to grant but Agamemnon denied (6.37). On that occasion Agamemnon's hatred of the Trojans culminated in the desire to bring death to all of them, including the infant in the mother's womb (6.58). Given the poet's way of expressing Agamemnon's cruelty through its effect on children, there is an ironic justice when the pain of the injured Agamemnon is compared to labour pains (11.269).

Other birth images in the *Iliad* bear suggestive links to the Agamemnon images. Menelaos stands over the body of Patroklos like a heifer over her first-born calf (17.4). War gives birth to death, and Patroklos is first-born because with him the war begins in a radically different way. The simile also looks forward to the inadequacy of Menelaos as a protector: like the hind in the Agamemnon simile, the cow will be unable to guard her calf against assault. The retreat of Menelaos from the body is described in the simile of a retreating lion (17.109). The Aias takes over and protects the body

> like a lion over his young, when the lion
> is leading his little ones along, and men who are hunting
> come upon them in the forest. He stands in the pride of his great strength
> hooding his eyes under the cover of down-drawn eyelids.
>
> (17.133–6)

The relationship of this to the previous simile requires no comment. The final birth image once more casts Patroklos as the lion cub. But this time the cub is dead, killed by a hunter during the lion's absence (18.318). Grieving and seized by fierce anger the lion goes in search of the hunter. The simile describes the grief of Achilles as he keeps watch over the body of Patroklos, and it looks forward to his aristeia on the following day. The precise internal shadings of the group are noteworthy: the cub or calf is seen alive as long as the body of Patroklos is fought over and in need of protection. The death of the cub is reserved for Achilles, in keeping with the perspective that governs the representation of Patroklos' death.

The theme of Patroklos as the child of war is linked to the Agamemnon images through the suppliant scenes, which are restricted in the *Iliad* to Agamemnon and Achilles. Thus all Iliadic similes that deal with birth and the fate of the very young are related to the pivotal events—the wounding of Menelaos and the killing of Patroklos—that set the war on a course of savage destruction. Aeschylus showed himself a very good reader of Homer when he figured the hubris of Agamemnon in the omen of the eagle devouring the young of the hare (*Agamemnon*, 115).

Some curious features occur in similes that show a lion and a carcass. A fairly elaborate version occurs when Menelaos' joy at seeing Paris is expressed through the image of a lion who finds a carcass and will not let go of it in despite of hunters and hounds (3.23). A second and sketchier version occurs when Hektor hangs on to the body of Patroklos like a hungry lion whom herdsmen cannot frighten away from a carcass (18.161). In Book 16, Patroklos and Hektor fight over the body of Kebriones like lions over a dead deer (16.756). The three similes share the only Iliadic occurrences of the word *peinaō*, 'to be hungry'. The similes of Books 16 and 18 are easily related to each other since they occur at the beginning and end of a narrative stretch that leads from the death of Patroklos to the rescue of his corpse. If we add to these similes the lion–boar simile (16.823), we get a short chain that transforms Patroklos from equal opponent through noblest of the vanquished into mere body. The simile in Book 3 at first resists integration into any pattern, and the potential identification of Paris with a carcass seems to humiliate him even more than he deserves. One is tempted to shrug it off as one of those similes that do not fit very precisely, but for a curious verbal echo between Books 3 and 17. The same line is used to describe the near-success Menelaos and Hektor have in dragging Paris and Patroklos to their side (3.373 = 18.165). Were it not for the intervention of Aphrodite, Paris would suffer the ignominious fate of being dragged away by Menelaos—not unlike a carcass being dragged away by a lion. If we now recall the prominent and ironic role that Menelaos plays in the fighting over the body of Patroklos, we begin to see a thematic connection between the carcass similes. Because Menelaos does not fulfil the expectation raised in the first lion-carcass simile, Patroklos must die and almost suffers the fate of being dragged away like a carcass.

Not all lion similes fit into such elaborate contexts. Two similes of a lion chasing away other predators are applied to Hektor and Aias without any apparent relationship (11.474, 15.271). The two Aiantes carry off the slain enemy Imbrios like two lions carrying off a goat (13.198). The simile bears no relation to, but neither is it interchangeable with, another carrying simile: Menelaos and Meriones carry off the body of Patroklos, like mules dragging a ship's mast down a rocky mountain path (17.742). This version of the felled-tree simile emphasises the value of the thing carried rather than the valour of those carrying it.

The lion does not always get his way. He may be beaten back; he may be injured or killed; he may survive on one occasion only to be killed later. Nine similes focus on temporary setback or ultimate defeat. Two similes describe a lion under pressure from dogs and men. They are both used of Menelaos when he leaves the body of Patroklos, the first time threatened by Hektor, the second time ordered by Aias (17.109, 657). The second simile is also used of Aias in conjunction with the donkey simile to describe his reluctant retreat—one of the rare instances in which a simile is repeated verbatim (11.548).

Only once is the lion killed outright. In Book 5, Krethon and Orsilochos have the temerity to face Aeneas, and they are compared to young but full-grown lions who kill sheep and cattle until their time comes to be killed (5.554). On two occasions the outcome of the lion's attack is left open but the possibility of death is explicitly stated. The similes refer to Hektor (12.41) and Sarpedon (12.299), both of whom die in turn. On a third occasion, Patroklos is compared to a lion whose courage brings death to him (16.752). The proleptic function of these similes is unmistakable.

Twice the lion is injured. The first time Diomedes, grazed by Pandaros, is compared to a lion whose fighting rage is tripled by his wound: he wreaks havoc among the sheep and escapes without further harm from the terrified shepherd (5.136). The other injured lion occurs in the final and longest lion image in the *Iliad*, which describes Achilles as he embarks on his aristeia and confronts Aeneas, his first opponent:

> From the other
> side the son of Peleus rose like a lion against him,
> the baleful beast, when men have been straining to kill him, the county
> all in the hunt, and he at the first pays them no attention
> but goes his way, only when some one of the impetuous young men
> has hit him with the spear he whirls, jaws open, over his teeth foam
> breaks out, and in the depth of his chest the powerful heart groans;
> he lashes his own ribs with his tail and the flanks on both sides
> as he rouses himself to fury for the fight, eyes glaring,
> and hurls himself straight onward on the chance of killing some one
> of the men, or else being killed himself in the first onrush.
>
> (20.164–73)

The simile refers to the entire aristeia of Achilles rather than to the specific encounter with Aeneas. It clearly connects with the simile of Book 18 about the grieving lion stalking the killers of his cubs. It is a fuller and more serious version of the Diomedes simile, just as Achilles is a fuller and more serious version of Diomedes. The wound of Diomedes at the hands of Pandaros repeats the wound Pandaros/Paris inflicted on Menelaos. The wound of Achilles is the death of Patroklos, another and more fateful repetition. The lion both times responds to the pivotal nature of the wound, but the five-line description of his response, culminating in the image of the tail furiously lashing ribs and flanks, far exceeds the power of the simple phrase 'stirred up the lion's strength' (5.139). Finally, this simile, too, is proleptic: like Hektor, Sarpedon and Patroklos, Achilles is a lion who will die.

CONTRAST AND SIGNIFICANCE IN THE ILIADIC IMAGE

The typical simile families stay close to the world they illustrate, and within a narrow range of subject-matter they show a high degree of subtle differentiation that is very responsive to simile placement. There are other similes that are no less responsive to narrative context but operate through contrast rather than through resemblance. The heifer and her calf (17.4) or the woman in labour (11.269) come to mind as examples. One of the most affecting similes in the *Iliad* compares the head of a falling warrior weighed down by his helmet to a poppy bent down by rain and the weight of its fruit (8.306). Discrepancy is also the point of two similes that stress the difference between men and gods. The bow-shot of Pandaros, elaborately prepared and disastrous in its final consequences, fails utterly of its intended result, for Athene deflects the arrow like a mother brushing away a fly from her baby (4.130). When Apollo destroys the wall he does so with the ease of a boy tearing down a sandcastle (15.362).

Most of the contrast similes are drawn from the human world and are deeply suffused with ironic pathos. This effect derives from their relation to the common simile families that compare the warrior to an animal. The power and frequency of such similes blur the dividing-line of man and animal: it is a highly charged moment in the poem when Apollo questions the humanity of Achilles and says that in his treatment of Hektor he behaves like a savage lion (*leōn d' hōs agria oiden*, 24.41). In contrast to the blurring function of animal images, similes drawn from the human sphere measure the loss of the warrior's humanity by drawing a line between him and other men. We find this effect when Achilles likens the weeping Patroklos to a little girl begging her mother to be picked up (16.7). Similarly, Hektor considers the possibility of negotiating with Achilles and rejects it in an image that epitomises the world of human conversation from which he is now excluded:

> There is no
> way any more from a tree or a rock to talk to him gently
> whispering like a young man and a young girl, in the way
> a young man and a young maiden whisper together.
>
> (22.126–8)

The most powerful effect of this kind occurs in an image that is not a simile. The race of Hektor and Achilles takes them from the walls of Troy to the springs, one hot, the other cold, where the Trojan women washed their clothes 'before the coming of the sons of the Achaeans' (22.156). The topographical detail, transformed into a vignette of deepest peace, measures the distance of the warrior from ordinary humanity. Such images, whether or not they occur in similes, perhaps come closer than any other feature of style or narrative to suggest an answer to the question: What is Iliadic about the *Iliad?* Three points suggest themselves. First, as Paolo Vivante has said, the poet knows 'where to look and what to ignore—how to focus his vision upon the vantage points of reality'. Homer's descriptive mastery is less a matter of technique than of the choice of the image in the first place. To focus on the springs is the stroke of genius in the last example, and time and again we observe that Iliadic effects derive from the manner in which the poet simply takes note of certain things, such as Hektor's spear in Paris' house, the lyre on which Achilles plays when the delegates arrive, Andromache's headgear, the flowers she embroiders or— a significant contrast—the loom on which Helen weaves the sufferings of the Achaeans and Trojans.

Second, the image, by virtue of being noticed, is endowed with a significance that does and does not point beyond itself. Jasper Griffin has written about the 'intrinsic symbolism' of certain Homeric gestures and images. Vivante states the same point more fully:

> It was the genius of Homer to draw his images true to life, and at the same time endow them unwittingly with a symbolic significance. Symbolic of what? we may ask. Certainly not of any superimposed value, but of a stress or mode of being which appears native to the objects themselves.

The women at the spring evoke a world of peace and are 'allegorical', in the literal sense in which all poetry is all-egorical, that is, 'says something else' beyond what it says. But the Iliadic image possesses to an eminent degree the quality many theorists consider the secret of the poetic image:

it resists the interpretation it invites. It is not opaque, but it cannot be interpreted away. Whatever thought is inspired by the women at the spring, our gaze never abandons them. The poet creates significance by foregrounding his image—hence the traditional admiration for the plasticity and lucidity of Homeric narrative—and this foregrounding has an arresting power that keeps the reader from abandoning the lively concreteness of the image.

Third, the significant and arresting image is part of a whole of which it is one extreme and which is conveyed in its wholeness as a contrast of polar opposites. This is an example of the pervasive tendency in Greek culture to think of the cosmos, the order of things, as a balance of opposites. The Iliadic totality, however, is unbalanced and moves towards its destruction in one extreme. In the static image of the shield of Achilles war and peace are evenly balanced, but in the narrative war and destruction prevail. Hence the poignancy of such scenes as Hektor's reminiscence of the conversation of boys and girls, the description of the women at the spring, or the flashback to Andromache's wedding: the poet celebrates beauty and order at the point of their destruction. The greatest example of this technique is, of course, the encounter of Priam and Achilles where the characters share the poet's vision of an order about to be destroyed.

DAVID MARSHALL

Similes and Delay

In the middle of a dramatic battle scene in Book Five of the *Iliad*, we are told: "Diomedes/ felt like a traveller halted on a plain,/ helpless to cross, before a stream in flood/ that roars and spumes down to the sea. That traveller/ would look once and recoil: so Diomedes backed away . . ." At moments such as this the reader or listener must halt, hesitate, back away (at least for a moment) from the dramatic action of the narrative. Like the traveller that Diomedes resembles, one must delay one's journey through the course of the narrative, at least for the time and space it takes for a simile to run its course. Most of the similes in the *Iliad* give us pause in this way. Readers have observed the incongruity which makes many of the similes seem ironic or even subversive in descriptions of the epic's heroes. It has also been noted that the similes appear to be in dialogue with the epic narrative, offering tableaux of nature and domestic life that both stand as a counter-story to the account of the Trojan war and add to the encyclopedic fund of knowledge transmitted in the Homeric epic. My concern, however, is not with the content or the didactic and polemical purposes of the similes; I am concerned, rather, with the ways in which the similes in the *Iliad* tend to work against the epic narrative itself, how they serve to impede the advancement of the dramatic action. I will suggest that similes and narrative are engaged in a struggle that is like the most serious of the struggles acted out in the poem.

Published in this volume for the first time. Copyright © 1985 by David Marshall. From a paper presented at the annual convention of the Modern Language Association, New York City, December 1983. Translations by Robert Fitzgerald from *The Iliad*, Garden City, N. Y.: Anchor Books, 1975 and A. T. Murray from *The Iliad*, Cambridge: Harvard University Press, 1924, identified in the text as M.

Let us return to the traveller halted at an overflowing stream, backing away from his destination. Even in the most straightforward of Homeric similes, the image of the simile expands so much that it threatens to eclipse the ostensible referent of its comparison; but often in the *Iliad,* one doesn't know what the literal referent of a simile is until the famous "like A . . . so B . . ." formula is completed. We may forget Diomedes for a brief moment while picturing the traveller, but at least we know where we're going, so to speak. Often we are given a description before we know what (by comparison) it is describing; as a result, the frame of the simile tends to fade into the background until the formula comes full circle and returns us to the main line of the dramatic action. We almost forget that we are in the middle of a simile as the narrative appears to veer off in an unexpected direction. Recall the famous description of Paris running through Troy: "Think how a stallion fed on clover and barley,/ mettlesome, thundering in a stall, may snap/ his picket rope and canter down a field/ to bathe as he would daily in the river—glorying in freedom! Head held high/ with mane over his shoulders flying,/ his dazzling work of finely jointed knees/ takes him around the pasture haunts of horses./ That was the way the son of Priam, Paris,/ ran." We might be left with a vivid image of Paris in all his vitality and glory; for a moment, however, the stallion threatens to run away with the narrative.

Furthermore, in other similes the referent and the object of comparison are more difficult to picture at once than are Paris and the stallion. Consider this simile, which occurs at the height of a battle scene in Book Four as a warrior is reeling in the dust: "A poplar/ growing in bottom lands, in a great meadow,/ smooth-trunked, high up to its sheath of boughs,/ will fall before the chariot-builder's ax/ of shining iron—timber that he marked/ for warping into chariot tire rims—and seasoning, it lies beside the river./ So vanquished by the god-reared Aias lay/ Simoeisios Anthemides." What happens to the battle as we try to picture this poplar in a meadow—and the three future stages of its life that are non-consecutively described for us? It is not merely that the epic narrative comes to a halt; we seem to find ourselves in the middle of another story, as in this description of a battle scene in Book Eleven: "at the hour/ a woodsman takes his lunch in a cool grove/ of mountain pines, when he has grown arm-weary/ chopping tall timber down, and, sick of labor,/ longs for refreshment—at that height of noon/ Danaans calling fiercely back and forth/ broke the Trojan line." These expansive moments of description feel almost like *non sequiturs,* at least insofar as they don't follow the story-line of the epic narrative. Like the tableaux that are pictured on the shield of Akhilleus—those pictorially static images which in the description of Book Eighteen take on the linear and temporal dimensions of stories—the similes of the *Iliad* tend to transform themselves from illustrations to narratives. As the Homeric simile unfolds, it acts like a digression; it delays and deviates from the story-line, holding the dramatic action in suspense while it elaborates its own alternate narrative time and space. The simile causes the reader or listener to swerve from the progressive plot of the epic; it threatens to derail or at least to sidetrack the train of events and actions that propel the narrative forward. Time and time again, if only for brief or not so brief moments, the reader or listener is turned away from the linear sequence and destination of the epic narrative. The narrative is interrupted, disrupted, stalled, delayed.

As we know, the *Iliad* is preoccupied with delay. As much as the poem is about the wrath of Akhilleus, it is about the delay of Akhilleus. Akhilleus delays because the end of his story is unspeakable. He claims to have two stories, two destinies, but both of them have the same ending: "the doom of death" (M,I,411). One destiny would postpone death, the other would accept it sooner rather than later. Akhilleus spends the entire poem trying to accept and trying to delay the end of his story: the destination inscribed in his destiny. He steps aside from the fighting that will lead to his death but in doing so he acts out his death, causing his comrades to experience his loss and his absence, as if he were dead. After they beg him to give himself back, Akhilleus allows Patroklos to enter the battle in his place, in his armor, not only as his stand-in but as his double, his similitude. Patroklos is meant to impersonate Akhilleus, to personate him, and through Patroklos' death Akhilleus can act out his own death, both mourn for himself and accept his destiny. But first he must bring another similitude of himself to death—this time Hektor in the armor of Akhilleus. By killing Hektor Akhilleus moves forward his own death, yet he refuses to let Hektor's body be consigned to death, just as he delayed in granting funeral rites to his other substitute, Patroklos. Priam finally convinces Akhilleus to allow Hektor to be consigned to death, but only after asking him to imagine his own death, to think of the father from whom Akhilleus has inherited his mortality. Akhilleus must allow his stand-ins to reach the unspeakable end that he has been delaying and rehearsing throughout the course of the narrative.

It is a critical commonplace that, in the *Iliad*, death is not to be avoided or escaped. Akhilleus, Hektor, and even Zeus himself (in regard to Sarpedon) must come to this conclusion. Yet despite its measured advance toward the end, the epic itself avoids relating the death of Akhilleus; it continues the delay and avoidance of the man who delayed by playing the lyre and singing "of the glorious deeds of warriors" (M,I,397). It is as if the epic narrator (call him Homer if you like) finds it "morally speaking, impossible" to go "straight-forward" to the end, at least without numerous "deviations from a straight line." The narrator of the *Iliad*, like Akhilleus, seems to want to delay, to turn away from the inevitable linear progression of the epic. The problem is that to enter narrative is to enter time, to begin or to take up the line that leads to the inevitable yet unspeakable end. To escape narrative would be to escape time, to back away from death: the destiny and destination prescribed in the story-line. Similes speak this desire to avert and divert the advance of the narrative, to suspend linear time by offering alternate and digressive versions of moments that veer away from the main story-line rather than going forward. Through potentially endless substitutions, similes enact a wish to go forward and to stand still at the same time.

At the end of Book Twenty-one, Apollo deflects Akhilleus' resolution to achieve his end by "taking Agenor's likeness to the last detail" and leading Akhilleus off in pursuit of a similitude, a simulacrum of the man he is after. When Akhilleus discovers that he has been following someone who is merely *like* his target, he bitterly complains to Apollo, "most cruel of all gods . . . thou hast now turned me hither from the wall" (M,II,455). Fitzgerald's translation nicely interprets the situation: his Akhilleus complains, "you have put me off the track, turning me away from the wall." The likeness he has followed has sidetracked Akhilleus, derailed him, as it were, just as the likenesses of the similes sidetrack and derail the train of the narrative. The key word here, however, is *turned*: when Akhilleus complains of having been turned, he uses the verb *trepein*, of which the noun form is *tropos*. He has been turned from his destination by a likeness, a similitude; he has been sidetracked because he has been troped. Like the reader or the listener, Akhilleus has been delayed by troping. (Immediately following his complaint, as he runs toward Troy Akhilleus is troped again by a simile that compares him to a horse and an unusually long simile that compares him to a star.)

Throughout the course of the *Iliad* similes allow us to turn away from the narrative, if only for a moment. In this sense the subtle battle between the similes and the narrative is like the peculiar plot that holds back both the narrator and the hero of the *Iliad*, even as it carries them forward.

Chronology

c. 4000 B.C.	Dawn of Bronze Age in Crete.
c. 3000 B.C.	Beginning of northern invasions of Greece.
c. 2000 B.C.	Unification of Minoan power in Crete.
c. 2000–1700 B.C.	Achaean invasion.
c. 1600 B.C.	Destruction of Phaestos and Cnossos in Crete. Palaces rebuilt. Greek linear script replaces hieroglyphs.
c. 1600–1400 B.C.	Strong Cretan influence in Greece. The shaft-grave dynasty at Mycenae.
c. 1400 B.C.	Second destruction of Cretan palaces. Rapid wane of Minoan power.
c. 1400–1200 B.C.	Great age of Mycenae. Development of Mycenaean trade in Egypt and Eastern Mediterranean. Trade with the West.
1287 B.C.	Battle of Cadesh between Egypt and Hittites; decline of both powers.
c. 1250–1240 B.C.	Trojan War.
c. 1180 B.C.	Troy destroyed by Mycenaeans.
c. 1150 B.C.	Destruction of Mycenaean centers in Greece.
c. 1100 B.C.	Successive waves of Dorian invaders penetrate Greece. "Dark Age" begins. Use of iron introduced.
c. 800–500 B.C.	Development of the city-state from monarchy. Ionian School of lyric poetry.
776 B.C.	First Olympic Festival.
c. 750–650 B.C.	Composition of *Iliad* and *Odyssey*.

Contributors

HAROLD BLOOM, Sterling Professor of the Humanities at Yale University, is the author of *The Anxiety of Influence, Poetry and Repression* and many other volumes of literary criticism. His forthcoming study, *Freud: Transference and Authority*, attempts a full-scale reading of all of Freud's major writings. A MacArthur Prize Fellow, he is the general editor of *The Chelsea House Library of Literary Criticism*.

MILMAN PARRY was Assistant Professor of Greek at Harvard University at his death in 1935. His work on the oral composition of the Homeric epics revolutionized Homeric studies.

RACHEL BESPALOFF was a French philosopher and essayist of Russian origin, and author of *Cheminements et carrefours: essais de l'art et de philosophie.*

MAURICE BLANCHOT is one of the major French novelists and literary critics of this century. His work, which first appeared in the 1930s, has been highly influential on French literary and philosophical writing.

MAX HORKHEIMER, founder of the Institute for Social Research in Frankfurt, was Professor Emeritus of Philosophy and Sociology at the University of Frankfurt at his death in 1973.

THEODOR W. ADORNO worked with Max Horkheimer at the New York Institute for Social Research and later taught at the University of Frankfurt until his death in 1969.

SIMONE WEIL taught Homeric philosophy, mathematics and Greek language and literature in England until World War II, when she was dismissed from her teaching post under discriminatory laws. During her teaching years she traveled to Germany, Spain and France to work with labor groups and among factory laborers. After her dismissal and a brief stay in the United States she traveled to France, where she contracted tuberculosis; she died in England in 1943.

E. R. DODDS was Regius Professor of Classical Languages and Literature at Oxford University.

ERICH AUERBACH was Professor of Comparative Literature at Yale University at his death in 1957.

BRUNO SNELL is one of the major European scholars of classical literature. His book *The Discovery of the Mind* is a comprehensive study of the tradition that goes from Homer through Virgil.

ADAM PARRY, son of Milman Parry, was Assistant Professor of Greek at Yale University at his death in 1972.

CEDRIC H. WHITMAN was Eliot Professor of Greek at Harvard University at his death in 1978.

THOMAS GREENE is Professor of English and Comparative Literature and Chairman of the Department of Renaissance Studies at Yale University.

ERIC HAVELOCK is Sterling Professor of Classics Emeritus, at Yale University.

NORMAN AUSTIN, the author of *Archery at the Dark of the Moon: Poetic Problems in Homer's Odyssey,* is Professor of Classics at the University of Massachusetts, Amherst.

HERMANN FRÄNKEL was Professor of Classical Literatures at Stanford University until 1953, when he became Professor Emeritus.

JAMES M. REDFIELD teaches at the University of Chicago, with appointments to the Committee on Social Thought, the Department of Classical Languages and Literatures, and the College.

DOUGLAS J. STEWART teaches classics at Brandeis University.

GREGORY NAGY is Professor of Greek and Latin at Harvard University.

MARTIN MUELLER is Professor of English at Northwestern University.

DAVID MARSHALL is Assistant Professor of English and Comparative Literature at Yale University.

Bibliography

Adkins, A. W. H. "Homeric Values and Homeric Society." *Journal of Hellenic Studies*, vol. 91 (1971).

Amory, Anne. *Blameless Aegisthus. Mnemosyne*, supp. vol. 26 (Leiden, 1973).

———. "The Gates of Horn and Ivory." *Yale Classical Studies*, vol. 20 (1966).

Armstrong, J. "The Arming Motif in the *Iliad*." *American Journal of Philology* , vol. 79 (1958).

Auerbach, Erich. *Mimesis: The Representation of Reality in Western Literature.* Princeton: Princeton University Press, 1953.

Austin, Norman. *Archery at the Dark of the Moon: Poetic Problems in Homer's Odyssey.* Berkeley: University of California Press, 1975.

Bassett, S. E. "Achilles' Treatment of Hector's Body." *Transactions and Proceedings of the American Philological Association*, vol. 64 (1933).

Bespaloff, Rachel. *On the Iliad.* The Bollingen Library. New York: Harper Torchbooks, 1947.

Bowra, C. M. *Tradition and Design in the Iliad.* Oxford: Oxford University Press, 1930.

Carpenter, Rhys. *Folktale, Fiction and Saga in the Homeric Epics.* Berkeley: University of California Press, 1946.

Clarke, Howard, ed. *Twentieth Century Interpretations of the Odyssey.* Englewood Cliffs, N.J.: Prentice-Hall, 1983.

Clarke, Howard W. *The Art of the Odyssey.* Englewood Cliffs, N.J.: Prentice-Hall, 1967.

Dodds, E. R. *The Greeks and the Irrational.* Berkeley: University of California Press, 1951.

Eichholz, D. E. "The Propitiation of Achilles." *American Journal of Philology*, vol. 74 (1953).

Fenik, Bernard, ed. *Homer: Tradition, and Invention.* Cincinnati Classical Studies, vol. 2 (Leiden, 1978).

———. "Typical Battle Scenes in the *Iliad*: Studies in the Narrative Techniques of Homeric Description." *Einzelschriften*, vol. 21 (Wiesbaden, 1968).

Ferrucci, Franco. *The Poetics of Disguise: The Autobiography of the Work in Homer, Dante, and Shakespeare.* Translated by Ann Dunnigan. Ithaca: Cornell University Press, 1980.

Finley, M. I. *The World of Odysseus.* New York: The Viking Press, 1954. Revised edition, 1965.

Fränkel, Hermann. *Early Greek Poetry and Philosophy: A History of Greek Epic, Lyric and Prose to the Middle of the Fifth Century.* Translated by Moses Hadas and James Willis. New York: Harcourt Brace Jovanovich, 1973.

Friedrich, Rainer. "On the Compositional Use of Similes in the *Odyssey.*" *American Journal of Philology,* vol. 102 (1981).

Greene, Thomas M. *The Descent from Heaven: A Study in Epic Continuity.* New Haven: Yale University Press, 1963.

Griffin, Jasper. *Homer on Life and Death.* Oxford: Clarendon Press, 1980.

Harrison, E. L. " 'Last Legs' in Homer." *Classical Review,* n.s. 4 (1954).

Horkheimer, Max, and Theodor W. Adorno. *Dialectic of Enlightenment.* Translated by John Cumming. New York: Continuum, 1982.

Kirk, G. S. *Homer and the Oral Tradition.* Cambridge: Cambridge University Press, 1978.

———. *The Iliad: A Commentary.* Vol. 1, Books 1–4. Cambridge: Cambridge University Press, 1985.

———, ed. *The Language and Background of Homer.* Cambridge: Cambridge University Press, 1964.

———. *The Songs of Homer.* Cambridge: Cambridge University Press, 1962.

MacCary, W. Thomas. *Childlike Achilles: Ontogeny and Phylogeny in the Iliad.* The Bollingen Library. New York: Harper Torchbooks, 1947.

Macleod, C. W., ed. *Homer: Iliad, Book XXIV.* Cambridge: Cambridge University Press, 1982.

Moulton, Carroll. "Homeric Metaphor." *Classical Philology,* vol. 74 (1979).

Mueller, Martin. *The Iliad.* London: George Allen & Unwin, 1984.

Nagy, Gregory. *The Best of the Achaeans: Concepts of the Hero in Archaic Greek Poetry.* Baltimore: The Johns Hopkins University Press, 1979.

Nelson, Conny, ed. *Homer's Odyssey: A Critical Handbook.* Belmont, Calif: Wadsworth, 1969.

Page, Denys. *Folktales in Homer's Odyssey.* Cambridge: Harvard University Press, 1973.

Parry, Adam. "Have We Homer's *Iliad?*" *Yale Classical Studies,* vol. 20 (1966).

———. *The Homeric Odyssey.* Oxford: Clarendon Press, 1955.

———. "The Language of Achilles." *Transactions of the American Philological Association,* vol. 87 (1956).

———. "Language and Characterization in Homer." *Harvard Studies in Classical Philology,* vol. 76 (1972).

Parry, Milman. *The Making of Homeric Verse.* Oxford: Oxford University Press, 1971.

Redfield, James M. *Nature and Culture in the Iliad: The Tragedy of Hector.* Chicago: The University of Chicago Press, 1975.

Scodel, Ruth. "The Autobiography of Phoenix: *Iliad* 9:444–95." *American Journal of Philology,* vol. 103 (1982).

Scott, J. A. *The Unity of Homer.* Berkeley: University of California Press, 1921.

Segal, Charles. "The Theme of the Mutilation of the Corpse in the *Iliad.*" *Mnemosyne,* supp. vol. 17 (1971).

Snell, Bruno. *The Discovery of the Mind: The Greek Origins of European Thought.* Translated by T. G. Rosenmeyer. New York: Harper and Row, 1960.

Stanford, W. B. *The Ulysses Theme: A Study in the Adaptability of a Traditional Hero.* Ann Arbor: University of Michigan Press, 1968.

Stewart, Douglas J. *The Disguised Guest: Rank, Role, and Identity in the Odyssey.* Lewisburg, Pa: Bucknell University Press, 1976.

Taylor, Charles H., Jr., ed. *Essays on the Odyssey: Selected Modern Criticism.* Bloomington: Indiana University Press, 1963.

Vivante, Paolo. *Homer.* New Haven: Yale University Press, 1985.

Wade-Gery, H. T. *The Poet of the "Iliad."* Cambridge: Cambridge University Press, 1952.

Whitman, Cedric H. *Homer and the Heroic Tradition.* Cambridge: Harvard University Press, 1958.

Woodhouse, W. J. *The Composition of Homer's Odyssey.* 1930. Reprint. Oxford: Clarendon Press, 1969.

Acknowledgments

"The Traditional Epithet in Homer," "The Traditional Poetic Language of Oral Poetry " and "The Traditional Metaphor In Homer" by Milman Parry from *The Making of Homeric Verse: The Collected Papers of Milman Parry* edited by Adam Parry, copyright © 1971 by Oxford University Press. Reprinted by permission.

"Priam and Achilles Break Bread" by Rachel Bespaloff from *On the Iliad* by Rachel Bespaloff, translated by Mary McCarthy, copyright © 1947 by The Bollingen Foundation. Reprinted by permission of Harper & Bros.

"The Song of the Sirens: Encountering the Imaginary" by Maurice Blanchot from *The Gaze of Orpheus* by Maurice Blanchot, translated by Lydia Davis, copyright © 1981 by Lydia Davis. Reprinted by permission of Station Hill.

"The Concept of Enlightenment" by Max Horkheimer and Theodor W. Adorno from *Dialectic of Enlightenment* by Max Horkheimer and Theodor W. Adorno, copyright © 1972 by Herder and Herder, Inc. Reprinted by permission of the Continuum Publishing Corporation.

"The Iliad, or the Poem of Force" by Simone Weil from *The Iliad, or The Poem of Force* by Simone Weil, translated by Mary McCarthy, copyright © 1945 by Dwight Macdonald. Reprinted by permission of Pendle Hill.

"Agamemnon's Apology" by E. R. Dodds from *The Greeks and the Irrational* by E. R. Dodds, copyright © 1951 by the Regents of the University of California. Reprinted by permission of the University of California Press.

"Odysseus' Scar" by Erich Auerbach from *Mimesis: The Representation of Reality in Western Literature* by Erich Auerbach, copyright © 1953 by Princeton University Press. Reprinted by permission.

"Homer's View of Man" by Bruno Snell from *The Discovery of the Mind: The Greek Origins of European Thought* by Bruno Snell, translated by T. G. Rosenmeyer, copyright © 1960 by Harper & Row. Reprinted by permission.

"The Language of Achilles" by Adam Parry from *Transactions of the American Philological Association,* copyright © 1956 by the American Philological Association. Reprinted by permission.

"Geometric Structure of the *Iliad*" by Cedric H. Whitman from *Homer and the Heroic Tradition* by Cedric H. Whitman, copyright © 1958 by the President and Fellows of Harvard College. Reprinted by permission.

"Form and Craft in the *Odyssey*" by Thomas Greene from *The Descent from Heaven: A Study in Epic Continuity* by Thomas Greene, copyright © 1963 by Thomas Greene. Reprinted by permission of Yale University Press.

"Epic as Record versus Epic as Narrative" by Eric Havelock from *Preface to Plato* by Eric Havelock, copyright © 1963 by the President and Fellows of Harvard College. Reprinted by permission of Harvard University Press/Belknap Press.

"The Function of Digressions in the *Iliad*" by Norman Austin from *Greek, Roman and Byzantine Studies*, copyright © 1966 by Duke University Press. Reprinted by permission.

"The New Mood of the *Odyssey* and the End of Epic" by Hermann Fränkel from *Early Greek Poetry and Philosophy: A History of Greek Epic, Lyric and Prose to the Middle of the Fifth Century* by Hermann Fränkel, translated by Moses Hadas and James Willis, copyright © 1973 by Basil Blackwell. Reprinted by permission of Harcourt Brace Jovanovich.

"Achilles," "The Hero" and "Landscape and Simile" by James M. Redfield from *Nature and Culture in the Iliad: The Tragedy of Hector* by James M. Redfield, copyright © 1975 by The University of Chicago. Reprinted by permission of The University of Chicago Press.

"The Disguised Guest" by Douglas J. Stewart from *The Disguised Guest: Rank, Role, and Identity in the Odyssey* by Douglas J. Stewart, copyright © 1976 by Associated University Presses, Inc. Reprinted by permission of Bucknell University Press.

"Poetic Visions of Immortality for the Hero" and "The Worst of the Achaeans" by Gregory Nagy from *The Best of the Achaeans: Concepts of the Hero in Archaic Greek Poetry* by Gregory Nagy, copyright © 1979 by The Johns Hopkins University Press. Reprinted by permission.

"The Simile" by Martin Mueller from *The Iliad* by Martin Mueller, copyright © 1984 by Martin Mueller. Reprinted by permission of George Allen & Unwin.

"Similes and Delay" by David Marshall. Published for the first time in this volume. Copyright © 1985 by David Marshall. Printed by permission.

Index